The Art of the Potter

REDWARE AND STONEWARE

Edited by Diana and J. Garrison Stradling

Main Street/Universe Books

New York

Articles included in this volume, or excerpts from such articles, are printed as they appeared in the following issues of *The Magazine* ANTIQUES:

Part I. On the Digging of Potteries, September, 1974; A Late Seventeenth-Century Pottery Kiln Site Near Jamestown, May, 1963; Earliest Yorktown Pottery, May, 1958.

Part II. Ceramics in the South, February, 1951; Pottery at Old Salem, July, 1965; A Note on Early North Carolina Pottery, January, 1935; Early Slip Decorated Cannister, March, 1926; Pennsylvania Potter, July, 1965; Slipware and Redware at the Philadelphia Museum of Art, October, 1959; Henry McQuate, Pennsylvania Potter, November, 1925; A Maker of Pennsylvania Redware, June, 1946; Early Pottery Lighting Devices of Pennsylvania, May, 1940; American Pottery Lamps, August, 1953; Mehwaldt, A Pioneer American Potter, September, 1922; Grandfather's Thumb, January, 1923; The Roof Tiles of Zoar, February, 1934.

Part III. The Bayleys: Essex County Potters, Part I, November, 1938, Part II, January, 1939; A Puzzling Pot, June, 1941; The Brooks Pottery in Goshen, Connecticut, January, 1940; The Exeter Pottery Works, July, 1932; The Osborne Pottery at Gonic, New Hampshire, February, 1931; Lyndeboro Pottery, February, 1928; Early Pottery of New England, January, 1922; New England Pottery in the Collection of the Smithsonian Institution, September, 1957; American Pottery at Old Sturbridge Village, September, 1955.

Part IV. A Checklist of New England Stoneware Potters, August, 1942; New England Pottery in the Collection of the Society for the Preservation of New England Antiquities, May, 1960; New Light on Boston Stoneware and Frederick Carpenter, June, 1972; The Fentons—Pioneer American Potters, October, 1923; Portrait of a Potter-Musician, July, 1941; The Facts About Bennington Pottery, January, 1924; A Strange Face From Whately, August, 1925; The Crafts Pottery in Nashua, New Hampshire, April, 1931; The Norwich Pottery Works, October, 1923; The Stoneware of South Ashfield, Massachusetts, September, 1934.

Part V. The Pottery at Huntington, Long Island, April, 1923; Batter Jugs, August, 1925; An American Pottery, December, 1941; Remmy Family: American Potters, Part I, June, 1937, Part II, September, 1937; The Cheesequake Potteries, March, 1944; A New Jersey Stoneware Jar, July, 1937; The Potters of Poughkeepsie, July, 1966; Nathan Clark, Potter, July, 1951; The Potters of Albany, December, 1944; Notes on New York State Pottery at Albany, August, 1958; Stoneware Made by the White Family, June, 1971; Ohio Pottery Jars and Jugs, October, 1933; Specimens of Ohio Pottery, October, 1937; Early Decorative Arts in Ohio, January, 1946; Stoneware of Ripley, Illinois, November, 1949; A Pottery Pig, January, 1939; More Information on Pottery Pigs, March, 1939; Information on Anna, Illinois, Jug, November, 1938.

Part VI. The Making of a Flower Pot, August, 1935; The Methods of Early American Potters, April, 1924; European Folk Pottery, October, 1933.

First Edition

Library of Congress Catalog Card Number 76-56872

ISBN 0-87663-960-0, paperback edition
ISBN 0-87663-285-1, hardcover edition

Published by Universe Books, 381 Park Avenue South, New York City 10016. Produced by The Main Street Press, 42 Main Street, Clinton, New Jersey 08809.

Printed in the United States of America

Contents

IV STONEWARE—NEW ENGLAND

V STONEWARE—NEW YORK AND WEST

VI THE POTTER'S CRAFT

Introduction

There have been so many articles on the subject of The Art of the Potter *from the inception of* The Magazine ANTIQUES *to the final issue of the bicentennial year, that it has been impossible to crowd them between the covers of this book. What is to be found here, therefore, are the authoritative writings concerning the hand-made pottery, the stoneware and the redware made in America, with the remainder left for possible inclusion in a second volume.*

During the seventeenth and eighteenth centuries trained potters arrived on these shores and set about plying their trade as they had learned it from generations of craftsmen, be it on the Continent (with the common denominator, the Germanic traditions) or in England.

The settlers from Central Europe—the Germans, especially—did not assimilate, but maintained their identity in separate, tightknit communities, cherishing and fostering the traditions they had known at home, holding on to them in many cases long after they had evolved out of use in the homeland—a phenomenon which sociologists refer to as "cultural lag."

So it was that the Germans in Pennsylvania treasured the tradition of sgraffito decoration—a technique which had originated in Italy and spread to Switzerland, Germany, and France. In America it seems to have been reserved for special gift pieces which were often dated and inscribed with the names of recipient and of maker. Displayed with pride on the shelf or mantel and handed down through generations, these objects have survived in far greater proportion than the more mundane wares designed for daily use, although thousands of utilitarian wares were made for every piece that has survived. The earliest date found on Pennsylvania ware is 1733.

There has been much speculation, but never an adequate explanation, as to why sgraffito decoration does not occur in New England ware, and the practice of slip trailing, rarely. When such touches do appear, they are often confined to names and to simple designs, occasionally in two or more colors. It is often suggested that the austerity of life and of the people who settled New England made such ostentation unpopular. Yet the folk potteries in the West of England did produce sgraffito and slipware in all of its forms—trailing, combing and marbling—throughout the seventeenth century and into the eighteenth.

The absence of these decorated wares is all the more puzzling when one realizes that the slip and sgraffito pieces of North Devon were heavily exported to America from 1635 until the end of the century, and that Barnstaple and Bideford, the principal points of manufacture, were centers of the Puritan population in England. Enormous quantities were shipped to New England, Maryland, and Virginia, but the great export trade came to an end by 1700, changing tastes in this country, as in England, dictating a shift to the white salt-glazed stoneware of Staffordshire and the delft of Lambeth, Bristol, and Liverpool. It can only be assumed that the vast majority of New England potters, working in the eighteenth century in a developing domestic industry, followed the dictates of fashion. The potters of other areas, many of them of German extraction, were less affected by these developments.

Slip trailing developed to a high art in America, especially in the Moravian communities such as Bethlehem, Pennsylvania, and even more so in Wachovia, North Carolina, where, in the closed communities of Bethabara and Salem, master potters set up shop under the supervision of the congregations. The master potter Gottfried Aust arrived in Wachovia in 1755.

There were, of course, potters of English extraction in eastern Pennsylvania, primarily in Bucks and Montgomery counties, coexisting with the Germans. Such men as Joseph Smith and Abraham Weaver gradually adopted the techniques of their neighbors, even to the use of sgraffito, but usually with English words integrated into their designs. The English potters of Chester County were predominantly Quakers who, in supplying the needs of the "Plain People" generally shunned the use of ornament in their wares. Yet the Vickers family of Chester County did list "green enamelled ware," and made the occasional piece with a simple sgraffito wreath surrounding a data, a name, or a phrase such as "Apple Butter."

Potting in rural America was a seasonal trade—taking second place to farming in Pennsylvania, revolving around the weather in New England. The part-timer was called a "bluebird potter" in Pennsylvania; in New England the small operation—its staff of one to three men—was more often than not a cottage industry, supplying the needs for storage jars and dairy utensils, sometimes even the tableware of home and neighbors without fanfare or advertisement.

Potting was an occasional trade; partnerships were as a rule shortlived, potters leaving the craft to become full-time farmers or merchants. Historically, there seems to be an association between dry-goods merchants, whose names frequently appear as the mark on stoneware and who often placed special orders for the types of containers they needed. Other such merchants went to the extent of providing the financial backing for potteries; just as often, potters are found to have given up their trade to become salesmen, probably maintaining an interest in the pottery while selling their wares in the shop.

Potting was an itinerant trade and has been one since the days when master potters, alleging to know the secret alchemies, peddled themselves and their formulae across Europe and England. Their wanderlust took them across America as well, following every migration of settlers into the South and West. Seldom having the funds to set up on their own, sometimes working in the employ of an entrepreneur, training his sons to take over some day, moving on to other areas where the demand for their wares would be greater—the average potter was forever on the move.

An entry in the Harwood Diary at the Bennington Museum mentions that the stoneware on hand must await firing because the decorator had not yet arrived. The hand of the Bennington stoneware artist betrays his presence at potteries as far west as Rochester, New York, and as far east as Charlestown, Massachusetts. There does not seem to have been a rigid apprenticeship system, but the trade was kept in families. It is possible to trace family names back through generations of potters to the old country. The incredibly influential Osborn family and their style of potting can be traced from its source in Danvers to Somerset and Essex, Massachusetts; to Exeter, Dover, Louden, and Gonic, New Hampshire; to Wiscasset, Newcastle, and Biddeford, Maine; to Providence, Rhode Island; and into New York State. Potters' sons married daughters of potters—William Crolius, in 1724, and John Remmey, in 1736, each married a daughter of a Corselius whose stoneware pottery is shown on a 1730 map of New York City. In New Jersey, Morgans married Van Wickleses; Warnes married Lettses.

In the shaping of an American ceramic tradition, much more than familial ties and cultural precedents were to come into play. The potter found in the New World different clays, certain coloring oxides unavailable and others plentiful, his tools cruder, perhaps only a softer type of brick available with which to build his kiln, forcing him to modify his wares. He began to simplify his techniques and adapt his methods to the materials he had available and, as he adapted, so his clientele found that they had different needs. Certain forms evolved as answers to the daily needs of the community. As well, crosscurrents of other cultures were felt, sooner or later, with the result being a hybridized ware in America, different from, though certainly influenced by, that of any other nation in the world.

Concern about a major health hazard, however, was to drastically change the course of the infant American pottery industry. Public outcry against use of lead glaze began to be heard as early as 1785, when one report in the *Pennsylvania Mercury* catalogued the frightening list of afflictions caused by its mixture into food, the effects of which were most deadly to country people and to the poor who used such earthenware dishes almost exclusively. The writer went so far as to suggest a bonus or exemption to those potters who would produce salt-glazed stoneware.

It was a gradual process, but the use of lead-glazed ware declined steadily and, by the beginning of the nineteenth century, stoneware manufacturers were producing utensils for farm and dairy, bean pots, pudding and bundt pans, chamber pots and spittoons. Neither the materials nor the skills were at first available anywhere except in the New York area. The fine grained "blue" stoneware clay was to be found only in a geologic stratum underlying much of Staten Island and the Amboys of New Jersey, with smaller beds in Huntington, Long Island, and in Pennsylvania. Clay mining developed in New Jersey as a major industry, and the Amboy clays were shipped up the Hudson River to the Albany area and also overland to Bennington and elsewhere in New England, westward on the Erie Canal after its opening in 1826, and by sea to coastal points up and down the Atlantic seaboard.

So many potteries were established on the upper Hudson that a trade association called the "Albany Convention" was formed to regulate prices. A price list of the E. & L. P. Norton pottery of Bennington, Vermont, is headed "Adopted by Convention at Albany, N.Y., May 24, 1865."

Along with the change from earthenware to stoneware came modifications in form and interior glazes. In New England the first shapes to be introduced by potters were ovoid—the nearer to spherical the earlier they are likely to be. Straight cylindrical crocks were produced in the mid-nineteenth century; "beehive" shapes—jugs with straight sides and curved shoulders—were last to come. As for interior glazes, the use of slip from the Albany area is believed to have been introduced there around 1800, slowly spreading in use from its point of origin.

As no attempt has yet been made to correlate shapes and techniques with the dating of marks in Pennsylvania, the South, and westward into Ohio, etc., it is impossible to make anything but a general statement of a random nature: that many Pennsylvania potters continued using ovoid forms well into the nineteenth century and never seem to have adopted Albany slip for linings; that potters in Ohio and points westward continued until late in the century to produce ware of all types and decoration. The situation may have been somewhat the same in the South. A price list of S. Bell & Son of Strasburg, Virginia, of about 1882 lists both "bulged jars" and "straight jars."

The high point of stoneware production occurred around 1840. As the widening industrial revolution made other sorts of manufactured ware available for storing food, potters steadily reduced their production. During this period cobalt decoration grew more exuberant and skillful. More and more potters, however, found themselves producing sewer pipe and chemical stoneware and fire-clay products such as gas logs.

In an effort to diversify and to cut rising costs, Albany slip began, around 1848, to be used by increasing numbers of potters as an exterior glaze, frequently on stoneware pitchers with press-molded relief designs. The introduction of German "lager" beer in the 1870s gave a final surge of life to the industry. The decorative arts became permeated with brew. Potters such as Noah White, in Utica, New York, began turning out every imaginable accessory—coolers, pitchers, mugs, tankards. During the craze, around 1890, Charles Wingender and his brother William established their business in Haddonfield, New Jersey, and were in production until 1954. Press-molded and slipcast forms proliferated, often embellished with German toasts and were so similar to the foreign product that most people today believe they were all made in Germany.

Toward the end of the century, Bristol glaze began to be used on stoneware crocks and utilitarian wares at most major stoneware potteries from Bennington to Utica to Akron and even in the South. The difference went undetected by the public and it was easier and cheaper to produce. The rather mealy-surfaced opaque white or gray ground was adopted for the blue-sponged and blue-stencilled wares produced in the Middle West at the beginning of the twentieth century.

During the whole period of stoneware production, redware continued to be made. Its use gradually diminished to the supply of unglazed flowerpots and was adapted to architectural terra cotta tiles, enamelled bricks, and garden ornaments. And like the stoneware producers who began to lavish cobalt decoration on their pieces in the mid-nineteenth century, the rural redware potters grew more exuberant and inventive with decoration in the hope of capturing the attention of new customers.

Then came "folk art."

The products of our native potters had once been considered of no value, "common as clay." These objects, like the "dirt dishes" of the South, were looked down upon. Then, in the 1920s and '30s collectors began seeking the lowly examples of the potter's craft, having found that they suited a modern aesthetic sense and could be called "art." Slightly later, looking for redware and stoneware, made in a manner that suggested skills handed down from generation to generation; collectors found that they could call it "folk."

At present many have come to feel that the useful among the early wares makes them too predictable, too everyday to be referred to as "folk art." Certainly, art was the last thing in the mind of the potter. Therefore special attention is given today to whimseys, presentation pieces, gifts that the potter made for a newly married neighbor or for his grandchildren. This has meant better times for the handful of "folk" potters who have been struggling to make a living selling crocks and jars. Lanier Meaders of Mossy Creek, Georgia, the last "folk" potter using modified ash and lime glazes in the United States, has turned to making electric lamp bases and to the production of marvelously grotesque face-jugs that have found an every-widening market among "folk art" enthusiasts. His business has picked up, though he can't understand why. "If you can use it, they don't want it," he was heard to say. "If you can't use it, they'll pay anything for it."

Growing knowledge of many of the American decorative arts can be traced through successive issues of *The Magazine* ANTIQUES. In glass, for instance, one can follow a progression of increasingly sophisticated articles from 1922 up to and beyond the publication in 1941 of the subject's magnum opus, *American Glass,* by George and Helen McKearin. In ceramics, on the other hand, an excellent survey had appeared as early as 1878—in *The Ceramic Art* by Jennie J. Young—and the most comprehensive book yet written, *The Pottery and Porcelain of the United States* by Edwin AtLee Barber was published first in 1893.

By the time the first issue of ANTIQUES appeared in 1922, Jennie Young and Barber were no longer available to contribute material. Lura Woodside Watkins, indefatigable researcher, and Arthur W. Clement, whose books *Notes on American Ceramics* (1944) and *Our Pioneer Potters* (1947) are landmarks in the literature, did, however, make major contributions to the magazine over the years. Nevertheless, we must view the collective output of ANTIQUES as we would the middle episodes of a movie serial or a play in which much of the important early action has occurred off-stage. Otherwise we might take the inordinate number of pages devoted to the potteries of Bennington, Vermont, as an indication of their relative importance in our ceramic history rather than as a measure of collector enthusiasm at a particular point in time.

This perspective on the magazine also helps to explain why certain subjects seem to have been neglected or overlooked. There is here very little published touching on the sgraffito and slipware of Pennsylvania, but few authors have been interested or brave enough to tackle the subject seriously since the publication of Barber's *Tulip Ware of the Pennsylvania-German Potters* in 1903.

It does not explain, however, the lack of information on Southern stoneware or why the comments of Arthur W. Clement in his survey of "Ceramics in the South" are almost everything to be found on the colorfully glazed redwares of the Bells and their potting neighbors in the Shenandoah Valley. For further information on this subject the reader is urged to consult *The Shenandoah Pottery* by A. H. Rice and John Baer Stoudt, and *Folk Pottery of the Shenandoah Valley* by William E. Wiltshire, III.

Because of what has gone before and what is yet to come in this field of research, it has been impossible to produce in one volume a truly definitive anthology. Everything has been done, however, to make it as accurate as possible. Each article on pottery published over a fifty-five year period has been weighed in the balance, and, where fallacy or fancy proved greater than fact, discarded. Photographs have been checked for accuracy. People too often misattribute objects in their collections on the basis of pictures in books. More than one article has been left out because pottery of now questionable origin was shown that destroyed its credibility. In a few instances, misleading pictures could be removed and have been. In the case of Donald Webster's "The Digging of Potteries," pictures unrelated to the text were omitted for space considerations, and will be used in the next volume.

Since most early American pottery is unmarked, provenance is at best a risky undertaking. Family legend or the survival of a piece of pottery in a house or town has too often be used as the basis of attribution. Censuses were too often dependent on the memories of landladies; city directories were compiled in an age when spelling was often whimsical; genealogies demonstrate best the perpetuation of first names, each father handing on the same set of names to his sons, the possibility increasing geometrically with each generation that an infinite number of cousins will all have the same name.

All assumptions should be regarded with suspicion for what they are: the urge to answer every question, the need to put a fitting end to every story; many of those involving potters are clearly legendary. Few writers are willing to reserve judgment until all the shards have been counted.

The result of the editing—the sifting, sorting and checking—is a matter for the reader to judge. In the final analysis the amount of useful and accurate information seems extraordinarily high. Of primary importance, however, has been the opportunity of taking the information in this collection of articles from the pages of the past and placing it into the hands of readers who have new insights and enthusiams to bring to it. If this book excites the imagination and causes even one reader to contribute something in the future to our knowledge of American ceramics, it will have been an unqualified success.

I Unearthing the Past

The state of Virginia has proved an archeological bonanza. Worked under the auspices of the United States National Park Service, the State of Virginia, and a galaxy of private foundations, the digs near Jamestown, at Green Spring, at Yorktown, the finds at Glebe River,[1] and near Carter's Grove, have proved the existence of potters at work in colonial America as early as 1630 or '40. Archeology has fired the imaginations of an entirely new group of scholars, and some of the most exciting news of American ceramics is to be found, in recent years, in the periodicals of the various archeological societies.[2]

There is much work that might be done elsewhere, as indicated by the finds of Lura Woodside Watkins in New England and Robert J. Sim in New Jersey, working on their own in the 1930s and 40s—but amateur digging can spoil a site for any kind of scientific interpretation. Ruined pots and shards found in upper layers of earth may only represent domestic refuse of later decades, and real clues may be hopelessly scattered. Far better for enthusiastic amateurs to hire one of the many trained archeologists from among the new generation of graduates, who will know how to supervise the dig and how best to interpret, record, and keep track of the finds so that the knowledge gained is not lost to the totality of information accumulating.

In May, 1958 *The Magazine* ANTIQUES published the J. Paul Hudson article, "Earliest Yorktown Pottery" (pp. 18–19), which stated the few facts known then—slender clues which launched an investigation still continuing today, one of the most exciting and complete stories yet to be revealed about American industrial history. Within a short time after the article was written, quantities of wasters of both salt-glazed stoneware and of lead-glazed earthenware were found to have been used as foundation for the roadbeds of the city, and, in fact, were so widely scattered that it seemed the entire town was a waster heap. As Hudson wrote, the only documentary clues known of the existence of a potter in Yorktown were the slighting mentions of a poor potter of earthenware in status reports of the royal governor, William Gooch, to the Lords Commissioners for Trade and Plantations. These began in 1732 and ended with the report of 1741: "The poor potter is Dead, and the business of making potts and panns, is of little advantage to his Family, and as little Damage to the Trade of our Mother Country."[3] (This date was inaccurately stated by Hudson as 1734.)

The mere mention of a potter, insignificant and inferior though he may have been, coupled with a recently discovered ledger entry of 1725 by the young trader John Mercer, noting a large purchase of earthenware from one William Rogers, was enough to launch C. Malcolm Watkins (now Senior Curator of Cultural History at the Smithsonian Institution) on the trail of any and all William Rogerses—eventually to locate the will and inventory of a merchant of Yorktown, who, at his death in 1739, had instructed his executors that "no potters ware not burnt and fit for sale should be appraised." Great quantities of both stone and redware, a horse-drawn mill, and forty bushels of salt left little doubt that here was *the* potter of Yorktown, but far from poor was he. Among his possessions were twenty-nine slaves, expensive furnishings—fifty-two pictures in the hall alone—lands and holdings in and out of town, one old boat, and a new sloop. This William Rogers of Yorktown—Gentleman, Captain of the Troop, successful brewer, merchant, and, from 1734, "Surveyor of the Landings, Streets and Cosways in York Town" (and thereby licensed to make use of his otherwise useless wasters in the laying of the city streets)—was, in fact, one of the wealthiest of colonial entrepreneurs.

The eldest daughter, Susannah, had married a British sea captain, Thomas Reynolds, who appears to have given up the sea and assumed management of the family enterprises; his appointment as Justice of the Peace is recorded in 1745. That the pottery was continued after Rogers' death in 1739 is evident in the Gooch report of 1741; it may have continued as long as 1750. The property, including the pothouse, was sold in 1760.[4]

It remained only to find the site of the kiln and to dig. Adjacent lots 51 and 55, each about a half acre, had been acquired by Rogers in 1711 and were still owned by him at the time of his death; it was believed that he had made his home on one of them. On lot 51 a tremendous waster heap was located in 1967, and, in 1970 the kiln was located, partially under a modern garage. A dig was organized under the direction of Norman F. Barka.

In October, 1972, with the excavation then only one-third complete, Barka delivered a paper at the Winterthur Conference on American Ceramics, summarizing the findings to date—findings which posed as many questions as they presented answers. The rectangular shape of the Rogers kiln seems to have no precedent in either the Staffordshire or the London stoneware kilns; if anything, it is most like London-area delftware kilns, and yet, no tin-glazed wares were found on the site. The kiln was used extensively for salt-glazed stoneware, but was also used for lead-glazed earthenware. Of the thousands of fragments, sixteen different shapes of earthenware and seven of stoneware were determined to have been made, but not necessarily simultaneously. Among the shards was found a complete redware porringer believed to have been made on the site—lead-glazed and Dutch in form, incised "A.G./1720"—giving a possible starting date to the Rogers pottery operation.[5]

Barka today reports that more than ninety different rim shapes have been discovered, with perhaps ten or fifteen fragments of each type from which to project their shape, and another kiln has just recently been uncovered on the adjacent lot 55. As work has continued on the site, and masses of fragments and information have accumulated, he is about to publish another updated summary.[6]

Of all the ware produced at Yorktown, there appear to be two distinct types: London-area salt glaze of the half-brown/half-tan "Fulham" type, and Germanic-influenced redware, with slip decoration and forms very similar to those found on the Continent. Both distinct types were handled with great care: saggers were used, and all ware appears to have been fired to the biscuit state, and then refired when glazed.

Ironically, the most provocative of the original clues, the swan-sprigged mugs—one of which is pictured by Hudson (p. 19) in a sagger with which it was not found—have not been provably linked with the Yorktown pottery. No more have been unearthed than the original nine fragments.

The production of the Yorktown pottery was enormous and would have been to the unknowing virtually identical with the imports from London. That such top-quality production could and did exist in colonial America in the first half of the eighteenth century, and that distribution was possible up and down the Atlantic coast and as far as the West Indies, may have been suspected but had certainly never before been confirmed by historians. C. Malcolm Watkins quotes a 1742 petition filed in Charlestown, Massachusetts: ". . . there are large quantities of [stone] ware imported into this Province every year from New York, Philadelphia, and Virginia."

Edward Ayres has made a careful survey of the Yorktown shipping records of the period 1725–50, and has tallied every instance where a ship was recorded to have left Yorktown with earthenware not carried in. Of the seventeen ships so listed, three departed for the West Indies, three to North Carolina, five to Maryland, and three to New England. The Connecticut-registered sloop *Friendship* landed in 1733 with earthenware, but left with "Virginia-made earthenware" (the only specific reference found by Ayres); and the sloop *Medford,* in 1735–6, brought earthenware from New England, but did not leave with any in its cargo.

Paradoxically, the royal representative in the colony, Governor William Gooch, the man charged with the protection of English mercantile interests, is found to have deliberately and consistently misled his superiors. With every belittling mention of "one poor Potters' [sic] work for earthen Ware" there appear mitigating words ". . . so very inconsiderable that there has been little less of that Commodity imported . . . ." Arlene Palmer's recently-completed study of the South Jersey glassworks at Wistarburgh describes a parallel situation, some thirty years later. Contrary to the fact that Caspar Wistar and his son, Richard, were among the most successful of colonial merchants, and that their enterprise, already twenty-nine years in existence, could hardly be termed a failure, the New Jersey governor, William Franklin, reported to Lord Hillsborough on June 14, 1768: ". . . A Glass House was erected about Twenty Years ago in Salem County, which makes Bottles, and a very coarse Green Glass for Windows, used only in some of the Houses of the poorer Sort of People . . . . It seems probable that, notwithstanding the Duty, Fine Glass can still be imported into America cheaper than it can be made there."[7]

This governor's report seems to have followed the outline suggested by his father, Benjamin Franklin, writing from London, who had advised him of the approach taken by other governors: "They are all very much in the same strain, that there are no manufactures of any consequence. . . . These accounts are very satisfactory here, and induce the parliament to despise and take no notice of the Boston resolutions . . . . You have only to report a glass-house for coarse window glass and bottles, and some domestic manufactures of linen and woollen for family use that do not half clothe the inhabitants, all the finer goods coming from England and the like . . . ."

Taken together, the Gooch/Franklin reports shed light on the possibility of a tacit agreement in official circles to keep silent regarding any extensive production in America, to give the appearance of compliance with the spirit of the British mercantile policy. Clearly, it seems that inferior colonial manufactures were tolerated, but that "all the finer goods" were to come from England at cost plus tax, a policy which our ancestors evidently resisted and circumvented. How ironic that, by the mid-nineteenth century, without the use of force, the conviction of American inferiority had become so firmly seated in the American psyche that merchants refused to stock domestic crockery or china unless it came marked with spurious British or French trademarks, or were left unmarked so that they might "pass." How many times have we heard it said and declared ourselves, "It's too good to be American; it must have been made in England"?

[1]Edward A. Chappell, "Morgan Jones and Dennis White: Country Potters in Seventeenth-Century Virginia," *Virginia Cavalcade* 24, No. 4 (Spring 1975).

[2]*Historical Archeology,* the journal of the Society for Historical Archeology is one example.

[3]C. Malcolm Watkins and Ivor Noël Hume, "The 'Poor Potter' of Yorktown," *U.S. National Museum Bulletin 249, Contributions from the Museum of History and Technology, Paper 54, The Smithsonian Institution* (1967).

[4]Conversations with Norman F. Barka, Associate Professor of Anthropology, College of William and Mary, and Director of Southside Historical Sites, Inc.; and with Edward Ayres, Research Historian for Southside.

[5]Norman F. Barka, "The Kiln and Ceramics of the 'Poor Potter' of Yorktown: A Preliminary Report," *Winterthur Conference Report 1972, Ceramics in America.*

[6]To be published in an early 1977 issue of the bimonthly *Archeology.*

[7]Arlene Palmer, "Glass Production in Eighteenth-Century America: The Wistarburgh Enterprise," *Winterthur Portfolio No. 11,* 1976.

On the digging of potteries

BY DONALD BLAKE WEBSTER, *Curator, Canadiana department, Royal Ontario Museum*

IN STUDYING EARLY pottery one sooner or later turns to archaeology to establish a reasonable and accurate connection between surviving objects whose provenance is not known and documentary research into potters and potteries.

The methods of excavating early potteries are determined largely by logic and experience.* Archaeological digging of this kind requires the background, money, time, physical facilities, and access to specialized analytical talent to glean all the information inherent in a site, and to assess fully and publish the results. Careful and often slow digging, keeping good records, and cleaning and reconstructing the artifacts recovered are essential. Moreover, the results of even a well-done dig left unpublished are useless to everyone but the digger.

Assuming the ideal, that a site has been undisturbed, former buildings may still be visible as mounds outlining foundations, for an abandoned pottery can easily become overgrown and covered with topsoil within half a century. Most undisturbed pottery sites have quantities of potsherds and sometimes brick lying on the surface, pushed up by frost and the growth of roots. The nature of these remains can provide a rough indication of what is likely to be found by excavating.

The underground remains of most North American pottery sites consist of production buildings, kilns, and waster dumps. Generally speaking, the buildings are archaeologically the least important of the three. Any structure could serve as a pottery shop, and shops and storage buildings were usually abandoned and empty before their demolition or eventual collapse.

The remains of kilns—usually only their brick or stone floors or bases—are most important. They indicate the kiln's shape and what type of draft it had, while the surrounding rubble usually provides clues to its upper structure. Remains or outlines of fireplace bases (generally two or four in North American earthenware kilns) are often evident, and sometimes traces of the vertical structure of the fireplaces are found as well. Alongside the remains of the kilns there are often setting tiles, stilts, wedges, and saggers which serve as evidence of firing techniques. Occasionally there are even shards and pottery dating from the time of the final firing of the kiln.

Stone base of a domed updraft kiln at the William Eby Pottery which operated at Conestogo, Ontario, from 1855 to 1907. The excavation was made in 1967 and 1968. The string grid, in half-meter squares, helps the archaeologist render the stonework on the site accurately on graph paper.

Partial vertical section of the waster dump at the William Eby Pottery.

Waster dumps, usually located near the kilns, contain pottery rejected for one reason or another during production. Over the years the piles often grew to between three and five feet deep and spread over an entire pottery yard, for the typical earthenware pottery was hardly a tidy operation. Because waster dumps always contain many essentially identical pots, all fragmentary, digging must be very methodical. The process is somewhat akin to working on ten thousand different jigsaw puzzles, each with pieces missing, but with a hundred thousand extra pieces thrown in which fit none of the puzzles. Objects found in and around a kiln can be associated with its last firings. This is not the case with waster dumps which, although far more productive of masses of material and reconstructible examples, are more difficult to dig and to interpret.

No two excavators agree on the best method for digging waster dumps, and indeed conditions probably vary too much for there to be a single, ideal method. Some prefer to dig every shard from the full depth of a five-foot square and depend on acres of table space and hundreds of hours to make something of it all. Others, without this sort of space or time, virtually reconstruct pottery in the ground with a trowel in one hand, a roll of masking tape on the other wrist, and a pile of paper bags alongside in which to put pots that have been taped together.

The primary drawback of waster dumps is that they represent only the pottery's rejects, not its full production. What is found in them is most useful for technical analyses of the pottery and identifications of types of objects made. They do not, however, offer valid clues to dates, total production, percentages of different types of objects made, or pottery successfully fired and sold.

Pottery thrown on a waster dump usually shows visible signs of why it was rejected. Much was discarded after the first, or biscuit, firing, and is discolored or misshapen owing to reduction or overfiring. Occasionally biscuit-fired earthenware was covered with lead oxide glaze before being discarded, but as this pottery was never refired, the glaze appears as a coating of orange-red powder. Stilts, saggers, pins, and other kiln furniture turn up in quantity in waster dumps. One also finds shards fused together or finished and distorted pots, indicating that all or part of a kiln load of stacked pottery collapsed during firing. Inappropriate glaze mixtures or glazes fired at too hot a temperature appear bubbled or discolored, while structurally weak pottery consistently shows fractures in the same places.

Information gleaned from kilns and waster dumps, when correlated with analyses of the glazes and bodies of pottery recovered, provides a very good over-all interpretation of the technical level of pottery operations. Moreover, there is no reason to doubt that recoveries from early pottery sites represent most of the forms produced at the potteries. The pottery excavated thus provides a reliable and precise key to attributing existing intact pieces.

Competent digging and particularly competent analysis of what has been excavated require a prior knowledge of what to look for and how to interpret the findings. A great problem is uncontrolled private digging or pot hunting by individual amateurs in spite of the fact that early pottery sites rarely produce intact objects. These and other such haphazard excavations should be prohibited by law, as they are in many places.

Archaeological exploration of industrial sites is not an end in itself, nor is it enough simply to report the results of a dig. Ideally, archaeological findings will be considered as only one of a number of analytical tools and correlated with historical and documentary findings.

---

*A good general introduction to archaeological techniques and the interpretations of finds is Ivor Noël-Hume, *Historical Archaeology* (New York, 1969).

AN ANTIQUES BOOK PREVIEW

A late seventeenth-century pottery kiln site near Jamestown

BY IVOR NOËL HUME, *Chief archeologist, Colonial Williamsburg*

"THERE IS LIKEWISE FOUND great Variety of Earths for Physick, Cleansing, Scouring, and making all sorts of Potters-Ware; such as Antimony, Talk, yellow and red Oker, Fullers-Earth, Pipe-Clay, and other fat and fine Clays, Marle, &c. In a word, there are all kinds of Earth fit for Use." So wrote Robert Beverley in his *History and Present State of Virginia* (1705). But not a word did he say of any potter in the colony who was making use of these abundant resources.

Because colonial Virginia was seated on a massive bed of natural clay, it has long been supposed that the colonists manufactured much of their own pottery. However, the records fail to support this contention and leave us with nothing more than a few hints that are more tantalizing than helpful. In 1622 Nathaniel Butler wrote that the "Furnaces for Glass and Pots [are] at a stay and in smale hope," a statement that has since been misquoted to read "the furnaces for glass and pottery are in decay." This does not necessarily mean the same thing, as the reference may well have been to siege pots associated with the Jamestown glassmaking project. Two years earlier the Virginia Company in London had prepared a list of tradesmen needed in the colony, and among these was an unspecified number of potters; but there is no record that they ever arrived. Later in the century we find a contract for the setting up of a pottery factory in Virginia's Northern Neck, but here again there is no evidence that the wheels began to turn. It is not until the second quarter of the eighteenth century that we find any direct and unequivocal documentary evidence that a potter was actually working in the colony. Consequently we are forced to rely on archeology for everything we know of pottery-making in Virginia in the seventeenth century.

Just as one swallow maketh not summer so one spoiled pot does not proclaim the presence of a factory. Although a few undoubted fragments of kiln refuse and occasional scraps of wasters have been found at Jamestown, the evidence for pottery factories in the town or, indeed, on the island, is thin to the point of transparency. There is no doubt that pottery was being made in Virginia in considerable quantities, perhaps as early as the second quarter of the seventeenth century, but as yet the sources of it have not been established with any certainty.

In the 1930's a well excavated at Jamestown yielded the most obvious waster found there, a large jar badly overfired and with its rim sagging into a wry and slightly melancholy smile. This was unquestionably a true waster, and the more adventurous authorities hailed it as a product of Jamestown—certainly a reasonable assumption, for there seemed little point in bringing so pathetic a pot from a factory site elsewhere. But as it turned out, that was exactly what had happened. Eventually the pot's quite different place of origin was discovered, not by brilliant Sherlock Holmesian deduction but through a combination of improbable coincidences.

During the summer of 1961 my wife and I, who had been spending our weekends on a beach on the Surry shore of the James River, sought a quiet spot on the north bank where the fishing might be better. The chosen place lay beneath a somewhat dangerously eroding cliff about three miles upriver from Jamestown. One day, while beaching the boat, my wife looked down and saw a fragment of an eighteenth-century German stoneware tankard lying at the water's edge. As a result of this small discovery I began to amuse myself by walking along the shore and picking up fragments of pottery. A close examination of these shards showed that the majority were of local manufacture and that a high proportion exhibited minor waster characteristics. On the strength of these finds a more serious examination of the shore was made, including skin diving in the river in the areas of the pottery's greatest concentration. The latter operation resulted in the finding of further wasters and the discovery of bricks and tiles lying in the river mud.

After we had established the possible location of a kiln on the basis of the shard concentrations on the shore below, five minutes of probing with steel rods along the top of the cliff revealed the potter's waster tip, or dumping ground. A series of test holes subsequently determined the extent of the surviving working area, although no kiln structure could be found. At that point we stopped exploring to make a careful search of the documentary records; but as always in James City County, this was unrewarding because the official court records were destroyed during the Civil War.

The only clue came from a 1683 survey of the Governor's Land (a tract assigned to that official) which showed that the site in question had been rented by one Edward Challis, who had come to the colony as an indentured servant in 1639 and had later acquired an acre of land at Jamestown; but there was no evidence that he was a potter or that he owned a pottery. However, we did learn that the shore line of the Governor's Land, was rapidly eroding even in the seventeenth century, a state of affairs that still existed in 1961. When in the autumn of that year, a large section of the cliff fell away, part of a refuse pit dug into the clay sixty yards east of the supposed kiln area was revealed. Excavated, the contents of this pit were found to comprise kiln refuse of a character quite different from that found in the main waster tip to the west: here the uneven thickness of the vessels' walls and their feeble rims suggested the work of a none-too-skilled apprentice. Because his products were concentrated at some distance from the main water area (although a few of his shards were present there) a picture emerged of a student potter setting up his own kiln under the wing of the master craftsman.

In December 1961 both the main waster tip and the secondary site were excavated by Colonial Williamsburg, but neither revealed any kiln foundations. From the former came quantities of waste products showing that the potter had been in business in no small way, producing jars ranging in height from eight and one-half to thirteen inches, as well as cream pans and bowls of various sizes, pipkins, jugs, dishes, colanders, and cups. So great were the quantities of fragments that it was possible to determine from the ratio of overfired to underfired shards which types of vessel had been fired in which parts of the kiln. In addition, these same clues indicated the variations of temperature either from firing to firing or in different parts of the kiln. Slabs of sandstone were found in the debris bearing the marks of pots that had stood upside down on them, while scraps of the stone were seen still adhering to broken rims. From this it was deduced that the chamber had been lined with pieces of sandstone instead of the gravel that would have been more suitable but was not readily available. Like the clay used in making the pottery, the sandstone was found exposed in the cliff face below the kiln site.

Although it was depressing to find that the kiln itself had almost certainly been eroded away, we were extremely fortunate in that we enjoyed the assistance of James E. Maloney, owner of the modern Williamsburg Pottery, who had served his own apprenticeship working a wood-fired kiln within a mile or two of the Challis site and using the same ocher-flecked clay. In moments of extreme frustration every archeologist is prepared to barter his soul for an opportunity to talk to the people who once inhabited his site. The presence of Jim Maloney could have been the answer to just such a wish: here was a man who had worked under almost exactly the same conditions as the Challis site potter and who had met with precisely the same difficulties. Maloney was thus able to tell us which structural fragments had come from which parts of the kiln, and to explain why the waster pots had warped and fired as they did. At the close of the project he completed his contribution by reproducing examples of the Challis pots, even to duplicating the consistent error that had caused many of the original potter's cream pans to lose their bottoms.

We had been stunned by the huge quantity of pan sides that had been found amid the wasters, while their bottoms had been stacked in piles and used as kiln props. It was almost as though the potter deliberately broke his pans just to make use of their flat bases, a most unlikely state of affairs. But when the bottom cracked out of Maloney's reproduction, he was immedi-

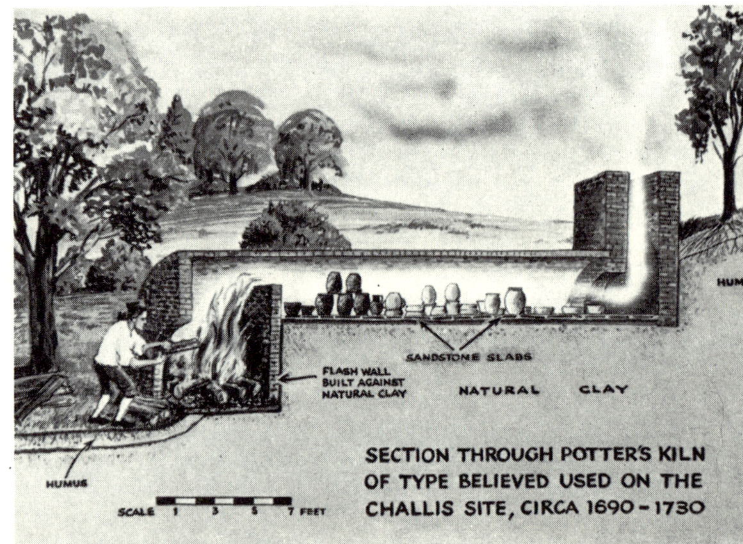

Artist's impression of the type of kiln that may have fired the Challis site pottery.
Illustrations by courtesy of Colonial Williamsburg.

ately able to determine the cause. It seemed that the angle of wall and base was very sharp and in shaping it there was a tendency for the craftsman's fingernail to make a small scratch around the junction, a scratch that developed into a major structural fault as the pan shrank in the kiln. This was obvious when Maloney pointed it out, but less easily explained was the fact that he discovered it at the first attempt, while the Challis potter turned out scores, even hundreds, of pans without, apparently, realizing the cause of the trouble.

The reproduced pots were fired in a modern oil-burning kiln and so their lead-glazed bodies emerged with an even color—an ideal that was probably never achieved by the colonial potter, the smoke from whose wood-burning kiln caused wide and uncontrollable variations of oxidation and reduction. Thus a single pot might come out of the kiln with its glaze color running the gamut from orange, through green, to deep purple. Similarly variations in temperature caused pots made from the same local clay to vary in body color from pale pink or buff to a dark gray. This taught us an immensely valuable lesson, and one that all collectors of coarse earthenwares should remember: it is impossible to determine the place of origin of a colonial pot on the evidence of the color of either body or glaze. Indeed, this is true of any simple earthenware, of any date, that has been fired in a wood-burning kiln. On the other hand, the manual idiosyncrasies of the potter that show themselves most clearly in the formation of such features as rims, feet, and handles, provide an inadvertent trade-mark which can reasonably be used in identification. Thus, the Challis site potter's products could be traced to Jamestown, and his waster to the filling of a well there.

Small jar and cream pan (restored), most common products of the Challis kiln site.

The presence of the Challis ware at Jamestown in contexts of the late seventeenth century, coupled with its total absence from the soil of Williamsburg, strongly suggested that the factory had ceased production by the beginning of the eighteenth century. Although no dating evidence was obtained from the main waster tip, our luck continued to hold. When the secondary area was cleared, a quantity of domestic refuse was found overlying the apprentice potter's waste, and in it were numerous wine bottles and a stoneware tankard made at Yorktown, all of which had been thrown away by about 1730. This find provided a terminal date (though one probably some years too late) for the potting ventures on the Challis site.

Reproductions of a Challis jar and pan, made by James E. Maloney of the Williamsburg Pottery.

Besides the objects already mentioned, the domestic rubbish included a splendid array of agricultural tools, equestrian fittings, cutlery, and miscellaneous metal objects—plus fragments of two lead-glazed earthenware bowls. Both of these last were made from the local clay, and both possessed rolled rims, forms frequently encountered in archeological deposits dating from the first quarter of the eighteenth century. We have no idea where in Tidewater Virginia these often-found bowls were made, and the craftsman is known to us only as the "rolled-rim potter." But if chance could yield the secrets of the Challis factory, why, chance may yet reveal the kiln of the rolled-rim potter, and- to mutilate the bard further—it may do so without our stir.

 This article is based on a chapter from Mr. Noël Hume's forthcoming book, *Here Lies Virginia,* to be published by Alfred A. Knopf Inc.

Earliest Yorktown pottery

BY J. PAUL HUDSON, Museum curator, Colonial National Historical Park, Yorktown, Virginia

Historic Yorktown—scene of the American and French victory over Cornwallis' British army in October 1781 which ended the American Revolution—can now claim the honor of being one of the few places in the southern Colonies where pottery (including stoneware) was made over two centuries ago, perhaps as early as 1700 and certainly by 1732, the year George Washington was born.

During the autumn months of 1956 three different localities in Yorktown yielded finds of pottery saggers, those receptacles of baked clay in which certain vessels were held while being fired in a kiln to protect them from coming in contact with the flames; and in the same places fragments of stoneware mugs, pitchers, and jugs were unearthed. Other objects found in association with the saggers, including clay pipes and wine bottles, were of types in common use in Virginia between 1690 and 1735.

Near one cache of sagger fragments the upper third of a mottled brown stoneware jug was found, a "waster" which had been discarded by the potter because it had cracked in the kiln. Glossy lead glaze covering part of its broken edge indicated that the crack had occurred before the jug was removed from the kiln, permitting glaze to run into the crack.

The saggers are cylindrical in shape, and in three sizes: six inches, seven inches, and eight and three-quarters inches in height. Each has three arches reaching two-thirds of the way up the receptacle and an open slot on the fourth side to permit the handle of a mug to extend outside. The purpose of the arches was to permit the entrance of the salt vapor when sodium chloride was thrown into the kiln.

Unearthed near the sagger fragments were circular stoneware disks, used for separating the saggers when they were piled on top of each other in the kiln. Small supports in the form of broken pieces of stoneware, used to reduce adhesion between the base of the mug or pitcher and the bottom of the sagger, were also excavated. Some of these were square, others had fairly sharp tops which prevented the glaze from adhering too much and left only a slight mark on the vessel after it had been fired.

Nine of the mug fragments unearthed were decorated in relief with a swan. As all were found within one hundred yards of historic Swan Tavern—which was operating in Yorktown as early as 1722—it seems likely that the mugs were made specifically for use in the tavern. Seven of the mug and pitcher fragments, including one waster, were impressed with initials *WR* surmounted by a crown. This monogram evidently referred to William III, who ruled England between 1689 and 1702.

Only two or three contemporary references uncovered thus far indicate that pottery was made in Virginia during the late seventeenth century or first half of the eighteenth. In 1688 the Rev. John Clayton wrote that he had made a pottery crucible in Virginia. This activity

The Swan Tavern, Yorktown, Virginia; known to have been used as a tavern as early as 1722.

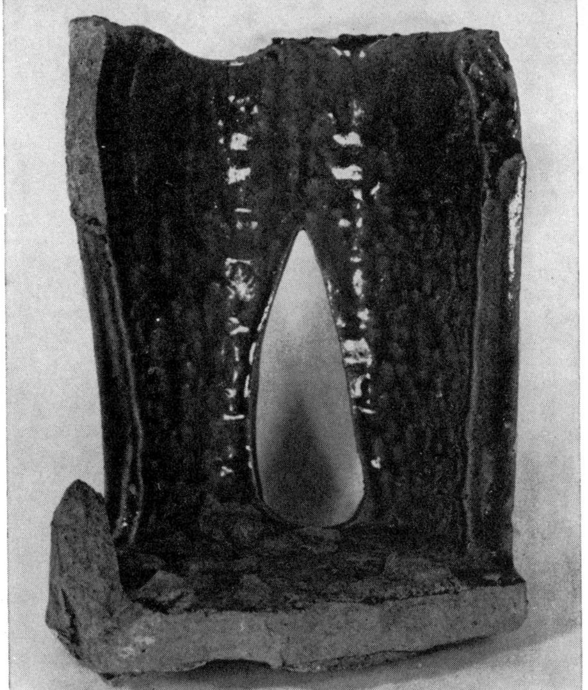

Incomplete sagger unearthed at Yorktown.

Mug in mottled brown saltglaze decorated with a swan in relief; found near the Swan Tavern.

was described in a letter Clayton sent to the Royal Society in London:

But to return again to the Nature of the [Virginia] Earth, which may be pretty well gathered from what I have already said; I have observed, that at five or six Yards deep, at the Breaks of some Banks, I have found Veins of Clay, admirable good to make Pots, Pipes, of the like of, and Whereof I suppose the Indians make their Pipes, and Pots, to boil their Meat in, which they make very handsomely, and will endure the Fire better than most Crucibles: I took of this Clay, dryed, powdered, and sifted it; powdered and sifted Potsherds, and Glass; three parts, two parts and one part as I remember, and therewith made a large Crucible, which was the best I yet ever tried in my Life; I took it once red hot out of the Fire, and clapt it immediately into Water, and it started not at all. (*A Letter from Mr. John Clayton, Rector of Crofton at Wakefield in Yorkshire, to the Royal Society, May 12, 1688, Giving an Account of several Observables in Virginia, and in his Voyage thither, more particularly concerning the Air.* Reprinted in Peter Force, *Tracts and Other Papers,* Washington, 1844, pp. 26-27.)

Mug in position in the sagger.

It is not known where John Clayton made his crucible, but as he spent much of his time on the peninsula between the James and York Rivers there is a possibility that the experiment was conducted in York County.

Another contemporary reference mentions the "poor potter" of Yorktown, meaning, perhaps, a poor craftsman rather than a poor man. Governor William Gooch, in a report to the Lord Commissioner of the Board of Trade in 1732, stated that:

The same poor Potter's work is still continued at Yorktown without any great improvement or advantage to the owner or any injury to the trade of Great Britain.

In 1734 Governor Gooch reported that "the poor Potter is dead," and hinted that the making of pottery in Virginia had ended.

The evidence uncovered to date, therefore—Governor Gooch's two reports, together with the sagger fragments and the pieces of salt-glazed stoneware mugs, jugs, and pitchers unearthed—seems to prove beyond a shadow of a doubt that pottery was produced at Yorktown during the 1700-1734 period.

Acknowledgment is made to Ivor Noël Hume, formerly of the Guildhall Museum in London and now chief archeologist of Colonial Williamsburg, who was the first to identify the sagger fragments found at Yorktown.

II Redware—The Germanic Influence

The Museum of Early Southern Decorative Arts in Winston-Salem, North Carolina, is currently conducting a field research program to locate and identify objects made in the South before 1821. And, having obtained microfilm of every available Southern newspaper published prior to that year, it has engaged a team of readers to extract and catalogue any pertinent information. The correlation of the two efforts should result in the production of a body of knowledge that will establish MESDA as *the* study center for the Southern decorative arts. More importantly, such intensive research should prove of invaluable assistance to the collector and student of Southern pottery. The questions now remaining for investigation are many.

For instance, recently some question has been raised concerning the origin of the two bottle forms illustrated in Arthur W. Clement's "Ceramics in the South" (pp. 22–24). On the basis of shards removed from excavations at Salem and Bethabara, North Carolina, it is felt that the potters of these areas rarely decorated their slipware with names, dates, birds or animals; yet the huge charger (p. 25) made by Gottfried Aust, presumably as a trade sign, has all three. Is this an exception to a general rule or is there much more evidence to unearth?

Anyone wishing to learn more about these slipware pieces should consult *The Moravian Potters in North Carolina* by John Bivins, Jr.

There are just as many questions concerning the redware of the North. In his article on Pennsylvania lighting devices (pp. 34–35), William J. Truax describes the pottery lamp in Figure 3 as a "signed piece." Even if the incisions in the lamp were meant to spell out the letters "I-S-I," there is no reason to call them the initials of the maker. Unusual pieces of pottery were often created as gifts, inscribed with the names or initials of the persons for whom they were intended. More common wares were sometimes marked with the name of a grocer or merchant, while the potter preferred to remain anonymous or place his own name or initials underneath. Collectors should be warned that not all pottery lamps are American and that many have been imported in recent years from Europe and the Near East.

Since the pottery of Jacob Medinger (pp. 32–33) is today collectible in its own right and no longer regarded only as an imitation of Pennsylvania-German slipware, it should be stated that he and William J. McAlister made a number of pieces of sgraffito in 1921, but started a more extensive production in 1924. These facts were reported by Oliver Christman in a catalogue relating to the loan exhibit of Medinger pottery in May, 1976, at the Great Pottstown Antiques Show.

A brief comment can be made about the "china teapot" described on the first page of Ada Walker Camehl's article (pp. 39–43) on Mehwaldt. It is not porcelain but English pearlware, of the type thought years ago to have been produced by the Bristol Pottery. An illustrated example may be seen on page 208 of *China Collecting in America* by Alice Morse Earle, New York, 1892.

Slip-decorated redware mug with inscription, "John Hildebrand/his mug." Attributed to the pottery of Friedrich Hildebrand, Tylersport, Montgomery County, Pennsylvania, ca. 1825–40.

Chocolate-colored vase and mottled brown pitcher. Both pieces of redware marked, "A. W. BACHER," presumably for Anthony W. Baecher, who potted near Winchester, Virginia, from 1870.

Red earthenware pitcher and jar, the pitcher incised, "Henry Schofield, Conowingo, Cecil Co." Mr. Schofield purchased a pottery just across the Maryland line from Pennsylvania toward the end of the century and worked there, seasonally, until the 1940s.

Redware reconstructed from fragments excavated at the site of Jamestown, Virginia. *Courtesy National Park Service.*

CERAMICS IN THE SOUTH

By ARTHUR W. CLEMENT

We continue our delving into Southern antiques this month with a consideration of ceramics. Mr. Clement, a trustee of the Brooklyn Museum, is a recognized specialist in American ceramics, author of Our Pioneer Potters.

The story of Southern ceramics cannot yet be told with any degree of completeness. This article must therefore be regarded merely as an attempt to gather together some of the information which is now available.

Virginia

In his *Briefe and True Report of the New Foundland of Virginia,* published in London in 1588, Thomas Hariot noted the presence in Virginia of clay suitable for making bricks. There is evidence that bricks actually were made at an early date in Jamestown. No pottery site has been found there, but fragmentary redware has been excavated by the National Park Service (Antiques, May 1936), consisting of simple bowls, pots, and plates, glazed on the inside only with a transparent orange or green glaze. It is the generally accepted opinion that this redware was made somewhere in the vicinity of Jamestown before 1700, and perhaps earlier.

Excavations have also been carried on at the site of the early settlement of Kicotan, at Hampton, Virginia, which became an English colony in 1619. An account of the findings of the Brittingham brothers at Kicotan has recently been published by C. Malcolm Watkins of the U. S. National Museum (*Norfolk-Virginian Pilot,* September 17, 1950). The pottery finds included two redware bowls similar to those found at Jamestown.

The earliest authentic reference to the making of pottery in Virginia is a recorded agreement dated November 2, 1677, between Dennis White of Westmoreland County and Morgan Jones, to be partners "in making and selling earthenware" for the term of five years.

There is no foundation for the assertion that there were "a number of small potters in Virginia who carried on a thriving business" by 1649. This is based entirely on an unsupported statement in an anonymous promotional tract, *A Perfect Description of Virginia (London, 1649).*

In 1688 John Clayton of Virginia, according to his own account, succeeded in making "a large Crucible, which was the best I ever yet tried in my life" (Peter Force, *Colonial Tracts,* Volume III): ". . . At the Breaks of some Banks," he wrote, "I have found Veins of Clay; admirable good to make pots, pipes or the like. . . . I took this Clay, dryed, powdered and sifted it, powdered and sifted Pot-sherds and Glass; three parts, two parts and one part, as I remembered, and therewith made a large Crucible . . . I took it once red hot out of the Fire, and clapt it immediately into Water and it started not at all."

It is not until well over a century later that we again find record of a pottery in Virginia, though it would seem that there must have been various ventures in the meantime. Between 1824 and 1887, pottery was made by Peter Bell and his sons Solomon and Samuel at Winchester and Strasburg, which has been exhaustively considered in *Shenandoah Pottery* by Rice and Stout. The Bells' redware is noteworthy chiefly for its brightly colored decoration, done in colored glazes or slips; their stoneware is dark gray, with decoration in blue.

There was a pottery at Alexandria, operated at first by John Swann. It was acquired in 1841 by Benedict C. Milburn, who continued with his sons to operate it for many years (Antiques, February 1945). Gray stoneware was made there, decorated with blue leaves, flowers, and other designs. Examples marked *Alexandria, D. C.* may be dated before 1846, when the Federal government returned Alexandria to Virginia.

The pottery made by Anthony W. Baecher at Winchester, Virginia, from 1870 to 1887 is so well modeled and glazed as to justify fully his designation as a master potter (Antiques, February 1944).

The Carolinas

At Bethabara and at Salem, North Carolina, very successful potteries were operated in the eighteenth century by Moravian congregations (Antiques, January 1935). The Bethabara pottery fired its first kiln in 1756, that at Salem in 1768. The potter at both was Brother Aust. That there was a great demand for his slip-decorated redware is shown by extracts

Earthenware Water Bottle, slip-decorated, dated 1800, by the Moravians at Winston-Salem. *Brooklyn Museum.*

Vase and Sugar Bowl, glazed earthenware, made by Anthony W. Baecher of Winchester, Virginia. *Courtesy Brooklyn Museum.*

from the records of both congregations, printed as a supplement to *Shenandoah Pottery.*

We have record of an ill-fated venture in South Carolina in the eighteenth century. In the *South Carolina Gazette* for October 4, 1770, Messrs. Bartlam and Company advertised that they were about to open a "China manufactory and Pottery" near Charleston. On November 20, 1770, they advertised for apprentices, and on January 31, 1771, the following advertisement appeared:

> John Bartlam, having opened his Pottery and China Manufactory in Old Church Street, will be obliged to Gentlemen in this Country or others, who will be so kind to send him samples of any kinds of fine clay upon their Plantations, etc., in order to make them Trials of. He already makes what is called Queensware, equal to any imported; and if he meets with suitable encouragement makes no doubt of being able to supply the demand of the whole Province."

The sad sequel to this promising beginning is related by none other than Josiah Wedgwood, in an *Address to the Workmen in the Pottery on the Subject of Entering into the Service of Foreign Manufacturers* (1783):

> About seventeen years ago, Mr. Bartlam, a master potter who had been unsuccessful here, went to South Carolina, and by offers made from thence, very advantageous in appearance, prevailed upon some of our workmen to leave their country and come to him. They took ship at Bristol and . . . they at last arrived safe and began a work near Charleston. This adventure being encouraged by the government of that province, the men, puffed up with expectations of becoming gentlemen soon, wrote to their friends here what a fine way they were in and this encouraged others to follow them. But change of climate and manner of living accompanied perhaps with a certain disorder of mind . . . carried them off so fast, that recruits could not be raised from England sufficient to supply the place of the dead men. In Mr. Goodwin's own words to me, whose son was one of them, they *fell sick as they came and all died quickly,* his son among the rest.
>
> Mr. Bartlam thus deprived of his whole colony returned once more to England, in order to raise some fresh supplies. In a little while by dint of great promises he prevailed upon four to go with him, but the event of this expedition was only more labor and more lives lost. For though the people there were disposed to encourage this infant manufactory, and the assembly of that state gave him at different times five hundred pounds to keep him on two legs as long as they could, yet all would not do; the work was abandoned and only one man returned to England, the rest, with Mr. Bartlam himself are either known to be dead or have not been heard of since.

The sole survivor was identified by Wedgwood in a footnote as "William Ellis of Hanley, who informs me that the wages promised were good enough, a guinea a week with their board, but they never received half of it."

There is an interesting connection between this ill-fated Charleston pottery and the one at Salem, North Carolina. According to the Moravian Church Diary (as translated in *Shenandoah Pottery*), William Ellis, the sole survivor, arrived in Salem on December 8, 1773. He stated that he understood how to make and glaze queensware. At Brother Aust's suggestion, the Moravian conference agreed to build a suitable kiln, and Ellis was to teach Aust what he knew about glazing. Such knowledge as Aust already had on the subject he had learned from another traveling potter.

By the following May Ellis succeeded in firing creamware and also stoneware. All the pieces had to be made by hand on the potter's bench. Ellis evidently did not stay in Salem very long, for the diary goes on to record that "the good man found our town too narrow for him, so for the present he has bid us a friendly farewell."

In the nineteenth century there were at least two pottery-making ventures in South Carolina. A pottery was established at Kaolin in 1856 by William H. Farrar, who had been a stockholder in Fenton's pottery at Bennington, Vermont. He believed that pottery should be made where the clay was found. Later managers included such able potters as Josiah Jones, formerly of the Cartlidge pottery at Greenpoint, New York, who brought with him to Kaolin some of the models which he had previously made for Charles Cartlidge. Examples of his corn pitcher made at Kaolin survive, in Rockingham ware and in porcelain. Others associated with the pottery were Decius W. Clark, also of Fenton's pottery, and Alexander H. Stephens, later to be vice president of the Confederacy, who was one of the financial backers.

Rockingham, white ware, and porcelain were made at Kaolin. The Brooklyn Museum has an exceptionally well modeled and glazed Rebekah-at-the-well teapot marked *S. P.*

POTTERY WHIPPET *(c. 1833).* By Solomon Bell, Winchester, Virginia. Length, 9½ inches; height, 6 inches. Semi-mat glaze of bright red-brown accented with touches of cream color. *Courtesy of John Ramsay.*

Co., which was made at Kaolin. During the Civil War, porcelain and stoneware telegraph insulators were supplied to the Confederate government, until the pottery was destroyed by fire in 1863 or 1864.

Another South Carolina pottery, operated by Colonel Thomas J. Davies at Bath, supplied the Confederate hospitals with a quantity of crude earthenware between 1863 and 1865. According to Barber's *Pottery and Porcelain of the United States,* this was "black or brown, clumsy, and entirely devoid of ornamentation." Some of the so-called monkey jugs are thought to have been made by slaves on Colonel Davies' plantation.

Georgia

Perhaps the most interesting episode in American ceramics is the story of Andrew Duché and his porcelain experiments at Savannah. In 1735, Duché was making redware at New Windsor, South Carolina, but on the urging of General Oglethorpe he removed his pottery to Savannah. He was making redware successfully there by 1738. Colonel William Stephens, the resident secretary of the colony, mentions Duché on May 27, 1738, in his regular report to the trustees in London. After commenting favorably on the dwelling house and kiln which Duché had built, Stephens continues:

> The master of it is a sober, diligent and modest man; he has baked off two kilns of handsome ware of various kinds of Pots, Pans, Bowls, Cups and Jugs fit for many uses, and tho it was a large quantity, they are found so convenient, that he does not want customers to take them off his hands, at a reasonable price. This however he seems to set no value on, in comparison of what may be expected; his next aim is to do something very curious, which may turn to good account for transporting, and he is making some tryal of the kinds of fine clay; a small tea-cup of which he showed me, when held against the light was very near transparent." (*Colonial Records of Georgia,* Volume 22, Part I, 1168.)

A few months later, Duché announced that "he had found out the true manner of making porcelain"—something no English-speaking person had ever done. He asked the trustees of the Colony to obtain a patent for him for fifteen years and to advance further moneys, but when one of the trustees asked him to duplicate in porcelain two cups which he sent, Duché replied that he could not until he had a suitable kiln.

With the aid of General Oglethorpe, Duché made a trip to England, in May 1743, in the hope of interesting someone there in his porcelain discoveries. There is circumstantial evidence that he was the man who furnished the Cherokee Indian clay to the proprietors of the Bow pottery which made the first recorded English porcelain in 1744.

Because of Duché's secrecy, and the conflicting claims and doubts which fill the Savannah records, it may never be known whether he did or did not make porcelain. There can be no doubt, however, that he was the first English-speaking person to recognize the porcelaneous quality of Cherokee Indian clay and to identify it as kaolin.

In the late nineteenth century there was a pottery industry in the eastern part of Crawford County, Georgia, according to the *Geological Survey of Georgia* (Bulletin Number 44). These potteries were operated by farmers, using primitive methods handed down from father to son. They made principally jugs, churns, and flower pots, with a mixture of impure kaolin and swamp clay or mud. The pieces were glazed with a mixture of lime and swamp mud, fired in small kilns, and sold at the pottery or peddled from door to door. In 1900, there were twelve of these potteries, but by 1927 only two were still operating. They had already lost some of their primitive character; both were using Albany slip, and one was shaping its flower pots on a machine.

An interesting note on the pottery now being made in the mountain regions of the Carolinas and Georgia is to be found in *Handicrafts of the Southern Highlands,* by Allen H. Eaton.

NORTH CAROLINA POTTERY. *Left to right:* Plate with cream ground, decorated in pumpkin brown and black; shaving dish with pumpkin-brown ground decorated in cream and black; plate dated *1812,* chocolate ground decorated in pumpkin brown, cream, and green; canteen bottle showing a bird that may be either a stork or an ostrich; plate with red-brown ground decorated in cream and green. *Diameter of plates,* approximately 13 inches. *Courtesy Joe Kindig, Jr.*

Pottery at Old Salem

An eighteenth-century potter's wheel in the Single Brothers' House, used by successive Salem potters and still used occasionally. Gottfried Aust was a potter in Wachovia from 1755 to 1788, at first with a shop at Bethabara, where his waster dump has yielded a rich reward of dated examples; in 1771 he moved his shop to Salem. The pottery was a sizable industry with three or four wheels going. Many objects such as heating stoves were made here because of the abundance of good clay and the absence of iron and glass. Succeeding potters carried on the craft until the twentieth century.

Four slip-decorated redware plates by Gottfried Aust, Salem's first potter (1755-1788), now in the Wachovia Museum. The large plate, 22 inches in diameter, was made with two loops on the back and hung outside of Aust's shop as a sign of his trade.

Tile stove in Salem Tavern. The Moravians made ceramic tile stoves of German type in various sizes, patterns, and colors. Instead of glaze this stove is finished with stove blacking; legs and base are of oak. These stoves were preferred to dirty and inefficient fireplaces and were less expensive than iron stoves, which had to be imported.

A Note on Early North Carolina Pottery

By Joe Kindig, Jr.

I HAVE never seen any *sgraffito* ware from North Carolina. All the decoration known to me is in slip. Nor have I seen any North Carolina plates bearing inscriptions, such as we frequently find in Pennsylvania. Such negative evidence, of course, does not afford proof that *sgraffito* and inscribed items were never made in North Carolina; but it is safe to say that they were, at least, very rarely produced. Furthermore, I have seen only one dated piece. It is marked *1812* in slip. A few pieces occur with initials scratched on the back, evidently before firing. The clay used apparently was very similar to that employed by the Pennsylvania makers of slipwares — light red in color, though perhaps a little lighter in tint than Pennsylvania clay. I have examined a few pieces whose body was almost white. Like that of Pennsylvania, North Carolina pottery is glazed on one side only.

The range of North Carolina glaze colors is wide, wider than will be met in corresponding Pennsylvania products. Backgrounds are usually of a light red as in Pennsylvania slipware; or a creamy white, very similar to the prevailing color of Pennsylvania *sgraffito* ware. Yet a third background varies from a dark reddish brown, through chocolate, to an almost black tone. Against such foundations the decoration is applied in slip of sundry hues. The light shades run from a creamy white to a rather dark yellow. Shades of green, red, brown, and black also occur.

The utensils made in North Carolina were, in general, similar to those produced in Pennsylvania. The majority of surviving items are plates and dishes ranging from about six inches in diameter to a rare maximum of fifteen and one half inches. In cross-section, a North Carolina plate almost invariably exhibits a wide rim and a fairly deep bouge. I have no recollection of finding any of the type, frequent in Pennsylvania, which approximate the form of a rimless deep dish. Of course, in Pennsylvania we find both types; but in North Carolina apparently we find only rimmed dishes (*Fig. 2*).

Fig. 1 — North Carolina Jug and Sugar Jars
Left to right: Cream ground with red, black, and green slip decoration. *Height*, 11 inches. Red ground with cream, green, and black slip decoration. Pumpkin ground with black and cream slip decoration. Note horizontal placement of handles on jars

Fig. 2 — North Carolina Lamp, Plate, and Mug
Left to right: Yellow-brown ground decorated in black, green, and cream slip. *Height*, 6 ½ inches. Black ground with cream, red, and green slip decoration. *Diameter*, 12 inches. Pumpkin ground mottled with black and cream slip

Next to plates, the most usual North Carolina pottery items are sugar jars. So, at least, these vessels are locally known, and I have found several that still contained some sugar. Collectors may term the large examples cookie jars and the small ones sugar bowls; but North Carolinians assure me that both were dedicated to the same sweet end. The lidded jars of Pennsylvania are of a different shape, with straighter sides, larger mouth, and proportionately more expansive lid. The handles of Pennsylvania jars are usually set vertically. North Carolina jar handles, on the contrary, are invariably horizontal and often extremely small. Pennsylvania lidded jars pass by various names, but I have never heard one referred to as a sugar jar. All the North Carolina jars that I have observed have been decorated with conventional ornament. Birds, flowers, animals, and the like have been notably absent.

Though plates and sugar bowls are the commonest articles of North Carolina decorated pottery, I have seen a few pitchers or jugs. The one illustrated in Figure 3 is an unusually pleasing example. I have also found a few Betty lamps like that in Figure 4. Flat, lidded shaving dishes partitioned into two divisions — one for soap, the other for water — were also made. Pottery flasks and small kegs, apparently for conveying liquid refreshment to workers in the fields, occasionally turn up. Other articles doubtless were made; but I have yet to meet surviving examples of them.

North Carolina potters were fond of conventional borders. In fact, I believe that they often surpassed their Pennsylvania contemporaries in the use of abstract forms. On the other hand, their use of floral motives, of which they were fond, is less convincing than that of their Pennsylvania cousins. Occasionally they introduced birds in the centre of plates, and, in one instance at least, a fish and two diamond-back terrapin. North Carolina potters did not approach the Pennsylvania craftsmen in variety of designs. It is solely in conventional decoration that they seem to have excelled. For such superiority the Brother Aust mentioned in the early records may have been chiefly responsible. The man was evidently a skilled potter and a trustworthy supervisor. It is unfortunate that nothing is known of his antecedents.

Early Slip Decorated Canister

By Rawson W. Haddon

Among the early products of the potter's art none, perhaps, are of greater interest than the slip decorated pieces made during the seventeenth and eighteenth centuries in Europe, and during the eighteenth and early nineteenth centuries in America.

Barber* states that the earliest dated piece of the latter known to him is a dish in the Pennsylvania Museum, Philadelphia, dated 1762. One of the earliest pieces of such ware, however, of which both date and maker are known, is a tea caddy, also discussed by Barber, which is now in the Terry collection in the museum of the Mattatuck Historical Society, Waterbury, Connecticut.

Its brown earthenware body, about five inches square, the front of which is covered with yellow slip which has been cut away to show some crude designs by bringing out the dark color beneath, is covered with rich dark glaze. The design on the front consists, among other things, of a tree bearing large objects, probably unknown to horticulturists, but resembling, in some slight measure, enormous blackberries, save for the fact that quite as many are square as are round.† The enormous size of these fruits may be judged by comparing their dimensions with those of the two weird birds of unknown species which repose beneath the shade of the extraordinary tree. It has been suggested by visitors to the museum that these fowls must, undoubtedly, be catbirds; and the face (if face it may be called) of the beautiful right-hand specimen would seem to bear out this conjecture. The tail of this bird, too, might have been studied with great interest and to some good purpose by the writing masters of the last century. Within the curling branches of the tree occurs the following inscription:

Esther Smith
Her Tea
Cannister
Sept. 6th
17 67

Slipware Tea Canister (*1767*)
Made by Joseph Smith of Wrightstown, Bucks County, Pennsylvania. The earliest known piece of American pottery whose authorship may confidently be ascribed. Size about 5 inches square. *In the Terry Collection, Mattatuck Historical Society.*

Barber is authority for the statement that this canister was made at the old Smith Pottery in Wrightstown township, Bucks County, Pennsylvania, which was erected, in 1763, by Joseph Smith and which is known to have produced such pottery. Joseph Smith had a sister named Esther, who was born in 1727; but, as she was married to Thomas Lacey in 1748, the canister could hardly have been hers. Barber's suggestion is that, as Smith was married in 1743, he may have had a daughter Esther, named for the sister, and that the canister was made for her.

The process of inscribing clay vessels such as this, either by impressing the material before glaze was applied, or by scratching through the wet glaze so as to expose the body of the ware, was extremely simple—as simple as marking a piecrust or as tracing patterns through the frost on a window pane. But it was by no means freely utilized. Early clay ware was cheap stuff, and there was seldom time for adorning it with special designs. Where these occur they generally reveal either a gift piece or a bit of self-expression on the part of some potter in whom for the moment political sentiment or the mere spirit of play was demanding outlet. Yet if all the early American earthenware which carries inscriptions of one kind or another could be brought together it would make quite a showing; more than that, it would posses qualities of extraordinary interest.

*Edwin A. Barber, *Pottery and Porcelain of the United States*, New York, 1893.

†A large proportion of these Pennsylvania designs appear to be reminiscences of European prototypes, which, in their time, were derived from the Orient. In these latter the eastern pomegranate and the artichoke played an important rôle. The fruit of this pottery tree may be identified as belonging to one or the other of these decorative types of fruit.—Ed.

Pennsylvania potter

THOSE INDISPENSABLE CRAFTSMEN of nineteenth-century America, the small local potters who worked mainly in redware, are as apt as not to be completely unknown today. Thanks to Frank J. Schmidt, director of the Historical Society of York County, we can now record the name of one of these—Henry Miller of York, Pennsylvania—and show some examples of his work as well. Like so many of his fellows, Miller did not mark his work; these pleasantly potted pieces are identified by their present owner, the potter's granddaughter.

Mr. Schmidt provides the following biographical data: "Miller was born August 20, 1826. We are not sure of the date of his arrival in America, but we do know that when he was naturalized, in September 1851, he rejected allegiance to the Elector of Hesse, Germany. His name appears in the first York city directory of 1856. Later directories and an 1876 atlas of the county show his pottery as in Freystown (or Frystown), then a small settlement just east of York and now along East Market Street within the city limits. He died in York on June 28, 1880."

Mug made by Henry Miller (working in York, Pennsylvania, from 1856; d. 1880); redware with green glaze. Height 5 inches. *Collection of Mrs. Ivan Gerber; photograph by Paul Galbreath.*

Side-handled pitcher by Miller; redware with dark brown glaze. Mrs. Gerber owns an almost identical pitcher with a clear glaze. *Gerber collection; Galbreath photograph.*

1965

Pennsylvania Pottery in the Philadelphia Museum of Art

Plates ornamented with sgraffito designs were cherished as ornaments, for the incised decoration rendered them impractical for use. Here the peacock, a frequent Pennsylvania-German motif, is perched on the tree of life, flanked by tulip and sunflower. Signed *R.G.* (probably R. Graber, Upper Hanover township, Montgomery County) and dated *1812*. By this time, potters no longer bordered plates with inscriptions.

Sgraffito plate made by Georg Hübner, pale gold in color, dashed with green. The formal placement of the triple tulip spray in its low ornamental urn is typical of this potter, working in the 1780's and 1790's probably in Montgomery County, who incised his motifs and lettered bands with great authority. Inscription, translated, reads: *Since no plaster can heal me, will you flee with me to the beautiful shelter of Heaven?* Formerly in the collection of Arthur Sussel.

Oval dish with fluted rim and scalloped edge. The sgraffito decoration is an urn holding a flowering stalk and the inscription, a favorite one of old-world potters: *Out of the earth, with understanding, the potter makes everything.* The work of Samuel Troxel, Upper Hanover Township, dated *July the 17th 1823.*

1959

Ceramic buttermolds are unusual. This piece, of brownish clay with two circular faces, was turned on the wheel, and glazed only on working surfaces. The ubiquitous six-point star symbols are balanced by deeply cut hearts, in which small rosettes are stamped for added ornament. Diameter, 4¾ inches.

Horse with detachable rider; made of red clay, speckled and glazed. Modeled freehand by one Jacob Fretz, who signed and dated it in 1809. Undoubtedly European in conception, as mounted horsemen were for many decades a common theme of German potters. Height over all, 9 inches.

Lidded and lined bowl covered with deep chocolate glaze and ornamented with pierced work of diagonals, dots, and interlacing arcs. Such pierced pottery is of ancient lineage. Pieces like this may have been made as demonstrations of skill by potters newly arrived from Germany in the mid-nineteenth century. Diameter, 8⅞ inches.

Ceramic whistles shaped as birds are an ancient toy, made by European potters during several centuries. This late eighteenth-century peacock is colored in pale buff and brown with dashes of green; sgraffito markings designate feathers. Height, 6¼ inches.

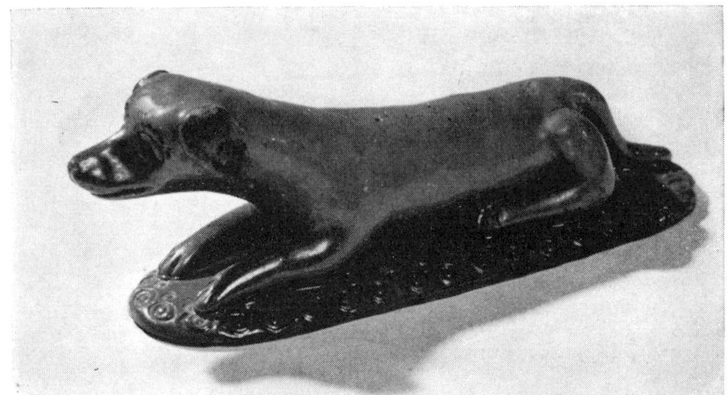

Small ornaments such as birds, cats, and dogs were specialties of certain potters, sometimes itinerants, in the nineteenth century. They were usually modeled freehand in red clay, coated with shiny glaze. Bases were embellished with borders impressed with stamps. Length, 5½ inches.

Henry McQuate, Pennsylvania Potter

By Rhea Mansfield Knittle

Fig. 1—Henry McQuate, Potter (*1826-1899*)
Born in Lancaster County, Pennsylvania, of Scotch and Irish parentage, McQuate produced pottery that was not devoid of individuality.

THE appraisal of almost every concrete object in life depends largely upon the viewpoint. A tree may mean many things to many people. A seascape, a fresco, a fan, a bit of lace, a pewter porringer—each is seen by different eyes at a divergent angle; and this is, perhaps, fortunate. For over a half century, eleven small specimens of earthenware accumulated dust as they stood in a somewhat negligible group on the upper shelf of an old pine corner cupboard. Semi-annually they were taken down and given a bath, and then put back again. One autumn day in 1924, a fresh pair of eyes beholding them discovered eleven lovely little examples of desirable American pottery, crying for recognition, wanting to be made much of, and hungry for little pats of appreciation.

These miniature bits of earthenware displayed an unusual variety of form, glaze and decoration; and, strange to relate, they did not conform to any known potter's product. They did not typify New York, New England or Pennsylvania; yet they epitomized, in ensemble, the traditions of various sections, and justified the use of that overworked adjective "distinctive."

The little examples, too small for any practical use, ranged in color from a deep chocolate to a tawny hue. Some were decorated with incised patterns; others were stippled here and there, in haphazard fashion, with a soft colored green, quite suggestive of early Chinese pottery. A tiny inkwell had many faceted sides; but the *chef-d'oeuvre* of the group was a beautifully modeled and glazed covered jar, four and one-half inches in height, whose handles, by a certain vital twist, gave evidence incontrovertible that an artistic soul had rejoiced in their fashioning.

Standing these pieces, like toy soldiers, in a row, I was reminded of a gathering of the clans. My interest was aroused: speculation: research: now, information.

Henry McQuate, for it was his pottery that fashioned these alluring bits, was born in Lancaster County, Pennsylvania, February 15, 1826. His father came from Ireland; his mother from Scotland. Emigrating to America in the early part of the nineteenth century, the pair settled in the south central part of Pennsylvania. When Henry was but a youth, the family moved to Lebanon County, in the same state, and here, in 1847, the young man was married to Mary Garmon, a native resident, whose parents had come from the low country of Germany.

Although born in the United States, Mary Garmon, like many others among her individualistic people, never learned to speak the English language, nor did she attempt to have it taught to her children. The husband and father, under these circumstances, acquired a Pennsylvania-German vernacular, mixed here and there with Scotch and Irish dialect, a combination, which, even at the present time, has left many provincialisms of a peculiarly provocative nature in the speech of some Pennsylvanians and Ohians of similarly mixed heredity.

To this union of Henry McQuate and Mary Garmon were born two sons and five daughters—John, Henry, Amanda, Carolina, Susan, Mary Ann and Emma—several of whom are still living.

In the year prior to his marriage, McQuate had united with the German Baptist church at Lebanon, and remained a faithful follower of the Dunkard, or "Tunker," faith throughout life. His wife, typical of the section and the period, was interested solely in her home, church and children, and wore, on all occasions, the simple dress demanded at the time by the adherents of her sect. The Dunkards were quite averse to having their pictures taken, a form of worldly vanity frowned upon by their religious elders; but, fortunately, in latter years, after their coming to Ohio (a state where half a dozen rigid sects have spread their wings), they listened to the persuasions of the children, and a "family group" resulted. The portrait reproduced is from this lone photograph.

Henry McQuate started his pottery industry about three miles west of Myerstown, Lebanon County, Pennsylvania, and, as near as can be remembered, in 1845. Not large at any period of operation, the plant required, at the most, three or four helpers, and the work turned from its wheels was excellent of its kind.

The method of decoration was in itself, quite outstanding, for a green slip was frequently used as a final individual touch over the warm, rich, reddish brown glaze. The ingredients for this color were ground in a mortar. Then the component parts were mixed in a large earthenware bowl, and were applied with a brush of no great size, or were stippled on the object. Occasionally the snake decoration was employed; frequently a dotted pattern; while, more rarely, an incised or *sgraffiato* method, so popular with the early potters of Pennsylvania, offered a pleasing variant. For this last manner, small awls or pointed instruments were used, the decoration generally being confined to a simple border.

The two staples turned out by McQuate were milk jugs and cider or vinegar jugs, the latter containers also being quite commonly used to carry water into the harvest fields, the clay body having a tendency to keep the water cool. These vinegar jugs, like the other ware, were of reddish brown body and glaze, emphasized generally with the green slip, and withal, quite pleasing to the eye.

In my inquiries I was particular concerning a certain point; "Did they not, even occasionally, employ a blue tone for decorative purposes?" Never any other color than

Fig. 2 — A Group of McQuate Pottery

The covered jar in the middle of the upper row is four and one-half inches high and establishes the scale of a group of items made for a child. The bowl (*No. 1*) has a tawny glaze stippled with green. The mug with handle (*No. 4*), with reddish brown glaze, is finished in the form of a gallon milk jug. Numbers 3 and 5 have a bright chocolate brown glaze.

this soft, somnolent green, stamping the McQuate pottery with individuality, which set it decidedly apart from the general run.*

The scarcity of remains from this plant is due primarily to the brief period of its operation, for the works closed down about 1859. Commercialization ended its career by bringing stoneware vinegar and cider jugs upon the market. With these it was impossible for the little pottery to compete. It was obliged to stop its wheels, and draw the fires—the same old story.

Henry McQuate then turned farmer; and, in 1871, with other Dunkards, we find him and his family coming to Ohio, where they lived industriously in a rather communal manner, cultivating one of the richest and most productive sections to be found in the state.

McQuate passed away in Ashland County, Ohio, March the 29th, 1899, at the age of seventy-three years.

The circumstance to which these miniature pieces of pottery owe their preservation is interesting. Amanda, the eldest daughter of the McQuate family, when a little girl, took a keen delight in watching all the operations at the plant, and became quite a favorite with the potters. She attempted in various ways to help, no doubt at times quite hindering production. But, from her father down, they allowed the youngster to daub, dabble and mold to her heart's content. The helpers, too, formed playthings and various odds and ends for the appreciative child, expending upon them the elements of thought and skill which have given these pieces their special charm.

The majority were long since broken; but, when the McQuate family emigrated westward to their Ohio home, Amanda, disobeying her mother, who had told her to relegate the "rubbish" to a convenient heap, secreted some toys among the family clothing. Thus, like Falstaff, they escaped, and for over fifty years stood complacently upon the top shelf of the old pine cupboard. Then a pair of eyes recognized their quality, and they now grace several carefully chosen collections.

*The implication is that McQuate produced no stoneware, which is salt glazed and not infrequently carries a blue underglaze decoration.

JACOB MEDINGER (*above*) "kicking the wheel." Photograph courtesy *Pottstown News.*

JACOB MEDINGER'S storeroom and wheel (*above, left*).

A MAKER OF PENNSYLVANIA REDWARE

By CORNELIUS WEYGANDT

IT WAS THROUGH NEW little jars of redware, glazed inside but unglazed outside, that I first became aware that we had a potter of the old sort still firing his kiln within thirty miles of Philadelphia. Our farmer from upper Montgomery County brought us apple butter in such jars, of pint and quart size. When I asked him where he found them, he said: "Oh, in country stores up beyond Collegeville." He did not know the potter's name, or where he had his kiln, but he had heard it was "somewhere up in 'the Stone Hills,' north of the Perkiomen Creek."

This was back before 1914. Then one day midway the 1920's, I heard again of this old potter and learned that he was still "kicking the wheel" near Neiffer, in Montgomery County. His name was Jacob Medinger and his father, William, had been a potter before him.

I had been gathering up redware now for some years. The commoner forms were fairly reasonable in price in the 1920's. They were of appealing shapes, and there were interesting decorations on pitchers and mixing bowls and pie dishes. I learned of strange designations – reversed chicken foot, wave motif, the triune lily, symbolic of the Trinity. At auctions I saw the decorated platters with their soldiers on horseback, their peacocks and tulips, and I happened on Doctor Edwin Atlee Barber's *Tulipware of the Pennsylvania German Potters* (1903), a good book long out of print. My collection was large enough when I discovered Medinger for me to know how good was his potting, how closely he adhered to the traditional forms of the Pennsylvania Dutch potters.

By the time of his death in 1932, hopelessly burned by a back draught from the fire under his kiln, I had acquired nearly a hundred pieces of his redware. Besides the ones that were decorated, some by himself, some by Mrs. Medinger, and the more elaborate ones by William J. McAlister, a woodcarver then living at

LIMERICK POTTERY
P. O. ADDRESS, R. F. D. NO. 2, SCHWENKSVILLE, PA.
NEIFFER, PA. March 10 1926
MR. Cornelius Weygent
BOUGHT OF
JACOB MEDINGER
MANUFACTURER OF
ALL KINDS OF EARTHENWARE. CIDER MADE
IN SEASON

5	Pie Dishes @	250	1250
3	" " "	50	150
3	" " "	25	75
1	Dish "	40	40
1	Black Pitcher	60	60
1	Carved "	150	150
1	Large "	140	140
			1865
	Paid 10 Pid	70	70
	Jacob Medinger		1735

RECEIPTED BILL from Jacob Medinger to "Cornelous Weygent," dated March 10, 1926.

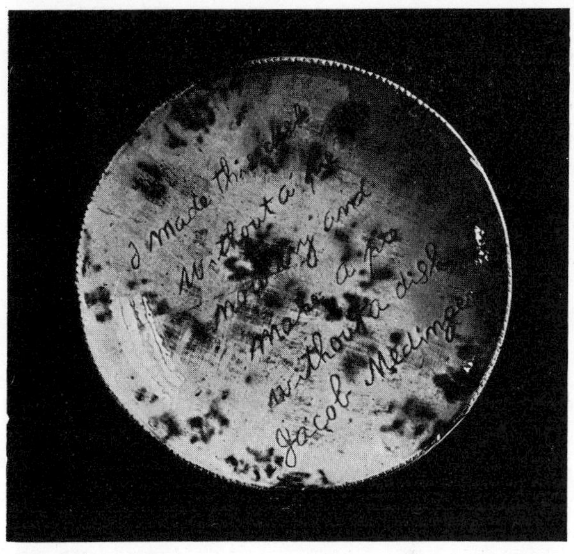

Pie Dish by Medinger (*left*). Signed, and with the legend, "I made this dish/ Without a pie/ now try and/ make a pie/ without a dish/ Jacob Medinger."

Peacock Plate (*right*) decorated by William J. McAlister, after George Huebener.

Bergey, Medinger stamped out little pie dishes and apple-butter jars on a machine, molded pie dishes on clay models, and turned perhaps twenty sorts on his potter's wheel. I have pitchers of various sizes from creamers to water pitchers, and of various glazes, jugs, sugar bowls, mixing bowls, milk pans, flower pots, hanging baskets for flowers, candlesticks, and cups and saucers.

A bird with uplifted wings that he had modeled for this burning of March 1932, and that came through the firing in good shape, was adjudged his work nearest akin to sculpture. An inkwell with a dog in black glaze he talked of several times to me as the best work of his father, but it was not in his house at those times our conversation turned to it. A bluebird on its box that Jacob had done for me came to grief in the firing.

I have twenty-four of the decorated pie dishes, of twenty-one designs. I have a duplicate of the nine-inch pie dish with the three birds on it, which is after a decorated platter by Samuel Troxel, who potted in the early nineteenth century. I also have a duplicate of the old nine-inch pie dish with a plant in a flowerpot and four flowers on the plant, and one of the big thirteen-inch plate with nine tulips cut through the slip to the redware beneath. The white slip laid over the redware base looks yellow through the red lead painted over it, which turns to yellow glass in the kiln. The plate with two eagles back to back is after another old-time potter, George Huebener (*c. 1792*). The peacock plates, too, are after Huebener. The bird-and-heart plate is after Joseph Smith, another potter of a century and a quarter ago.

Which of the three aforesaid, Jacob, Mrs. Medinger, or McAlister, did this or that one of the pie plates with original designs, I am not sure. A horse in harness with a swallow in flight above it I have never seen on old platters. Only on one other pie dish have I come on a rabbit. The pie dish with the cow upon it is the only one of its kind I know. Elsewhere I have come on the cow in Pennsylvania Dutch decoration only on butter molds.

That the historians of our American folk culture may have detailed data for the last pottery in Pennsylvania Dutchland with an unbroken descent from the past, I reproduce a receipted bill of a purchase of twenty-five items nearly twenty years ago.

On his little farm in a sunken bowl of the "Stone Hills," an ice pond, a clay pit, a potter's shop, a kiln, and a cider mill, besides his house and little barn, made Jacob's twenty-three acres a busy place. He had the gift of making grafts grow, and delighted in the old-fashioned apples and pears and peaches which his orchard bore. Like his father before him, Jacob was a handy man. He had made the pickets for the neat fence that surrounded his home yard. He kept everything in apple-pie order. Jacob Medinger burned his pottery three times a year, in winter, spring, and summer. In the fall he was busy with his cider making, folks from far and near bringing their apples to him to be pressed. What he most prided himself on was his November cider. That turned hard, and, drunk in moderation, was a boon to the discriminating.

A Cupboard filled with Medinger's pottery, in the author's house.

Fig. 1 — Heart-Shaped Saucer Lamp. Attributed to David Spinner, who plied his trade at Melford in Bucks County from 1800 to 1811. This lamp is a mere three inches long, with a single wick channel. Its heart shape suggests that it may have been a wedding present

Fig. 2 — Spout Lamps. Of the same red-brown tone as Figure 1. From Berks County. *Left*, quite apparently copied from a mug; three inches tall; spout of the same length. *Right*, probably modeled after a teapot or jug; stiff, straight spout. Height, 4 5/16 inches; spout 3 1/2 inches long

EARLY POTTERY LIGHTING DEVICES OF PENNSYLVANIA

By WILLIAM J. TRUAX

PENNSYLVANIA pottery occupies an unquestioned place in the domain of antiques. Indeed, since much of it has been unmistakably earmarked by time, we may be sometimes inclined to look upon the whole colorful category as a survival from the distant past. Yet Jacob Medinger, the last of the old-school Pennsylvania potters who were responsible for much of the ware that collectors prize today, died but a decade ago. The craft of making redware pottery in the early manner survived in Pennsylvania because of the rather astonishing fact that the people, though in constant communication with other parts of the changing continent, clung tenaciously for over two centuries to many early methods, customs, and superstitions. Yet, while they perpetuated the customs of their forefathers that seemed to them sound and good and appropriate, they shrewdly adopted new designs that came to the pottery kiln, and sometimes the happy combination of old and new lifted the products of their craft into the realm of art. One writer has observed that almost any antique found in any one of the original states has its counterpart in the Dutch country of Pennsylvania, but that the counterpart always reveals the characteristic local touch.

Fig. 3 — Candlestick. An amusing example in lighthouse form, whose wide saucer might support a betty lamp. Incisions in the sides form the letters *ISI* so that this combination candlestick and lamp stand might be classed as a signed piece. So many potters claim these initials, however, that they are not an exact identification. This piece was made in Lebanon County. The glaze is very dense, with green and dark-brown spots running through it, and slip of yellowish brown. Height, 7 1/8 inches; top diameter, 4 15/16 inches

Fig. 4 — Betty Lamps. In pottery, with wire hangers; both have pottery wick channels. The hanger of the right-hand example springs from the back, as in metal lamps of the type. This lamp, 4 7/8 inches long, is of dull brown pottery. It was once displayed in the Berks County Historical Society. *Left*, 3 3/8 inches long; bright, yellowish-brown glaze

Though the Pennsylvania potter spent the greater part of his days in making more or less standard commercial products such as pie plates and crocks, he expressed his individuality in the fashioning of numerous odd objects that are to us utterly delightful. Whistles in the form of birds — a whistle could hardly be caged more appropriately; small houses to be used as children's banks; flowerpots with fine pie-crimped edges, designs on their sleek sides, and often an inscribed date; and tremendous dishes for the bride-to-be, abundantly and happily adorned with a medley of tulips and love birds and inscriptions, all in rich, bright colors — such varied objects we find today, a persistent monument to the play spirit of the industrious potter of yesterday.

Lighting devices seem to have offered a special invitation to the personal touch. That the Pennsylvania potters produced lamps of almost every conceivable design is evident from the great variation in extant specimens. The majority of these are of redware glazed in plain colors. Their lack of elaborate decorations may be due to the small surface of the pieces. Occasionally fine specimens turn up with variegated or speckled glaze or with ornamentation in slip. Others, though lacking distinctive coloring, are unusual in form, and sometimes excellently proportioned. No two are alike, and the forms were frequently copied from unrelated objects that caught and pleased the potter's eye. Most of them embody the simplest principles of illumination, providing a receptacle for grease and a channel for holding the wick in place. Still, as some of the illustrated examples testify, more complex devices are to be found.

To the collector of old lighting fixtures the matter of date is important. Yet, in the case of these pottery devices, unless a piece is dated or bears the individual and unmistakable mark of a certain potter, it is difficult indeed to say when it was made. And such identifying marks are rarely found. According to John Ramsay's *American Potters and Pottery*, the eastern Pennsylvania counties of Chester, Montgomery, and Bucks became a pottery-making center before the middle of the eighteenth century; the first recorded pottery in the district was built in 1740. It is generally accepted that the earliest potteries were in Chester County, and several collectors and dealers with whom I have discussed the subject feel that pottery was being made there soon after 1700, if not before that date. So far as I know, however, there is not one existing example of Pennsylvania pottery earlier than a platter inscribed *1733*.

While some of the lighting devices here pictured are of a type used in this early period, I am not credulous enough to believe that any of them can boast an age of two centuries and more. The persistence of old patterns, and the primitive character of many late pieces that were turned out simultaneously with superior work, make the task of dating with any accuracy almost impossible. It is safe to say, however, that the lamps here illustrated represent the century of potterymaking between the years 1770 and 1870. The forms are characteristic of what the collector may expect to find, though the condition of the members of this group is above the average.

Pottery lamps are being copied today, but the discriminating collector will soon learn to differentiate between old ones and new. The latter have a lighter, more porous body, and lack the patina that comes only with age. The fact that old lighting devices in Pennsylvania pottery are not half so numerous as specimens in metal or glass only adds zest to the collector's chase.

Fig. 5 — Grease Lamp. The molding of the standard resembles linen-fold paneling; three small knobs decorate the handle. Height, 7 ¼ inches; base diameter, 4 ⅞ inches. The color is light brown. This lamp has the characteristics of Berks County production

Fig. 6 — Grease Lamp. Short, open-top, saucer-base example covered with a glaze almost black in color. Though discovered in western Pennsylvania, it may be an Ohio piece. Height, 4 ⅛ inches; diameter of base, 5 ¼ inches

Fig. 7 — Candlestick. While not particularly appealing in design, this piece has the distinction of an inscription, incised in the base: *W.A. and A.D. No. 22, 1866*. The known list of potters fails to throw light on this bold marking. This stubby specimen was found in Montgomery County. Height, 2 ½ inches. The scalloped saucer base is 5 ¼ inches in diameter. The glaze is speckled brown and green

Fig. 8 — Three-Wick Lamp. Shape possibly inspired by a quill holder and ink pot, which it resembles. The wick tubes, and the known fact that the well once contained oil, not ink, prove that it is a lamp. The other lighters here illustrated could have been outfitted with wicks made from a piece of oil-soaked rag, but this piece calls for the solid round wick used in camphene lamps. Discovered in Berks County. Height, 2 inches; diameter of bowl, 4 ⅞ inches

5

American pottery lamps

BY LURA WOODSIDE WATKINS

Fig. 1. Lamp of unglazed red earthenware made at Morgantown, West Virginia, by John W. Thompson, probably before 1840. Height, 5 inches. *The Smithsonian Institution, United States National Museum.*

EVERY LARGE COLLECTION of American lighting devices includes one or more pottery grease lamps. These are primitive affairs, usually with a simple open reservoir on a standard, a saucer base, and a handle or handles. The greater number have a slight beak in the bowl-like reservoir where the wick may rest, others have spouts, while a very few have wick supports.

Such fat lamps are now comparatively rare, but in their day they were probably rather common. They were fashioned by local potters who made a business of supplying household utensils of whatever clay was available. Red-burning clay was the material most often used, but lamps were also made of stoneware. Most surviving specimens date from the first half of the nineteenth century.

Almost all the lamps of this type have been found in areas of German settlement, principally in Pennsylvania and Ohio, among the Moravians in North Carolina, and to some extent at a late period in Tennessee. It is more than probable that all American pottery lamps, even when made by potters of British descent, originated among the German settlers. This theory is bolstered by the fact that no pottery lamps of any kind were made by the hundreds of clayworkers of English descent in New England. Neither do they appear to have been produced by any of the numerous English and Irish potters whose histories have been recounted by Arthur E. James in *The Potters and Potteries of Chester County, Pennsylvania.*

Judging by the probabilities alone, the German settlers would have made the style of lamp familiar to them in their homeland. That they actually did just this we know for the reason that similar lamps were in use among the peasants of northwestern Europe, in Hungary, and in Sweden. Continental lamps differ in the respect that they usually have a pouring lip in the saucer base, but they show the ancestry of our American examples.

The lamp shown in Figure 1 is referred to by Walter Hough in his *Collection of Heating and Lighting Utensils in the United States National Museum* as having "English ancestry." By this he probably means that it was descended from an English lamp type known as a "Cornish chill," examples of which are to be found in the Penzance and Truro museums in Cornwall. One of these Cornish specimens has the lip in the base found on Hungarian and Swedish lamps. There is evidentally a relationship between the Cornish and Continental types, but the latter, brought to us by German immigrants, are more likely to be the originals of our own clay lamps.

Hough obtained the lamp shown in Figure 1 in Morgantown, West Virginia, from a daughter of John W. Thompson, the potter who made it. Thompson's father had taken his family over the mountains from Bel Air, Maryland, in 1785, and John became an apprentice in the first pottery west of the Alleghenies, founded by one Foulk at the very beginning of the settlement. This pottery supplied the demand for household wares then so expensive to obtain from Baltimore or other seacoast sources of supply. Thompson succeeded to Foulk's business and continued to make redware until about 1840, when the manufacture of stoneware was begun. The lamp illustrated must have been made between 1800 and 1840. Hough surmises that it may have been a potter's lamp. Although it was perhaps designed for the potter's own use, we now know that it is a type often repeated in the middle Atlantic states. It is most primitive in construction, being simply a lipped saucer on a stand with saucer base and a handle.

A similar example, made in Tennessee of stoneware clay, was illustrated by H. C. Mercer in *Light and Fire Making.* He says of it: "From the boat-shaped earthen lamps of ancient Rome, from the green majolica ones of candlestick shape used by the Moors of today, to this miniature boat-shaped one of stoneware set upon a stemmed dish, in which opossum or 'coon' fat might have burnt for the Tennessee moonshiner, where I found it two years ago in the hill country of White County, Tennessee, there is no change of character or make." He further adds: "There J. T. Goodwin baked it for me of blue clay in 1895."

Such instances of a lamp by a known maker are rare. A lamp that was sold at the auction of the Alfred B. MacClay collection in 1939 was marked on the base, *J. L. Blaney, Cookstown, Pa.* This lamp must have been made between 1825 and 1854, since Cookstown had different names before and after those dates. Needless to say, such a marked lamp is a priceless rarity.

Fig. 2. Stoneware lamp glazed with Albany slip, found in Ohio. Height, 5½ inches. *Author's collection.*

Fig. 3. Lamp with globular reservoir, glazed red earthenware, attributed to Pennsylvania. Height, about 5 inches. *The Smithsonian Institution, United States National Museum.*

Fig. 4. Lamp with two handles and spouts, dark brown glaze. Height, 6⅞ inches. *Henry Ford Museum.*

Fig. 5. Lamp with a true spout, dark brown glaze. Height, 5¾ inches. *Henry Ford Museum.*

Fig. 6. Lamp with fully developed spout, glazed red earthenware. Height, 2¼ inches, length, 4¾ inches. *Author's collection.*

At the pottery centers of Bethabara and Winston-Salem, North Carolina, Moravian potters were working as early as 1756 and as late as 1830. Lamps from this area have a light red earthenware body and are decorated with a combination of brown, black, cream, and green slips on a yellow-brown ground.

The large stoneware lamp in Figure 2, with a lipped open reservoir and an Albany slip glaze, was found in Ohio. John Ramsay illustrates an almost identical example in his *American Pottery* (page 158). Albany slip glazing on stoneware was a nineteenth-century technique, and these lamps may have been made about 1840. A pair of lamps of a similar shape were made and used in a rural community in Tennessee as late as 1905.

A number of grease lamps have reservoirs of globular form. The one shown in Figure 3 has a slight lip for a wick rest. It is attributed to Pennsylvania and is distinguished by a rudimentary decoration of tooled straight and wavy lines. Some globular reservoirs are slightly closed in at the top, and have chunky projecting spouts to serve as wick channels. An example with two handles and two spouts is in the Ford collection at Dearborn, Michigan (Fig. 4). The spouts, of triangular shape, are simply contrived. A similar lamp, owned by Mrs. Rhea Mansfield Knittle, is shown in John Spargo's *Early American Pottery and China* (plate 31).

Lamps with true spouts are great rarities, probably because they were difficult to make. Since the reservoirs of all these lamps were turned on the potter's wheel, they are fundamentally cups or bowls adapted to the purposes of illumination by the addition of lips or spouts. A lamp with a true, albeit rudimentary, spout is shown in Figure 5. This displays the novel feature of a reservoir partly closed to prevent the spilling over of oil or grease. A more fully developed spout may be seen on the lamp in Figure 6, which has the wick opening on the upper surface of the beak. Here, as rarely, no stand was provided, and the result is a lamp as primitive as those of ancient Greece or the Near East and not much different from some of them. A lamp of this type, provided with a carrying handle, was illustrated in an article by William J. Truax in Antiques for May 1940. Mr. Truax also showed an example with a deeper reservoir, which might possibly have been intended for a lamp filler.

Another class of pottery lamps is equipped with tubular or gutter-shaped wick supports, which allowed any surplus grease to drip back from the wick into the reservoir itself rather than onto the outside of the lamp. A notable example of this type is that shown in Figure 7. Its wick tube is a perfect cylinder at the outer end, but is opened and spread apart towards the center of the bowl. The lamp with rudimentary spout in Figure 8 has a ceramic trough or channel (the more usual form) inside.

At least four examples of pottery Betty lamps with interior wick supports are known, all from Pennsylvania. One, illustrated in the article by Mr. Truax, has a handle and was not designed for suspension. The lamp in Figure 9 has a punched opening in the tab at the back for the accommodation of a wire or string. Two others of unique form appear in the group shown by Mr. Truax. One is complete with the regular type of twisted iron handle and hook so familiar on iron Bettys; the other has been pierced at the sides in a wholly original manner for an iron suspending wire and hook.

The Bettys are the aristocrats of American pottery lamps and must have a strong appeal for those who like to reflect upon old customs and ways. They represent the successful attempt of their makers to provide a wanted necessity when the usual materials were not at hand. All these lamps, in fact, must give us added respect for the ingenuity of those masters of the wheel.

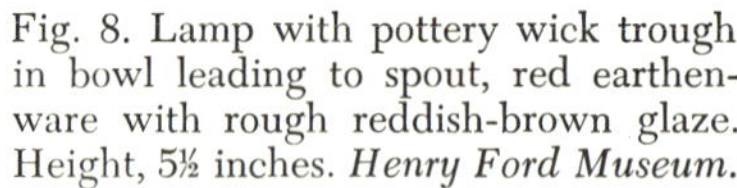

Fig. 8. Lamp with pottery wick trough in bowl leading to spout, red earthenware with rough reddish-brown glaze. Height, 5½ inches. *Henry Ford Museum.*

Fig. 7. Lamp equipped with pottery wick tube in bowl, the standard partly hollow, red earthenware with dark brown glaze. Height, 7 7/10 inches. *Landis Valley Museum.*

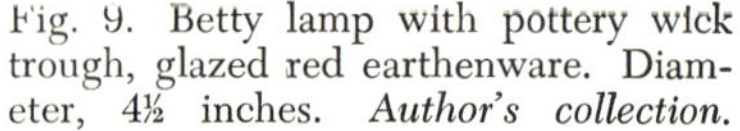

Fig. 9. Betty lamp with pottery wick trough, glazed red earthenware. Diameter, 4½ inches. *Author's collection.*

Fig. 1 — Fragments of Chandelier and Piece of Tile Stove
The decorative elements here seem characteristic of the period — about 1860. Note particularly the various applications of the acanthus motif on the tile at the right.

Mehwaldt, a Pioneer American Potter

By Ada Walker Camehl

(Illustrations from the author's collection)

I AM one of that company made illustrious by the membership of Horace Walpole and the gentle Elia. "China's the passion of my soul," and I love, as did Charles Lamb, the vari-hued and quaintly-drawn creatures "in this world before perspective," which I find upon the tableware of the early housewives of my country.

Much besides pottery do I gather from my quickly-made acquaintanceships over a broken teapot or a Nankin bowl. Tales of pioneer life and hardship, sidelights upon familiar incidents of our national history, together with ever personal stories of the great human comedy, are poured into my ears as I seek at farmhouse door, or in country kitchen, for ancient treasure. "Those plates were on the table the day father entertained Governor Clinton and his party when they stopped here on a coaching tour through New York state to inspect the canals," explained a lonely old woman, with conscious pride.

"I carried that teapot in my hands when we moved down from the farm, for fear the little swan would be broken off from the cover," said an aged housewife, with the feminine love for a China teapot glowing in her faded eyes:— and there stood the dainty piece of Bristol still intact, with the graceful little swan still mounting guard over the fragrant Bohea. May its future owners be as gentle with this fragile treasure!

But the story I have to tell is a hitherto unexploited romance of the pioneer days of our country, a tale of transplanted old-world enterprise, which failed to take deep root in the land of its adoption. I came to the knowledge of it quite by accident, through a chance remark. During a china-hunting tour through the Niagara river region, a German woman, with whom I had bargained for ancient treasures and heirlooms, handed me a small mottled, reddish-brown pitcher, saying:

"You may have that pitcher. It was made by my father many years ago, over at Bergholtz."

I carried the little, plebeian brown pitcher home, placed it with my more showy lustres and rich blues, kept in memory the information as to its origin, and resolved to follow up the trail.

The result of subsequent investigations has been my discovery of the fact that, not five miles from the spot where the Frenchman LaSalle launched the Griffon, the first sailing vessel on the Great Lakes above Niagara Falls, a German potter in the middle of the last century set up his wheel, and, using the clay of the neighboring fields, for nearly forty years fashioned, with his own hands, a variety

Fig. 2 — Covered Crocks and Various Other Mehwaldt Dishes

Fig. 3 — Inkstand and Pen Tray
In the eclecticism of its design this seems to belong to the Civil War period.

of crockery and tableware which, for honest workmanship and artistic merit, deserves a place beside the wares of any American potteries of his day.

In 1808, in Bruessow, a German village near Berlin, was born Charles August Mehwaldt. He came of a line of potters; for his father and his grandfather before him had spent their lives at the potter's wheel. After he had learned the trade, young Mehwaldt, as was the custom of the country, passed several years as a journeyman potter, his *wanderjahre* in search of experience taking him over Russia and into the Holy Land. On his return to his home, he found the country in a state of political unrest. Greater liberties were being demanded by the people, while free America, beckoning across the sea with an alluring hand, was welcoming many citizens of all classes to voluntary exile.

Fig. 4 — A Memorial Wreath in Earthenware, Colored After the Firing

In 1844, a man of wealth, Williams by name, gathered together several families from the neighborhood of Bruessow and brought the little band to the United States. They purchased a piece of land in western New York, on the Niagara frontier, cleared the timber and built a hamlet of log houses. In 1847, they erected the still standing German Lutheran church. Remembering the village of Bergholtz from which many of them had come, they named the new home New Bergholtz,—later dropping the "New."

Fired by the glowing accounts which came back to the Fatherland from this transplanted colony, a second company came together, in 1851, to follow the first. Among this group were the potter Mehwaldt, his wife, and their five children. They set out in a sailing vessel. The voyage lasted seven weeks, and, as seems to have been the not uncommon fate of sailing vessels during those years, the ship ran ashore and was wrecked upon a sandbar off Long Island. The passengers were rescued by means of a tub, which ran on a cable from mast to the shore, and the German party came on to Bergholtz, making the journey across New York State by way of the Erie Canal. Upon their arrival they found that the great cholera epidemic of 1851 had visited the settlement, and had taken away many of their former associates.

Here Mehwaldt bought a log house and two acres of land and set up his pot works. His outfit was of the most primitive description; a small brick oven in his back yard for firing the clay, and a wooden kick-wheel. These, with his hands and his Old-World training, were all his capital, and here he worked alone at his trade until he died in 1887, at the age of seventy-nine years.

The years during which Mehwaldt came to America and began his work belong to that period which has been called the dark ages of our nation's history. Human slavery was in practice. The Great West was a glittering lode-star to the adventurer. Railroad travel was in its infancy. American ceramic art had long been an established fact, and many potters had come from Europe to try our clays, among them James Clews and William Ridgway, authors of many of our best-loved old blue dishes. But "the staples of ware fabricated on this continent are few and not of a high degree of perfection," wrote Horace Greeley in 1853, concerning the specimens of American-made pottery at the Crystal Palace Exhibition in New York City. It was not until the event which proved to be the renaissance of the potter's art in the United States—the Centennial Exhibition of 1876—that this country fully awoke to the possibilities hidden in its soil.

As the Civil War drew near, Mehwaldt's sons were swept away with enthusiasm for their adopted country. "They

Fig. 5 — Bottle, Butter Dish and Mug
Not particularly subtle, but showing the hand of the potter in every line.

would go into the barn and sing patriotic songs all night long," said their sister, in telling me of her early life in her father's home. Finally, the three boys ran away and enlisted in the Northern army. Two of them met death on Southern battlefields; only the third returned home. As memorials to his dead soldier boys, the potter made two wreaths of clay flowers to hang upon the walls of the local church. With them hung the photographs and the war records of the soldiers, and an American flag. On a little shelf above these ornaments stood a bouquet of immortelles under a glass dome.

Upon these wreaths the potter seems to have lavished all the wealth of his artistic fancy. They are sixteen inches in diameter. The flowers were modeled from the common garden and wild flowers which grew about his home—the sunflower, rose, daisy, myrtle, zinnia, water lily, buttercup—all massed within a band of green leaves. Loving care and thought are felt in the modeling and arranging of these flowers, leaves, and buds, and each tiny petal and stamen were closely studied before being fashioned into clay. The colors were evidently put on after the wreath was fired. Now somewhat faded and soiled, they were once, no doubt, the nearest approach to the colors of nature which the potter could command. These wreaths are not only unique and interesting examples of our pioneer ceramic art, they are also mute witnesses to a tragic period in our national life.

For his church, Mehwaldt also wrought a huge chandelier of clay, which for many years was the chief artistic feature of the barn-like structure, and which is spoken of by the people of the village today as a marvel of achievement. This chandelier was about four feet in diameter and held two rows of candles. The large, round, central piece was surrounded by small scalloped saucers for holding the candles, and all were held together by festoons of colored clay balls strung on wires. I rescued several pieces of this chandelier, as well as a pair of tall pewter altar candlesticks, from a heap of discarded objects in the church loft. The chandelier was made of coarse, reddish clay, well-modeled and colored, and the fragments show considerable originality and skill in the design and making.

Mehwaldt produced quantities of chimney crocks, earthenware crocks of all sizes, butter-crocks, with handles, to be hung in wells to keep the butter cool; cooking utensils, candlesticks, all manner of tableware—platters, plates, sauce-dishes, cups and saucers, mugs, pitchers, sugar bowls, vegetable dishes, teapots, and teakettles,—all either of a reddish-brown color mottled with dark spots, or of plain, dark brown. This dark-colored tableware would have suited the country housewife in the story, who, weary with much dish-washing, drove to town one day for the express purpose of buying a set of dishes "that wouldn't show dirt."

Fig. 6 — Coffee Pot
Glazed only in part. Note the marks of the potter's wheel. An interesting example.

These dishes somewhat resemble the brown mottled ware of the Bennington potteries, which was made about the same time; but they lack the rich green and blue shades and the hard metallic glaze of the Vermont specimens.

Potter Mehwaldt also fabricated several German tiled stoves, and quantities of milk-pans. The pans were discarded, however, as soon as tin pans came into general use in the neighborhood. At Christmastime, he usually turned out many little dinner-sets for children, and toys made in the form of pigs, owls, roosters, and birds, with whistles in their tails. When these figures were filled with water the whistles gave out a variety of tones.

An inkstand by him displays more elaborate workmanship than the table dishes. It is nine inches long and five inches high. Above the large space for penholders are two receptacles resting in holes in the top. One of these is for ink, and the other has a perforated top through which to scatter the sand which was used in those days in place of blotting paper. Each end of the stand is decorated with a rose blossom and branch in relief, while from the front hangs a row of heart-shaped figures. I have also seen a large bread-mixing bowl, which he made, with the words, "Give us this day our daily bread," in German lettering around the outer edge.

The clay which Mehwaldt found in that section was of the common red kind, coarse in quality and calling for much working. "It was not like it was in the old country," said his son, in talking about the experiences of his early life. "It took father a long time to get the right mixture of sand. He had to experiment a great deal, and that meant a great loss. He first formed the wet clay into large lumps like cheeses, piled them on the floor of his workshop, and then took a circular knife and shaved them down very fine, and took out all of the stones and hard materials. He then worked the mixture on the floor with his bare feet. We boys helped with this, and it was pretty cold work in winter time. He then cut off small pieces of the clay and kneaded them on a table just as bread is kneaded. He had to get out every particle of stone or hard substance. All this was very severe work, and he said that, if he were a young man, he would get up some kind of machine to do this work."

"We children helped to grind the lead for the glaze," said his daughter. "There was a large stone in one corner of the workroom. From the ceiling a pole was suspended, with a flat stone on the end of it, and this pole had to be kept going round and round in order to grind the lead in the tub. My brother and I would stand on chairs and take hold of the handles and get it round and round. We would count 100 and then rest. How our arms used to ache! I can imagine I feel it in my shoulders yet, I was that tired."

Red lead was used for the glaze, also tea lead, which had been burned to ashes. Some of the lead was mixed with animal blood to give a darker glaze, and the mottled effect was produced by splashing the darker mixture upon the surface with a small brush. The potter either dipped the dishes into the glaze or poured the liquid over them from a cup. He tried to make blue ware and white ware, but was unsuccessful with the materials at hand.

Mehwaldt adopted no distinctive mark for his pottery. Several pieces have the letter M scratched in the biscuit, as if done with a sharp-pointed stick. The forms are simple and good and show little attempt at ornamentation. Several of the pitchers have rows of impressed lines around the top, while the more elaborate plates bear around the rim impressions which the potter made by pinching the soft clay between his thumb and forefinger, "just as we fix pie-crust around the edge of a pie," explained his daughter.

A little shop for the sale of these wares was attached to one side of the potter's house, and many orders were filled for the neighboring towns. The ware sold for a low price. "A plate could be bought for two cents," said his daughter, "and pitchers varied in price according to size. A good one could be bought for ten cents."

Today the settlement of Bergholtz consists of about 200 inhabitants, nearly all of German descent, with two German-Lutheran churches, a general store, a post-office, and a blacksmith shop grouped about a village green. Set down in the midst of a foreign race, these people still cling to their own national tongue and manners, and it was not many years ago that a traveler, passing through this village, imagined himself in another land when he saw upon the feet of several of the inhabitants the wooden shoes of the German peasant.

In a recent pilgrimage to the little village I found a man who was a small boy at the time when the potter came to this country, and who entertained me with stories of their long acquaintance. In his German-flavored English he told how many a time he had watched with Mehwaldt all night over the fires of the kilns. Soft wood was used for fuel, either pine or basswood, and the firing was an affair of over a day and a night, with constant watchers in attendance to maintain the required temperature.

"How sleepy we used to get watching the fires! If it got too hot, it bust; if it was too slow, they cracked," he said. The ruin of a kiln full of material was a serious loss in those days of poverty and struggle. He said that the American clay differed so materially from the clay which the potter had been using in Germany that much experiment and loss were necessary in order to get satisfactory results. He gave me a pantomimic account of the potter sitting at his wheel, kicking it with his feet to make it revolve, and pulling and shaping the wet clay with his hands. He said that, for two years before his death, Mehwaldt was unable to work, as he had injured his feet by the constant effort required to turn the wheel.

That there was no one to carry on the business after his death was a source of great disappointment to the potter. "He was proud of his calling," said his daughter, "and would tell how many generations of his family had been potters, and he did not want the business to die with him." Upon his death, however, the works were destroyed and the house sold. Today, nothing remains of the once flourishing pottery which stood for so many years in the village except the pieces of the peculiar mottled ware still upon the shelves of many homes for miles around.

Fig. 7 — Mehwaldt Pitchers
Here are some very snug and hospitable looking jugs. The only ugly one in the lot is the third in front.

Bergholtz Pottery
Cup and saucer showing mottled glaze characteristic of Mewaldt's tableware.

Grandfather's Thumb

By way of supplementing her article on Bergholtz pottery, which appeared in Antiques for September, Mrs. Camehl has favored the Attic with two interesting letters, one of them enclosing additional photographs and, therewith, much to the Attic's joy, an actual cup and saucer made by Mehwaldt in his rural establishment.

It is worth noting that this cup and saucer, like other tableware produced by Mehwaldt, are covered with a mottled tortoise-shell glaze; whereas his kitchenware was, in the main, of a monotone brown. In a recent visit to Bergholtz, Mrs. Camehl encountered a granddaughter of Mehwaldt, who remembered with satisfaction her youthful visits to her grandfather's home, where she and her sister always ate more out of the beautiful brown dishes of their grandfather's make than they would from their usual ware at home.

"She showed a small pitcher of hers that he made, and in explaining its formation in his hands she ran her thumb through the spout of the pitcher remarking 'That's grandfather's thumb'." This pitcher she would not part with; but Mrs. Camehl did procure a large bread-mixing bowl, eighteen inches in diameter and one and one-half inches deep, bearing around the upper edge, marked with a sharp stick, the following inscription:

"Alles ist ein Gottes Segen
Und an Seiner Gnad gelegen."

"All things come as the blessing of God
And manifest His Lovingkindness."

Surely Mehwaldt found comfort in an old-time religion of faith. Two of his sons killed in the war, the hope of transmitting his trade to his own posterity frustrated, his strength failing—for in his later days he lost the use of his legs from years of constantly kicking the wheel—yet he fixes this motto of submission on clay and adds the prayerful amen, with his initials. It reads like an epitaph. For the brave and faithful old German potter, none more fitting could have been devised.

More Bergholtz Pottery.

The Roof Tiles of Zoar

By E. J. Bognar

Except as noted, photographs from the author's collection

I DARE say that no one has visited Zoar, Ohio — that historic settlement which, for more than eighty years prior to its disbanding in 1898, thrived under a communal government — without remarking on the red-tiled roofs of the houses. Today only about twenty buildings, and most of them relatively small, are still covered with these rare old tiles. On the others modern roofing has superseded the earlier material. Such tiling as remains in place has endured with little deterioration for more than a century; though the collapse of roofs through decaying rafters has caused no little destruction. Indeed, it is sad to report that most of the dwellings in Zoar have been little cared for. Were it not for their originally sound construction, in which brick and heavy timbers were liberally employed, they would long ago have fallen into decay.

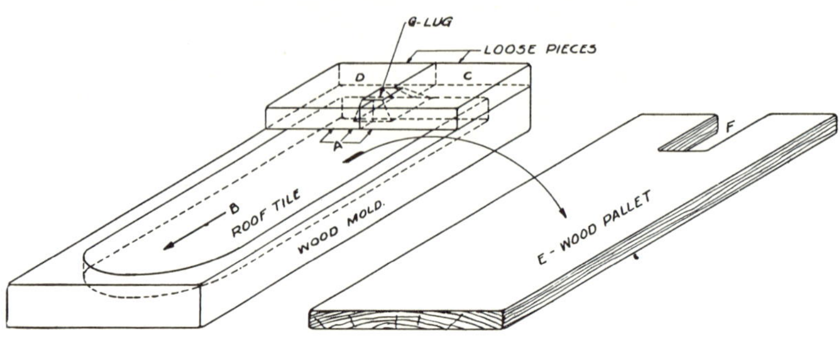

Fig. 1 — Diagram of Tile Mold and Pallet
The partly shaped clay was pressed into the wood mold at the left, and the "lug" formed by means of loose pieces applied at one end. On removal from the mold the tile was turned out on a pallet, such as that shown at the right, and was allowed partially to dry.
Sketch by the author

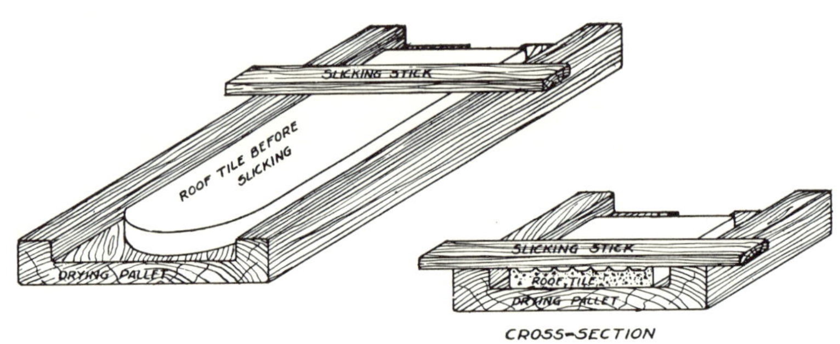

Fig. 2 — Simple Method of Decorating
Where decoration was not impressed in the clay from a design cut in the mold, the partly dried tile was placed in a troughlike pallet and fluted or grooved by drawing a slicking stick over its surface.
Sketch by the author

The first Zoar tiles were made about 1820, shortly after the founding of the town (*1817*). With some interruptions their manufacture continued until late in the 1840's. We are more certain of the beginning date than of that which marked the end of manufacture. All told, approximately two hundred thousand of these handmade tiles were produced by the Zoarites solely for their own use. In so far as known, none were distributed commercially. Of the total output, perhaps fifty-five thousand remain. The rest have been destroyed, or, in recent years, have been acquired by collectors who are attracted by their artistic quality and their historic significance.

Aside from their importance as mementoes of a vanished social experiment, the tiles of Zoar are interesting from a ceramic viewpoint. Handmade wares of similar design would do credit to any roof-tile plant today that cared to undertake their manufacture. Study of their composition reveals that they were molded from local alluvial clay such as may still be found in the flats at the southern extremity of the present village. This clay was doubtless dug by hand, casually picked over to eliminate pebbles and other large impurities, and then

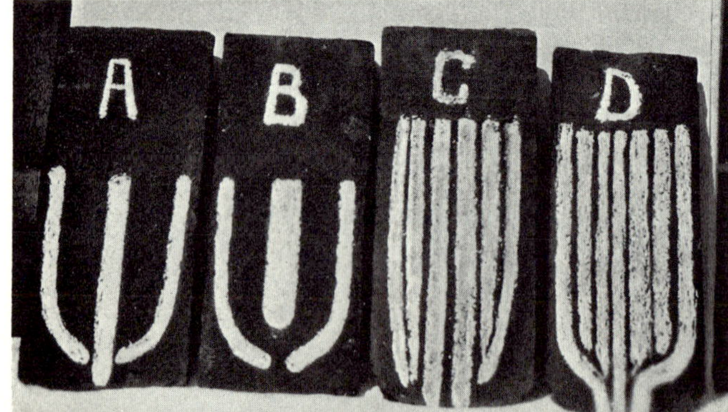

Fig. 3 — Major Types of Flat Roof Tiles
Types *A* and *B* received their pattern in the mold. Tiles of this type are always heavily sanded on the unprinted side, indicating that a liberal amount of sand was used in rolling the walk and that no slicking — which would have removed the sand — was done. Types *C* and *D* rarely show heavy sanding. Their pattern was produced with slicking stick and fingers, which scraped away much of the sand. The designs in this and succeeding photographs have been chalked to obtain greater clarity

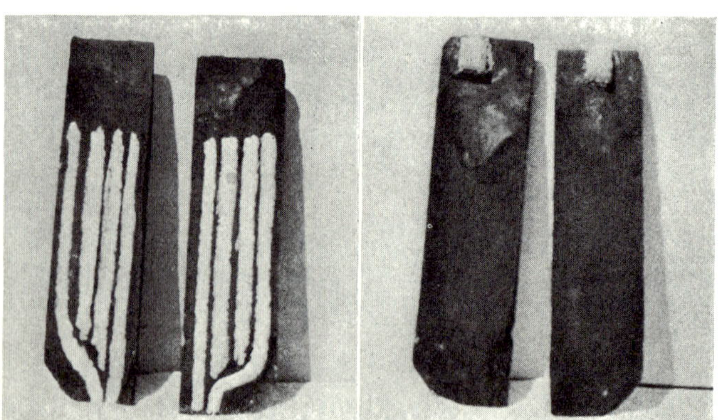

Fig. 4 — Half Tiles
Showing front and back, the latter exposing the lugs that kept the tiles in place when set

Fig. 5 — Dated and Initialed Roof Tile
Impressed *H G in Zoar 1829*. According to Mr. Breymaier, aged 72 years and one of the few survivors of the original community, the initials are those of Henry Gail

Fig. 6 — Dated and Initialed Roof Tile
Scratched *I.G.A. in 1832.* Initials are probably those of a member of the Ackerman family, prominent in Zoar history. *By courtesy of Mrs. Rhea Mansfield Knittle*

dumped on a large floor so that oxen tethered to a turnstile could knead the material as they slowly plodded about in their circuitous path. After the clay had been thus thoroughly trodden, it would be spaded, and probably stored in bins to be drawn upon at need.

Methods of Manufacture

Zoar tiles were formed in wooden molds; and the lug side was molded "up" (*Fig. 1*). The clay "walk" or "roll" (the piece to be molded) of the correct size was shaped by the molder on a table spread with a fine sprinkling of river sand. During this performance the sand, of course, would stick to the "walk," and when the latter was thrown into the mold would prevent the clay from sticking to the wood form. Careful study has revealed that, curiously enough, the lug was not applied after the tile was made, as has been supposed, but was molded directly into the tile by means of a "loose" piece that fitted into the top of the mold and was superimposed on the clay after the "walk" had been thrown into the form (*Fig. 1*).

A wire, or "bow," drawn in the direction shown by the arrow *B* in Figure 1, was used to cut the walk from the loose piece marked *C* and *D* in the illustration. The lug *G*, the reader will note, fitted into the gap *F* in the wood pallet *E*, onto which the tile was dumped and left until semi-dry. Tiles of type *A* and *B* in Figure 3 were allowed to dry completely in the mold or pallet before they were picked up to be burned in the kiln.

Tiles of these two types received their decorative pattern from designs cut in the mold itself. The more ornate tiles of the types *C* and *D* in Figure 3 underwent a different treatment. After their preliminary molding, followed by semi-drying on a pallet, they were laid in another pallet (*Fig. 2*), where their upper surface was scraped into crude flutings with the aid of a grooved "slicking stick." Obviously the slicking stick could incise only parallel lines. For further elaboration the molder used thumb or forefinger to impart a slight inward curvature to the outside flutes (*Fig. 3C*) or to develop a more complicated linear treatment. Worcester, in his monograph *Manufacture of Roofing Tiles* (Bulletin Number II, Geological Survey of Ohio), states that the patterns described were wrought solely by the molder's fingers. With this opinion I disagree. Having studied the Zoar tiles for ten years, during which time I have examined more than five thousand specimens, I am certain that the method was, as I have indicated, partly mechanical, partly free-hand. In fact, I find ample evidence that great care was exercised to ensure uniformity in size, shape, and ornament, by means of such simple devices as mold, pallet, and slip stick, before free-hand adornment was attempted.

The illustration (*Fig. 3*) shows the four major types of flat Zoar roof tiles. These types might be subdivided on the basis of slight variations in design, but such complicated analysis seems unnecessary. It should, however, be noted that half tiles were made to stagger joints on the roof (*Fig. 4*). But either they were not universally used or they have suffered more than their share of destruction, for I have found very

Fig. 7 (above) — Roof Tiles with Unusual Markings
Initials *M.L.B.* on the first of the group probably denote a member of the Breymaier family. Tiles *H* and *E* show interesting departures from usual ornament. The design of tiles dated *1828* and *1830* probably continued in use for a long period

Fig. 8 — Zoar Ridge Tiles

Fig. 9 — The Employment of Ridge Tiles

Fig. 10 — Zoar Ridge Tiles

few of them on the roofs.

To the whole and half tiles already mentioned must be added the nearly cylindrical ridge tiles that crowned the rooftree of a tiled building. These ridge tiles were all molded by hand in a cradle with the exposed side up. Some were finished without decoration. Others were marked with free-hand patterns executed with a stick or the molder's calloused finger-tips. Four distinct ridge-tile designs occur — just as we note four basic designs in the flat tiles.

Fig. 11 — An Early Residence of Zoar
One of the oldest in the community; restored, retiled, and ridged with original local tiles. Old ridge tiles are now scarce, and considerable hunting was needed to find the specimens illustrated

Of course, the most interesting of the Zoar tiles are the ones that in some respect depart from type, by virtue either of a special flourish scratched by the molder, or of impressed dates and initials. Dated and

Fig. 12 — Hearth Tiles or Bricks from Zoar
Made from an alluvial clay. Such tiles are to be found in the older dwellings and sidewalks about Zoar

Fig. 13 — Typical Wall Construction in Zoar
After the log-house days, buildings were framed in oak, the interstices filled with brick, and the surface stuccoed

initialed tiles are of particular interest, inasmuch as they help us to identify some of the old-time makers and perhaps to determine just when a given design was in popular use. I have made a special effort to collect unusual tiles of this description and am illustrating a number of the more significant ones.

Tile roofs are heavy, but the methods of construction employed by the Zoarites were adequate to sustain the load. In fact, they more closely approximated mediæval European methods than any other construction known to me on the American continent. A frame of stout oak timbers having been erected, the spaces between the posts and girts were filled with brick. The entire outer face of the wall thus constituted was covered with stucco. Had the brick filling only been concealed by this coating and the framework left exposed, the houses of Zoar would have borne a close resemblance to the half-timbered dwellings of Elizabethan England.

The roofs themselves were of heavy rafters on which were placed thin split hickory boards about two inches wide and three sixteenths of an inch thick, and of varying lengths, so spaced as to lie directly under the joints in the tile and prevent leakage of water. Save for these strips, no board or other provision against water seepage was employed. The tile rested on the rafters.

The tiles of Zoar, like the local brick, are rather porous. Their color is characteristically a dull deep red. They were burned in kilns near the place of their making, and I am of the opinion that with them were burned hearth tiles, pottery, and bricks. Of these last, large quantities — in two dominant sizes — were produced (*Fig. 12*). At a later time I may have something to say about the pottery of Zoar.

Editor's Note. The Separatists Society of Zoar was a communistic religious organization located at Zoar, on the Tuscarawas River, in Ohio. It was founded by two hundred and twenty-five German Protestant peasants, lead by Joseph Baumler (later called Bimeler), who emigrated from Württemberg in April 1817. Bimeler purchased 5,000 acres of farm land, portions of which each family was expected eventually to acquire, in return for labor. Diversity of ability made this scheme impracticable, however, and in 1819 the Zoarites organized into a community of property and effort. In 1832 the Society reached its highest membership — five hundred — and was incorporated under Ohio laws as "The Society of Separatists of Zoar," which had the powers and rights of a corporation. After its organization as a commune the Society steadily prospered, and, in time, built up several industries. At the period of its height, it boasted two flour mills, a saw mill, a planing mill, machine shop, tannery, dyehouse, stove foundry, cooper shop, woolen mill, brewery, slaughterhouse, blacksmith shop, tile works, pottery, and so on. The value of the property increased until, about 1875, the community was worth one and a half million dollars. But rival industries injured Zoar trade, the Zoarites themselves were not progressive, few new members joined the Society, and the younger members became increasingly interested in seeking their fortunes elsewhere. The decline continued until 1897, at which time the Society decided to disband and place its properties in the hands of a commission for equal distribution among the remaining members. This was completed in the fall of 1898. Life in Zoar was simple and serene. There was never a divorce in the community, and no member was every charged with a crime or felony. The Society, whose religious tenets were few and simple, considered ceremonies useless, engaged in no public prayer, and recognized no ordained minister. It did not seek additions, nor did it attempt to propagate its principles, either religious or economic.

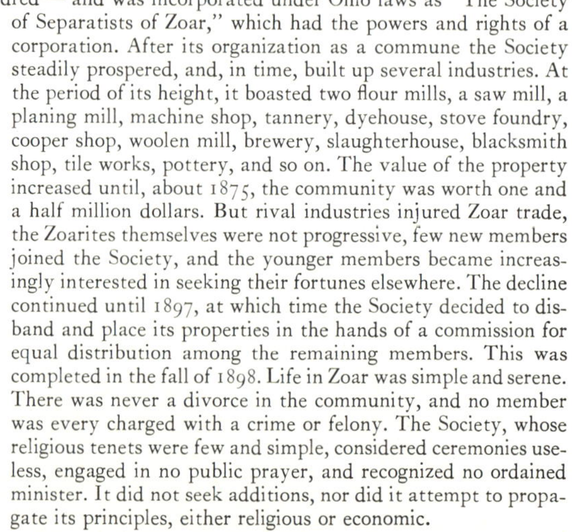

Fig. 14 — The Rarest Roof Tile of Zoar
Inscribed *Zoar/D:14/Juli/1824/C W M.* The initials are said to be those of Christian W. Mitchely

III Redware—The English Influence

While it is generally recognized that early New England redware was made in the English manner, and more specifically that fancy wares were stylistically related to the so-called "Metropolitan" slipware, now thought to have been made during the seventeenth century at Harlow in Essex rather than in London, Lura Woodside Watkins has noted an exception to prove the rule. In the last article of the following section (pp. 70–74), she mentions New Jersey potters who brought their methods to Norwalk, Connecticut, producing slipware plates that, she feels, cannot in many cases be distinguished from those of New Jersey or Pennsylvania.

Joseph Johnson Smith, on the other hand, states in *Regional Aspects of American Folk Pottery,* published in 1974 by the Historical Society of York County, Pennsylvania, that bat-formed plates from Connecticut differ in profile and coggling from those of Pennsylvania. "The Connecticut plate has a shallower, flatter curve to the side and less pronounced coggling," he says.

Anyone interested in visiting the Brooks Pottery, described on pages 57–59 by Lura Woodside Watkins, can do so at Old Sturbridge Village in Massachusetts, where the building was moved from Goshen, Connecticut. There it is serving once again as a pottery where redware is made according to the early methods.

Early New England pottery (probable date 1800–1850). The center item in the top row has been attributed to Barnstable, Massachusetts. The first item in the lower row has been similarly attributed. The small black glazed bowl in this lower row is credited to Whately, Massachusetts. Sources of the other items are unknown, beyond the possibility that they are in New England. Scale may be judged from the height of the largest specimen—the green jug of the upper row—which is 10 1/2 inches. These pieces were formerly in the collection of Mrs. William Whitman, Jr., and are now on display at The Bennington Museum, Bennington, Vermont.

THE BAYLEYS: ESSEX COUNTY POTTERS

PART I. *Chiefly Biographical*

By LURA WOODSIDE WATKINS

THE COMMON glazed redware used by our colonial ancestors is one of the most perishable of ceramic types. Its soft body is easily chipped; its glaze readily devoured by acids. Furthermore, since its use was limited almost exclusively to kitchen and dairy, it was not so carefully preserved as the choicer wares in the china cupboard. In consequence, only a small quantity of native pottery made before 1800 has survived, and we have had virtually no means of ascertaining what were the shapes, glazes, and styles of decoration employed by our earliest New England potters.

Pennsylvania potters have left us a record in the form of rare dated and inscribed pieces. Thus to mark redware was not customary in New England; so that determining the provenance of stray specimens has been largely a matter of guesswork. The only fact of which we are quite certain is that all pottery made of *native* New England clay *burns red.* The making of stoneware necessitated the importation of clay from other parts of the country.

During the last third of the 1700's redware potters were to be found in nearly every community in the settled portions of New England. One observer has stated that, in 1791, the output of common native pottery exceeded the current consumption. (*A Brief Examination of Lord Sheffield's Observations on the Commerce of the United States*, American Museum, Matthew Carey, 1791.) This was certainly true of Essex County in eastern Massachusetts, a centre of the clay industry since the establishing of the first potworks in Salem before 1640. Potters have plied their trade in Amesbury, Merrimacport, Newburyport, Rowley, Ipswich, and Gloucester. It is said that in the Danvers-Peabody district alone sixty workmen have been recorded. More than probably Danvers (until 1710 a part of Salem) was a training ground for many apprentices who later settled in the surrounding towns.

Obviously, the only reliable information about eighteenth-century redware must be drawn directly from the fragments of discarded or damaged objects such as were invariably left in the potters' dumps. Many such waste piles must be conveniently awaiting the excavator's shovel. Others must be buried beyond recall beneath various buildings. In 1934 my husband and I, by the merest chance, had opportunity to do some rather extensive digging at Newburyport, where, from 1764 to 1799, two generations of the Bayley family had worked as potters. The construction of a bypass under High Street had occasioned the removal of many dwelling houses and shops, including the whole block bounded by Summer, High, and Winter Streets. When we arrived upon the scene, a steam shovel had already ploughed the area, scooping away tons of earth, to a depth of twenty-five feet or more. On both sides of the cellar level of the demolished buildings the ground was still undisturbed. Running parallel with Summer Street, the shelf thus formed was ten or twelve feet wide; on the opposite side, six or eight. Below cellar level, the loosened earth sloped at a steep angle to the bottom of the cut.

The Bayley house and pottery shop had stood at the junction of High and Summer Streets. All that remained of the pottery dump when we began our work was a small segment of shelf, running back perhaps fifty feet. By stepping over the edge of the slope, we could dig in under the surface, which we were not allowed to disturb. At this point, we were about eight feet below the level of High Street. The quantity of earthenware that we managed to uncover in the short time at our disposal before the construction work was finished convinced us that an even larger amount had been eliminated by the steam shovel. In fact, the operator of the machine told us that he had been shoveling through pottery for two days. Nevertheless, our findings are, we believe, a distinct contribution to the history of native ceramics.

Since our discovery at Newburyport, we have also obtained a small supply of fragments from the shard pile of a still earlier Bayley in Rowley. This bit of history, therefore, really begins at Rowley, although in order to make the earlier data comprehensible the record of results should be set down first from the Newburyport angle.

THE BAYLEY FAMILY

The potting Bayleys were descended from James Bayley, one of the first settlers of Rowley. In 1668 James Bayley's son John married Mary Mighill and set up housekeeping in a tiny cottage on Wethersfield Street near the corner of Kiln Lane, a narrow way which took its name not from the pottery but from Deacon Mighill's lime kiln. The cottage referred to was enlarged in the next generation by Nathaniel Bayley. It continued to be the home of the Bayley family until 1902, when it was torn down.

Joseph Bayley, potter, one of the children of the enterprising Nathaniel, was the son in his generation who owned and occupied the enlarged dwelling. Born October 17, 1701, Joseph was nearly twenty-one at the time of his father's death. When he came of age, his uncles, Jonathan, Thomas, and James Bayley, who had an interest in the property, assigned their rights to him, and he was thenceforth head of the family.

FIG. 1—JOHN AND MARY (MIGHILL) BAYLEY'S HOUSE

Built in 1668 presumably for the newly married couple. Located on Wethersfield Street, Rowley, Massachusetts. Enlarged by Nathaniel Bayley, of the next generation. Torn down in 1902 after occupancy by six generations of the same family. From a woodcut of the 1800's; hence not altogether trustworthy

Joseph Bayley married Sarah Jewett June 12, 1725. For at least two years he had been pursuing his calling. The first mention of his name as a potter appears in a deed dated January 18, 1723. Even earlier he had finished his apprenticeship probably under one of the master potters of Danvers, and had been working independently. Four children were born to Joseph and his wife in Rowley, and two later in Newbury. They were Elizabeth (*1725*), Nathaniel (*1727*), Daniel (*1729*), Amos (*1731*), Joseph (*1735*), Hannah (*1742*).

In 1735 Joseph and his family ceased to reside in Rowley and moved to Newbury. Joseph lived until 1761. For twenty-five years he must have worked in Newbury, but as yet the precise location of his house in that community is unknown. It is certain that he owned a dwelling, for it is listed in the following inventory of his estate:

One Bed and Bedstead 74/
One timepiece 24/ apparel 26/8 Books 18/ pewter 12 pound 12/2 iron pots 6/8 Scales and weights 8/ Steelyard 1/6 Box iron 1/8 a Shovel and tongs 3/ 3 tramels 5/4 a warming pan 6/ a frying pan 4/ 4 old tables 8/ three Chests 8/8 2 Desks 7/4 Some old Chairs 4/8 a looking glass 2/4 Earthen and Glassware 4/ wooden ware 3/ a Saw 5/4 a Gun 6/ a lamp and skimmer 2/4 a Sieve and Candlestick 1/1 9 lb of flax 6/ old Iron 8/6 a Mortar 2/ three wheels 6/8 three presses and a plate 10/8
A stone 13/4
half a Kilnhouse and kiln utensils 9/ two Jars 1/6
a House 16 " " " "

FIG. 2 — THE BAYLEY HOUSE SHORTLY BEFORE ITS DEMOLITION
Apparently the farther end of the house as seen in this illustration represents the cottage of 1668. In the course of 234 years of use the building must have been subjected to sundry alterations in addition to those undertaken by Nathaniel. Here Joseph Bayley the potter (*1701–1761*) was born, and so, too, his son Daniel (*1729–1792*)

Joseph probably shared ownership of the kiln and kilnhouse with his son Daniel, who succeeded to the pottery business. His possession of three wheels may indicate that a third potter worked with them at one time or another.

DANIEL BAYLEY

Joseph's third child and second son was born June 27, 1729, in Rowley. He was only six years old when the family moved to Newbury, but he was probably making pottery before 1745. When he established the High Street shop (*1763*), he was an experienced workman. In 1763, the year in which Newburyport was set off from Newbury as a town, Daniel bought of Moses Ordway, for a little more than twelve pounds, the lot on the corner of High Street and the passage (Ordway's Lane) later known as Summer Street. This piece of land had a frontage of thirty-six feet and a length of sixty-four. Just across the lane were St. Paul's Church and its churchyard.

Here Daniel erected a dwelling house and a workshop. In a mortgage deed to Daniel Farnham, dated March 26, 1764, the property is described as "One Certain Dwelling House and Potter's Shop and Kiln adjoining and the Stone and Floor for grinding the Clay the Wheels Irons and Utensils to the Potters' business belonging and in said Shop together with about Ten Rods of Land on which the House Shop &c are Erected and Situated near Saint Paul's Church in Newburyport aforesaid."

MUSICIAN AND PUBLISHER

The story of Daniel Bayley is of unusual interest. More than a routine craftsman, Daniel could boast several accomplishments. He became the church organist and choir leader of St. Paul's, whose organ had been acquired a few years before from King's Chapel in Boston. His love of music turned his thoughts to the publication of psalm tunes. Finding the existing collections scanty and difficult to read, he proceeded to assemble old favorites and new. These he printed himself and sold from his house.

In this connection the name of Daniel Bayley is not unknown to bibliophiles. Indeed, these folk have disagreed as to whether Bayley actually did his own typesetting and presswork or employed a Boston printer. His first two published collections were little more than reprints, "printed for and sold by Bulkeley Emerson and Daniel Bayley." However, Daniel's assurance that *The American Harmony*, published in 1769, was printed and sold by the author may be accepted as the truth. In the inventory of his estate are listed "1 Printing press and Roll" and "Bookbinder's Tools" — evidence that printing was in fact one of his avocations. Thus Isaiah Thomas' claim to have made the first book printed in Newburyport seems to be refuted.

Evans' *Bibliography* and Currier's *History of Newburyport* yield a long list of Daniel Bayley's publications. To this may be added one more work, which I have found advertised in the *Essex Journal and Merrimack Packet*, under date of April 13, 1774:

> This day PUBLISHED, and to be SOLD by Daniel Bayley, at his House near the CHURCH And at the POST OFFICE Mr. Noble's Sermon on the nature, use and end of Music in the Worship of God, Preached at the North Meeting House, Newbury Port, February 8, 1774. At the same Place may be had Tansur's and Williams's singing Books, and a new Royal Harmony, Also Bibles, Spelling Books, Psalters, Primmers, Watt's Psalms, and Hymns, Tate and Brady's ditto, &c.

It has been said that Daniel Bayley was likewise a coppersmith. While I find no evidence in support of this tradition, other than lumps of copper unearthed on the pottery site and probably material for coloring glaze, I think it possible that our potter may have dabbled in metalwork. His inventory lists ten pounds of old copper, twenty-seven pounds of leaden weights, and seventy-seven pounds of pewter, besides the household garnish weighing thirty-two pounds. It may be, however, that these materials were taken in exchange for earthenware and later sold as opportunity permitted.

Judging by the items in his inventory, Daniel was a man of taste in dress and in the furnishings of his home. He was the owner of "Jacketts" of black velvet, broadcloth, linen, and fustian, of three coats, broadcloth, fustian, and "wooling," three pairs of breeches, a waistcoat, four caps, two hats, two wigs in a box, and a walking stick. His wife wore cloaks of silk and broadcloth, dresses of light and dark chintz, a "taffity" gown, a harebine gown, a "bussel" petticoat, bonnets, caps, and a lawn apron. It is easy to picture the couple after a hard week's work, setting forth on Sunday in gala attire.

The inventory also names the following items relating to Daniel's craft: "½ Potter's kiln and house — 5Li; 1 Stone and muffler 3/; ½ Of the clay knives 6/; Potter's shop and half loose boards 9Li; clay and raw ware 3/; 1 horse cart 3Li; empty casks and tubs 1Li. 4/." (A muffler is a small kiln, sometimes used for glazing.)

YOUTH AND MARRIAGE

At the age of twenty-one, Daniel was in Gloucester. There he married Elizabeth Dennen in April 1750. A child born the following year was christened Daniel. This infant must have suffered the fate of many colonial babes, for we find a second son, born in Newbury five years later, also endowed with the paternal name. Just how long Daniel lived in Gloucester is not known; I find no record of his residence between 1751 and 1753.

Here I must digress to narrate one of the strange coincidences of research. In Ravenswood Park, Gloucester, a tract of forest maintained for the public enjoyment, lies a row of three cellars on the "Old Salem Path," reputed to have been the direct road from Gloucester to Salem in colonial days. Among one of these ruins I had found some unusually large bricks. They were five by nine by two and one half inches, as compared with the ordinary house brick measuring four by seven (or eight) by two. In the opinion of Professor F. H. Norton of the Department of Ceramics at the Massachusetts Institute of Technology, my finds are kiln bricks.

On the basis of this clue, we secured permission from the park trustees to undertake some investigative digging. Near the cellar we found pottery fragments and kiln bricks scattered over an area the size of a large room. They were not more than a foot below the surface and were pretty thoroughly disintegrated. With them we recovered a few pieces of salt glaze, delft, and early creamware, none of them representing articles likely to have been made after 1760. Continuing our work in the hope of finding assurance that a pottery had once occupied the site, we finally came upon the needed evidence. It was a spur or crow's-foot — one of the triangular supports or stilts of clay formerly used for stacking bowls in a kiln.

The question of who may have owned the little pottery in the woods then arose. Neither recorded history nor the knowledge of the best-informed persons now living afforded the slightest clue. A study of county records, however, revealed the names of several landowners in the vicinity of the sparsely settled Salem Path. One of them was Daniel Bayley's elder brother, Nathaniel, who, as early as 1747, occupied a house in Freshwater Cove, where he raised a family, and in 1760 died of smallpox. Sudden recollection of Daniel's Gloucester marriage at last supplied a key to the mystery. Members of the Dennen family had owned land on the north side of the Salem road. Furthermore, Daniel's second wife, Sarah (Thomas) Stone, the widow of John Stone, was a Gloucester woman. In 1751 she was living in the same neighborhood. Various other names on deeds and mortgages added more links to the chain connecting Daniel Bayley with this romantic woodland ruin.

It is not difficult to reconstruct the story. In 1749 Gloucester's veteran potter, Joseph Gardner, who for more than fifty years had supplied the town with earthenware, passed on. Quite probably young Daniel, apprised of the event while visiting his brother's home, seized the occasion to strike out for himself in a new and favorable location. Either at the home of Elizabeth Dennen's parents or in a place of his own, he set up a kiln. Clay was plentiful near by at Dolliver's Neck; wood was abundant in the forest; and trade went by the door. The future looked bright. Then the smallpox horror descended upon Gloucester and created the wildest panic. Business was at a standstill. This misfortune, coupled with the loss of his child, perhaps from the dreaded epidemic, must have prompted Daniel to retreat to Newbury.

THE POTTERY IN NEWBURYPORT

Presumably on his return to Newburyport, Daniel went into business with his father, Joseph. His daughter Elizabeth was born in Newbury, April 2, 1753, and Daniel, his second namesake, July 15, 1755. In June 1765, only a year after he had built the High Street pottery, he lost his wife. Two weeks later Daniel announced his marriage intentions to Sarah Stone. Reading between the lines, one may perhaps find reason for his seemingly indecent haste. In 1760 he had lost his brother; in 1761, his father. Now his wife was gone, leaving him in a new home with two small children to care for. What more suitable than his marriage to a widow, already the mother of three children, whom he had known in his youth at Gloucester? With Sarah, Daniel lived out his days. Four other children came to swell the household: William, born May 9, 1766; Anna Thomas, January 6, 1769; Nathaniel, June 16, 1771; Mary, August 6, 1775.

THE
Essex Harmony
containing a new and concise
INTRODUCTION TO
Musick
To which is added
a Choice and Valuable Collection
of PSALM Tunes Suited to the
Different Measures of Either
Version Composed in Three and
Four Parts Carefully set in Score
by DANIEL BAILEY Philo Music
Newbury-Port Printed and Sold by
The Author sold also
Book Sellers In Boston 1770
A

FIG. 3 — TITLE OF "THE ESSEX HARMONY"
One of many collections of "Psalm tunes" printed by Daniel Bayley, who was a musician and printer as well as a potter. *Size of page*, 3⅜ by 5$^{13}/_{16}$ inches. *From the collection of Robert W. Lull*

Sarah Bayley died in 1792. A fortnight later her husband was laid beside her in St. Paul's churchyard. Today one may find the gravestones of the couple less than two feet from the southeast wall of the present church. As I stood at the spot one warm spring day, the music of the organ suddenly rumbled through the open window above; the ground shook, and with it, the bones of Daniel Bayley. I thought he must be pleased to have it so.

Daniel's namesake and his half-brothers, William and Nathaniel, all became potters. Daniel and William worked with their father until the latter's death, when the property was divided between the two young men. So exact was the partition that an imaginary line was drawn through the centre of the house door to a stake in the land behind. William was given the half of the house on Summer Street, with "the privilege to bake in the Oven in the North-west end of said house as long as the said chimney shall stand." Daniel inherited the other half, with a larger portion of the land, and the pottery buildings. The other brothers and sisters, after some family bickering, were each paid $100 from the estate. Nathaniel married Abigail Pilsbury of Newbury, March 2, 1793; had one child, born in Newbury in 1794; mortgaged a lot of land on "backstreet" in 1796; and thenceforth is heard of no more until he died of consumption in Newburyport at the age of seventy-eight.

It is, of course, impossible to distinguish the work of the elder Daniel from that of his sons in the pieces recovered from the Bayley pottery in Newbury. The enterprise must be judged as a family affair. Apparently the father was the moving spirit, for the business was discontinued shortly after his death. June 25, 1796, Daniel Junior mortgaged his share of the property, including the pottery buildings, to Caleb Stickney. Three years later, February 22, 1799, he died. William followed him in May of the same year.

The inventory of the older brother's estate lists "the kiln house and kiln, $20; 1 mill to grind clay, $3.33; about 200 feet shelve boards, $1.33; one kiln and one Quarter of Raw Ware, $12.50; Potter's Shop. $33.33; Two Wheels. $3.33;" and a few tools and implements. There is no evidence that any of the children of either brother followed their father's trade.

Thus before 1800 an industry which had flourished for eighty years, through three generations, passed out of existence. That it came to a sudden conclusion is one of the helpful circumstances in studying the wares recovered. *All the pieces excavated at Newburyport fall into the period from 1764 to 1799.*

Author's Note. Recently I have discovered that Joseph Bayley's land faced on Winter Street, formerly Bartlet's Lane, near the present site of the Newburyport railroad station. It was entirely removed during construction of the bypass.

THE BAYLEYS: ESSEX COUNTY POTTERS

PART II. *Their Products*

By LURA WOODSIDE WATKINS

A FEW words about the methods employed by early New England redware potters may aid in understanding the specimens found. Made from a native, blue, glacial clay, redware is so called because, when burned, it turns red like an ordinary flowerpot. Such clay is abundant in New England. The Bayley pottery was situated over a bed of this material, and clay pits were accessible only a few hundred yards away. Mixed with water in a revolving pug mill, until of the proper consistency, the clay was rolled into balls and stored for future use. Then, freed from pebbles, or, perhaps, screened for finer work, it was kneaded and shaped into blocks of convenient size. The essential material was then ready for the potter's wheel. The turning process has been well illustrated in ANTIQUES (January 1931), showing exactly how the most delicate bowls, as well as the heaviest jars, may be made. As the objects were formed, they were placed on boards and carried away to dry. Two or three days later they were ready for the glazing process.

Almost without exception, New England redware was coated with a lead glaze. This was a mixture of *sand, powdered red lead*, and *water*, which, when fired, produced a glassy surface. If the interior only of a piece was to be glazed, it was customary to pour some of the liquid mixture into the vessel, which was then, perhaps, given a few whirls on the wheel to insure an even coating. The surplus glaze was then poured out. If both exterior and interior were to be covered, the object was simply held by the base and dipped into the glaze tub, thus coating it.

Glazed redware is usually reddish or brownish in hue, the result of the natural body showing through the clear glaze. No added coloring matter was necessary to achieve reddish tones. In order to obtain a black or brown, varying quantities of manganese oxide were added to the glaze; for green, copper filings. The mottled effects to be observed in nearly all native pottery were occasioned by mineral impurities in the glazing substances or in the clay itself rather than by any intention on the potter's part. Such variabilities add greatly to the charm of these simple utensils and are an additional insurance against an exact likeness between any two pieces.

FIG. 4 — JUGS AND PITCHERS: DARK-BROWN GLAZE
a, Two-quart jug. *b*, Fragment of quart pitcher. *c*, Fragment of two-quart pitcher

FIG. 5 — PUDDING POTS, BAKING DISHES, AND LARD POTS

EIGHTEENTH-CENTURY FORMS

So little pottery dating from the eighteenth century is in existence today that we were surprised by the variety of forms revealed by our Newburyport discoveries. The following list of the articles that we found complete, or in fragments sufficient in quantity or size to show dimensions, is only partly representative of the things made in this one pottery. The measurements are given in inches, the width by the height.

Pudding pans — 8 ¼ x 5 ½ or 5 ¾; 8 x 6 ½; 7 x 4; 4 x 3
Lard pots (the deep jars also known as bean pots) — 6 x 7 ½; 7 x 8; 8 ½ x 11
Deep dishes, of all diameters from the size of a saucer 5 x 1 ⅜ to large pans
Bowls — 4 x 1 ½; 4 ¼ x 2; 4 ¼ x 2 ¼; 6 x 2; 6 x 2 ¾; 6 ¾ x 3 ¼; 7 x 3 ¼
Milk or bread pans, of various sizes, the largest 18 ½ x 4 ½
Bowl with flared rim — 4 x 2
Pitchers (body only) — 6 x 7; 3 x 4 ¼; 2 ¾ x 3 ½
Straight mugs — 3 x 4; 3 ¾ x 5 ¾; 3 ¾ x 6 ¼; 4 x 6 ½
A curved mug — 3 ¾ x 5 ¼
A porringer — 5 ¾ x 2 ¾
A washbowl — about 14 x 4 ½
Chamber pots — from 6 ½ x 5 ½ to 8 x 6 ¼
Jugs — one measuring 6 x 8 ½
Teapots
Beakers
Baking dishes, with steep sides

UNDECORATED WARE

The major proportion of utensils made in the Bayley pottery, and probably in other potworks of the period, was undecorated and purely utilitarian. Lard pots, pudding pots, and deep baking dishes were indispensable in the colonial kitchen. The lard pot (the shape so designated in pottery bills of a later period) is a straight-sided, open-mouthed jar, incurving toward the base. It is unglazed outside, but glazed within. On its outer surface it is well smoothed, but the telltale ridges left by the potter's fingers in turning are visible on the interior surface. Bayley's lard pots were sometimes lined with a coffee-colored glaze, or, quite as often, with greenish-black or mottled dark brown. It would be impossible to distinguish them from similar jars made in any one of a hundred New England potteries. These receptacles are also known as cream pots, and I have many times heard them called old-fashioned bean pots. They were suited to a number of purposes, but I think their primary purpose was to harbor drippings or other kinds of grease.

FIG. 6 — ALE MUGS
a, Small, with thin walls; brown. *b*, One-and-one-half pints; black. *c*, Quart; brownish orange, brown streakings. *d*, Dark brown

FIG. 7 — BOWLS
a and c, Small, with greenish and brown mottlings. *Diameter*, about 4 inches. *b* is 6 inches in diameter

On the other side of the excavation, near the corner of High and Winter Streets, we found jars of similar shape, slightly elaborated with tooled bands. They were peculiar in showing a glaze on the exterior of the base (*Fig. 10e*). I believe them to have been made at an earlier period than the others. An example of this type occurs among the Rowley fragments.

The deep pudding pots, somewhat slope-sided, like a flowerpot, were used for baking Indian puddings or similar mixtures. They, too, may have been antecedents of the modern bean pot. Unglazed outside, they were covered inside with a coffee-colored or greenish glaze. In one instance, we found fragments of this form in a true and brilliant green. The range of sizes may be observed in Figure 5. The jar in the top row was recovered from the dump without chip or scratch, although its unglazed surface, as in all other examples, is sand colored from long burial in the earth. A break in the body of any piece invariably shows its basic red color. Pudding dishes, broader but not so deep, were common. We have no entire example, but the fragments give clear evidence of form and size.

Huge pans for mixing dough or for setting milk were made in quantities in all potteries. Although not very strong, they were thick, and heavy to handle. Milk pans were ordinarily glazed inside with a perfectly plain glaze. The artistic soul of Daniel Bayley must have revolted against the dreariness of such objects. He varied the coloring with happy results. One large pan of which we have a part is gray-green with fine dark spatterings and patches of smooth color; another, smaller, is greenish or yellowish with rosy mottlings; and the largest of all, eighteen and one half inches in diameter, is a mahogany hue with contrasting areas of plain and streaked glaze. The effect was intentional.

It is perhaps impossible now to learn the exact purpose of the smaller slope-sided pans of the same shape. Their great variety within the limited range of Bayley's colors suggests that they progressed, on occasion, from the fireplace to the dining table. No doubt they were used for "pasties" or meat pies, or for the deep-dish apple pies still baked in the country. All Newburyport pans, either large or small, are unglazed outside, and many of them show clearly the parallel marks that were made by the potter's fingers when the pieces were turned on the wheel.

Numerous fragments of ware without glaze turned up in the wastepile. They are parts of jars or pots whose purpose is problematical. Even when washed with glaze on one surface, redware does not always hold liquids without oozing. Unglazed objects could certainly not be employed in cooking. Jars for cooling water were, however, unglazed. We found rims and bases of very large coolers, but the clay in them is so extremely coarse that I have hesitated to include water jars as a Bayley product. They are possibly of foreign origin.

With one exception, the remaining articles to be described are glazed on both inner and outer surfaces, their bases left plain. In the category of ware thus glazed, but without decoration, are jugs, mugs, bowls, and pitchers.

Jug fragments were so few in the Newburyport excavation that one might almost conclude that the Bayleys made none. It is more reasonable to assume, since jugs were probably the commonest article of pottery manufacture, that there were many such fragments in the tons of material carried away by the steam shovel. The pieces illustrated bear the closest resemblance to Bayley's other work. The jug in Figure 4 is virtually complete; it was found in a cistern-like cavity in the embankment, whence came some of the most interesting items recovered. The color is a mahogany brown with fine streakings. It will be noticed that the handle of one jug (*Fig. 10c, middle row*) rises from the shoulder of the piece, while that in Figure 4 springs from the neck itself. Whether this variation in practice is significant of period or only of the potter's whim is difficult to determine.

The mugs made by Bayley and his sons are handsome. Their height places them at once in the century of tall ale tankards. Compared with these fine drinking vessels, the cans of later days are stolid affairs, squatty and insignificant. In color, the Newburyport mugs range from a brownish black through browns, plain and mottled, to delightful shades of orange with fine streakings of brown (*Fig. 6c*). Occasionally a greenish hue may be noted. The black mugs are severely plain, with only a slight tooling at the base. They were doubtless ordinary tavern ware. One of them, partly restored, is a departure from the straight cylindrical form (*Fig. 6d*). In specimens with a lighter glaze we see the hand of the artist. These pieces are turned with very thin walls and decorated around the body with a broad band of six tooled ridges. There is good reason to believe that the more ornate items are of earlier origin. Joseph Bayley tooled his mugs at Rowley before 1735. The small example minus handle (*Fig. 6a*) is, from a technical standpoint, one of the finest pieces of redware potting I have seen. It is extremely thin, not only at the rim but also near the base, which is

FIG. 8 — FRAGMENTS OF VARIOUS VESSELS
a, Probably sugar bowl. *b*, Base of cream pitcher. *c*, Pitcher, about 4 inches in height; light green; incised. *d*, Base of tumbler. *e*, Shallow bowl with rim

FIG. 9 — BLACK-GLAZED ARTICLES
Cup, bowl, cream pitcher, saucer. *Height of pitcher*, 3 ½ inches. All are fine in form and delicately potted

sharply defined within. Only a highly skilled potter could so manipulate the rather coarse-grained and crumbly native clay.

A man who could make such mugs would have had no difficulty in turning the delicate bowls and cups shown in Figures 7 and 8. These are by far the most important Newburyport find. All of those pictured are largely restored, but even a great deal of patching cannot rob them of their charm. Several correspond in size to the larger English teacups of the period. For this reason, and because a matching saucer was found, we may not doubt that they were intended for serving tea. Accordingly we are presented with a new picture of the colonial table. Native wares must indeed have supplemented the wooden trenchers and the garnish of pewter, giving color to what otherwise would have been a dull equipment. Small pieces, delicately made, provided a satisfying substitute for the fine imported china that was beyond reach of the rank and file. That virtually none of the best redware has been preserved is easily understood when one considers the huge importations after 1800 of the gayer products of Staffordshire. The brown and yellow native pottery disappeared as completely and unostentatiously as do contemporary bowls and cups from our present-day kitchens.

The mottled and dripped effects in the small greeny-brown Newburyport bowls can be neither adequately described nor illustrated. They are ever different and ever pleasing. The large bowl in Figure 7 is mahogany brown outside and orange within. The interesting streakings on this and on other pieces may have been due to drippings of glaze from objects higher in the kiln. (Bowls were stacked for burning one within the other, with a three-pointed cockspur between each two. Three spur marks scar the glaze in the bottom of every one.) Some bowls are a true black in color. One (*Fig. 8a*) has a ledge inside the rim, suggesting that a cover once rested upon it. It was probably a tiny sugar bowl. In the same illustration may be seen the base of a tumbler or beaker and a low small bowl of graceful contour.

We found a number of reddish-orange fragments of small bowls or cups edged with a narrow line of light slip (*Fig. 10b, top row*). As befitted ware for the table, they were finished in a superior manner. In fact, the quality of the Newburyport "wasters" is so excellent that, in spite of the redware body, question of their native origin was raised. Doubts were allayed by examination of their bases. All are flat, like the bottom of a common jug; in no case does a rim appear, as on English cups and saucers.

Although the number of pitcher fragments proved small, we obtained enough examples to illustrate several sizes and forms. A little cream pitcher, black glazed (*Fig. 9c*), is about the size of a Jackfield cream jug and was probably inspired by some such prototype. In spite of the loss of its nose and its spottiness where the glaze has flaked away, this little vessel still retains its pristine charm. The half-pint pitcher (*Fig. 8c*) is notable not so much for beauty of form as for its light-green hue — shading into rose where the glaze is thin — and for the attempt at decoration with incised lines. Only two other instances of incised decoration came to light. The fragment in Figure 10, bottom row, which displays both straight and wavy lines, seems to be a part of a large straight-sided jar or crock. It is almost red in color, with brown spots. The other, unglazed, was apparently an experimental piece. Quart jugs, black or brown, must have been a common product. The example (*Fig. 4c*) which, though badly damaged, still sports its handle, shows the form. Another shape, thick and heavy (*Fig. 10c, top row*), was

FIG. 10 — FRAGMENTS OF VARIOUS ARTICLES
Top row: a, Teapot fragment. *b*, Jar rim and edge of small bowl. *c*, Base of pitcher or teapot. *d*, Teapot base. *e*, Glazed base of heavy unglazed jar.
Middle row: a, Jar rim. *b*, Teapot base. *c*, Jug fragment. *d*, Teapot cover. *e*, Handle.
Bottom row: a, Rim of large jar with incised bands. *b*, Fragment of washbowl, covered with light slip. *c*, Jar

either a pitcher or a teapot. It obviously had a handle, but its complete outline must be left to the imagination.

Half a cover and sections of black teapots showing strainer perforations were found (*Fig. 10*). Both resemble in size and shape a type of redware teapot made long after the close of the Bayley pottery; but there can be no question that they are pottery discards and, therefore, products of the eighteenth century.

SLIP-DECORATED WARE

Judging by our discoveries, slip decoration was practiced at Newburyport upon only three classes of utensils — deep dishes, chamber pots, and porringers. The fragments of chamber vessels far outnumbered the remainders of dishes, and only one recognizable porringer was found. Strangely enough, the Bayley family seems to have exerted its ingenuity upon humble and intimate toilet items rather than upon receptacles of more public utilization. Or, perhaps, our perspective was warped by finding an undue number of certain articles: we may have struck a discarded kilnful of them. At any rate, the collection is amazing, showing, as it does, a variety of necessities not usually handed on to posterity.

FIG. 11 — SLIP-DECORATED VESSEL
Greenish ground with yellow decoration

FIG. 12 — VESSELS, SLIP DECORATED AND PLAIN
The second was excavated intact

An explanatory word about slip decoration may not come amiss. Slip is a mixture of clay and water. When applied over a darker clay, it may be used to produce happily contrasting effects. The slip used on our native redwares was a white English pipe clay. It was trailed or brushed on the body of the ware, which was then coated with a clear lead glaze. Because of impurities in the glaze, usually a percentage of iron oxide, the decoration in the finished ware appears yellow. There is a tradition in Newburyport that the pottery was sent to England to be decorated. Such a belief is, of course, absurd. The truth is that the *materials* for decorating were brought from abroad.

The process of trailing the liquid slip has often been described. The creamy fluid was fed from a small clay cup through a quill spout in much the same way as a cook ices a birthday cake. In some potteries, two or three quills poured the slip in parallel lines, but that notion does not seem to have occurred to the Bayleys. In fact, a great deal of their slip work was done with a brush.

The restored mug in Figure 11 is an excellent specimen of free brushwork. The piece is unusual in color: a mottled yellowish green with light-yellow decoration. Figure 12*a* is a finely streaked brown. In this instance, the trailed slip had a little manganese in its composition, for it is dotted with brown. The effect may have been unintentional and responsible for the discarding of the pot. The simple crossing of wavy lines to be seen in Figure 12*c* was carried out on a light ground with green dots and mottlings.

Many fragments reveal a rosy red with strong yellow lines; others, a deep red or brown background. Several are glazed in dull light or dark green, which, in some cases, is pleasantly shot through with yellow or rose tones. Two mugs are lettered in a flowing script. Unfortunately, the key pieces are missing, and on one can be distinguished only the word *betwixt*. The other is marked with a name — apparently *Mary* (Daniel Bayley's daughter). This gift pottery probably came from the hand of William Bayley, who presumably expressed his youthful spirits in such capers.

Other chamber vessels without decoration were recovered almost in their original state. Figure 12*b* pictures a mug which was dug up intact, except for a few chips on the rim. It is a rich brown outside, and a brownish green inside. Black glaze was used both inside and out on some specimens, and upon others as an exterior coating only, with a green or brown lining. All the variations of glaze color possible with the material available were exhausted by the potters on these common objects.

Slip-decorated dishes were the poor man's china in the eighteenth century. The ingenuity expended in obtaining simple but effective designs indicates that they were not merely cooking dishes, although they could be used in the oven. In their day they were, no doubt, accepted without any appreciation of their artistic value. It is amusing to observe that similar wares from Mexico have a ready sale today among those who tire of mechanical perfection.

All the Bayley dishes are flat-bottomed and have sloping sides. (The Pennsylvania or Connecticut pieplate shape, made over a mold and notched along the edge, seems not to have been introduced into New England until about 1790.) The decoration was usually applied to the centre of the dish and around the slanting walls. It often took the form of straight or wavy lines, or, occasionally, a definite motive or repeat. Both brush- and quillwork were employed.

The pan in Figure 15 is one of our most important finds. It bears the initials *W B* brushed on — doubtless the work of William Bayley. The background color, now somewhat iridescent, is a greenish yellow with rosy tints where the glaze is thin. The yellow of the painted bands is dotted with green, which has flowed into the glaze here and there. Even in its wrecked state — several fragments are missing — it is a beautiful object.

Other examples range from chocolate brown through rosy tans to a real yellow. Speckles of green throughout the decorated portions frequently appear. A rim fragment in deep olive brown — the only one in that color — has the peculiarity of flaring back instead of curving straight up. This represents an earlier type than the other pieces.

One of our first discoveries was a shattered porringer. Unfortunately, its fragments were collected before we suspected the possibility of restorations, and portions were lost. The remainder is shown in Figure 17. In answer to the question whether or not the vessel is really a porringer, I have the evidence of an account book kept by one Preserved Pearse, of Swansea, Massachusetts, in the 1780's. Pearse made trips by boat along the Connecticut and Rhode Island shores, trading in return for other necessities pottery made in the region around Swansea and Somerset. In a long list of earthenware forms, corresponding closely to those made at Newburyport, he mentions porringers. Our example is a light yellowish brown brushed with yellow slip.

An unusual employment of white slip to cover the entire background is shown in the fragment of a washbowl in Figure 10*b*, bottom row. This process resembles the Delft technique, the intention being to produce a lighter-colored ware than would the natural glazed clay. The plain surface is varied by spongings of dark-brown glaze.

It would be tedious to discuss these and other fragments at greater length. Some have incising or peculiar coloring; others, oddity of form. There are rims of various jars, straight sided or bulbous, and portions of many a pitcher, mug, and bowl. Careful study of thousands of these potsherds makes it possible to identify with reasonable accuracy the objects of which they were a part.

THE POTTERIES AT ROWLEY AND GLOUCESTER

The knowledge acquired by examination of so great a quantity of wasters from the Daniel Bayley pottery enabled us to interpret the small findings at Rowley and Gloucester.

We guessed the approximate site at Rowley, because we knew that Joseph Bayley lived in the family homestead and presumably worked in a neighboring shed or barn. However, the ground thereabouts has been cultivated and recultivated, and the spot where the barn once stood is now concealed under a garage and a cement walk. Although small bits of pottery are strewn about the present yard and lawn, digging here and there has yielded nothing. The pieces we found were scattered over an acre of land east of the pottery site and two feet below its level, where they had washed downhill from the dump. A recent ploughing made possible the recovery of these fragments, which would otherwise still be hidden from sight by the overgrowth of turf.

Looking back to 1720, one must realize that virtually nothing is known about folk earthenware of that period in America, and relatively little about it in England. With this fact in mind, a higher value will be placed on the bits dug up at Rowley. That they are really pottery discards and not merely the broken shards thrown away by housewives is evident from their imperfections of firing, form, and glaze.

The most striking thing about Joseph Bayley's ware is its close resemblance to the work of his son and grandsons. Tradition, not fashion, determined the shapes and styles of the folk potters. Considering this work of 1720, which, in many respects, is identical with the craftsmanship of 1820, one is faced with the question of where our New England types of pottery originated. The answer is: in the Metropolitan slip-decorated ware of London. Metropolitan slip was dark brown with trailings of light slip. Its sole embellishment was usually a motto of Puritan character, such as: *Fear God, Obeay the King, Doe Well.* Our Puritan forebears who lived in southern England were doubtless familiar with such pottery, and our earliest American potters were trained in that tradition. Going further back, one might point out that the same technique was practiced by the Romans, who, however, left their wares unglazed.

Among the Joseph Bayley fragments is a black piece with design delicately trailed in light slip. It is apparently the *interior* of a small bowl. As noted above, only one example of dark glaze with decoration turned up at Newburyport. Parts of small bowls and other forms difficult to identify show that the early eighteenth-century potters made articles on the same diminutive scale as china of the period. There is one piece, jet black, which seems to be part of a tiny teapot. Black teapots were not unknown this early: they were imported to America in 1715. Therefore, there is no reason why a skilled native potter should not have tried his hand at them. The greater number of fragments is of ordinary milk pans, pots, jugs, and jars. Tooled mugs, very much like those in Figure 6, appear.

The large jar in Figure 16 I like to think was made by Joseph Bayley. It was found in the cellar of the old Bayley house when the excavation was cleared for building a new bungalow on the old foundation. A cracked and useless receptacle, it may have been discarded generations ago and left unnoticed by the later Bayleys who occupied the house.

Little may be said about Daniel Bayley's 1750 product, except that it shows the transition from Joseph Bayley's style to the freer experimentation of his son's later period. Among the Gloucester fragments are pieces of dark bowls decorated on the inside with light slip. There are mugs which might have been, and perhaps were, tooled with the same implements used by Joseph. There are fragments of dishes with a tracing of slip decoration, finer but less freely executed than that of the Newburyport examples. There are thin cups rimmed with yellow slip. The glaze colors are more generally dark, with little spattering or mottling, and green does not appear at all. As a rule, however, except for slight variations of form, the work remained virtually unaltered throughout three generations, from 1720 to 1799.

Author's note. Last summer I ascertained from a study of land records that Joseph Bayley's pottery in Newburyport stood on the southeasterly side of Bartlett's Lane (now Winter Street), approximately opposite the railroad station. The site had been entirely removed by excavation before our arrival. I learned

FIG. 13 — SLIP-DECORATED FRAGMENTS OF CHAMBER MUGS
First and third in bottom row exhibit lettering

FIG. 14 — FRAGMENTS OF DEEP DISHES
Light brown, tan, or yellowish ground; yellow slip

FIG. 17 (*below*) — SLIP-DECORATED PORRINGER
Yellowish brown, with yellow design. *Diameter*, 5 3/4 inches

FIG. 15 — SLIP-DECORATED PAN
Initials *W B*. Greenish yellow, brushed with green. Bands of yellow slip dotted with green. *Diameter*, 13 inches

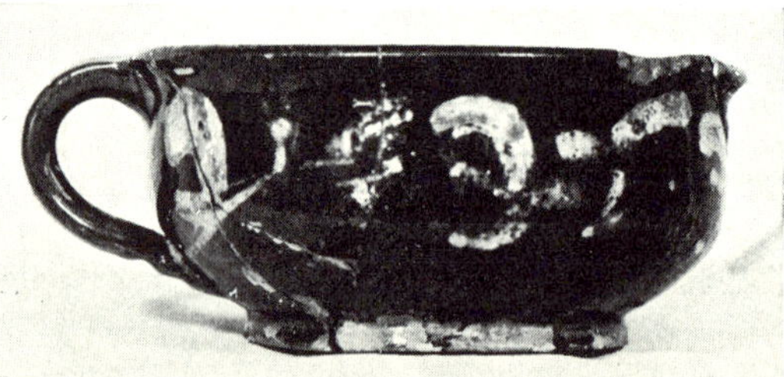

FIG. 16 — LARD POT
Found in the cellar of the old Bayley house. Perhaps made by Joseph Bayley. *Height*, 11 inches

also that, in the eighteenth century, a group of potters lived and worked on the Lane. Among them were Clement and Stephen Kent and Ebenezer Morrison, who later lived on Back Street, a stone's throw from High Street and from Daniel Bayley's pottery. Vestiges of Morrison's work still remain near the old burying ground, where he dug clay and presumably had his shop. The fragments of unglazed jars with glazed bases (first found near the corner of Winter and High Streets) may not have been discards from Daniel Bayley's pottery, but the work of some other potter. Although we picked up a few shards below the site of Joseph Bayley's shop, at the time they did not seem significant, since bits of earthenware were scattered over a large area. —*L. W. W.*

A Puzzling Pot

Rawson W. Haddon reports an interesting but puzzling redware jar which the Mattatuck Historical Society of Waterbury, Connecticut, has recently received as a loan from one of its members. Encircling its rotund body are the figures *1765–8*. The known facts about this piece of pottery are few. It was found near Norwich, Connecticut, and is said on apparently good authority to have been made there.

Certainly the color and interior glaze of the jar seem to justify attribution to the Bean Hill Pottery at Norwich. However, the date on the jar, if indeed the figures do indicate a date, is earlier than that of the establishment of any known pottery in Norwich or elsewhere in Connecticut, with the single exception of the John Pierce pottery in Litchfield, Connecticut. There work is believed to have commenced in 1753. It is a generally accepted fact that the making of earthenware in Norwich dates from about 1779, when Christopher Leffingwell commenced operations there at the Bean Hill Pottery. He was succeeded by his son-in-law, Charles Lathrop, in 1792. To the latter, pieces marked *Norwich* are attributed. In 1796 C. Potts & Son commenced operations as potters in Norwich, continuing until 1816.

The figures on this jar give the piece an unusual interest and raise a number of questions. It is possible that they do not represent a date at all, though it is certainly natural to assume that they do. Even if they do, the date is not necessarily that of the pot's making, but there must have been some reason for it. Still, no explanation presents itself. Obviously the jar does not commemorate a birthday. No event in Norwich history seems to call for exceptional recognition of the three years between 1765 and 1768. Even the most inept apprentice would not take three years to make one jar, nor would he in all probability have taken the trouble to record such slow progress. A plausible explanation may some day be forthcoming, but in the meantime the jar remains a puzzle.

Fig. 3 — Redware Jar. Found near Norwich, Connecticut. *Now on loan at the Mattatuck Historical Society. Illustration from the Connecticut Index of American Design*

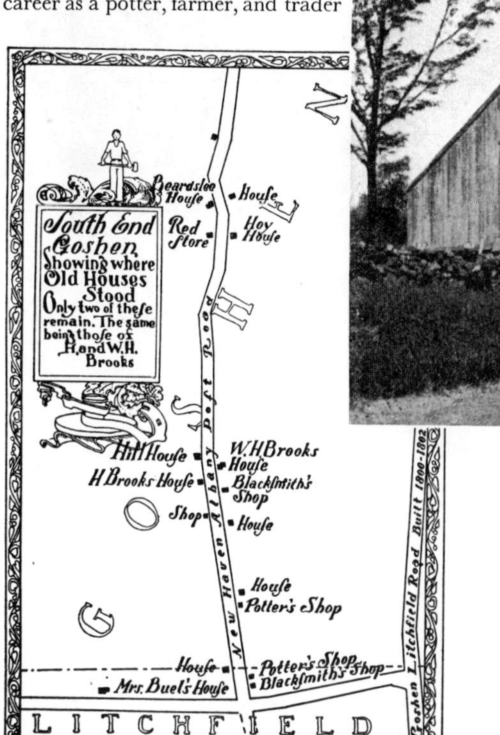

FIG. 1 — MAP OF SOUTH END, GOSHEN, CONNECTICUT
The Post Road is now the drive to the Brooks farm

FIG. 2 (*right*) — WORKSHOP AND HOUSE OF HERVEY BROOKS
In Goshen, Connecticut. Occupied by the potter from 1829 until his death in 1873, after a long and active career as a potter, farmer, and trader

THE BROOKS POTTERY IN GOSHEN, CONNECTICUT

By LURA WOODSIDE WATKINS

Illustrations from the collection of John Norton Brooks

HERVEY BROOKS has been listed as an early potter of Litchfield, Connecticut. Actually he lived just north of the Litchfield line, in a section of Goshen known as South End. This community was a trading post for craftsmen and peddlers, conveniently situated on the old New Haven-Albany post road, only a few rods west of the highway from Litchfield to Goshen.

Hervey Brooks himself wrote a history of South End in 1858, and in his account books, kept from 1802 until his death in 1873, he left an invaluable record. From these sources of information, and with the assistance of his grandson John N. Brooks, who still lives in the family homestead and who owns many products of his ancestor's skill, I am able to present a remarkably complete picture of the potter's career.

Litchfield and Goshen were early centers of the potter's trade. John Pierce is reputed to have worked in Litchfield in the mid-1700's. Jonathan Kettle (Kettell), son and grandson of Danvers potters, followed the family calling. He went to Goshen about 1780, and probably lived in what Hervey Brooks mentions as the "old Kittle place." John Norton, founder of the Bennington pottery in 1793, was a native of Goshen and probably learned his trade thereabouts. He was familiar with South End, for shortly before his departure to Williamstown, whence he proceeded, after a brief residence, to Vermont, he married Lucretia Buell, whose father's house is shown on the map (*Fig. 1*).

The pottery of Jesse Wadhams, in Goshen, stood a little more than a mile north of South End. Reverend A. G. Hibbard, in his *History of Goshen*, says that Wadhams "built a house on the west side of the turnpike, about 80 rods south of the south end of Long Swamp. Here he worked at his trade, which was that of a potter. He manufactured the red earthen ware from the common clay. This was between 1790 and 1810." Wadhams was the son of Seth and Anne (Catling) Wadhams. He was born August 22, 1773, six years before the birth of Hervey Brooks on October 26, 1779. He probably established his business shortly before his marriage to Polly Hopkins in 1795.

In that year Hervey Brooks, then a lad of only sixteen, went to live in South End. The inference is obvious that at first he was Wadhams' apprentice. Hervey was the eldest of the twelve children of Joseph Brooks, a native of Durham, and his wife, Amanda Collins, a Goshen girl. In South End he boarded with Captain Jonathan Buell, in the same house where Norton had courted his sweetheart. While the Buells were always considered residents of Goshen, their house had been built by mistake in two townships and stood squarely on the Litchfield line.

April 24, 1803, just after the account books begin, Hervey Brooks married Polly Taylor of Granville. Thenceforth, he led a life of almost ceaseless activity. When he was not working for Wadhams, he picked up odd jobs here and there. It is not quite clear whether at this time

FIG. 3 — SMALL JUG AND PITCHER
From the Brooks pottery

he had a kiln of his own: he may have done his turning in Wadhams' shop, buying materials to fill his private orders. In any event, a country potter's trade was never sufficient to take all of a man's time, and Hervey was apparently able to turn his hand to anything that came along. He entered bills in his book for haying, chopping and hauling wood, hoeing potatoes, spreading dung, grafting apple trees, picking apples, shingling, splitting nails, driving a horse to the mill, and even butchering a calf. He also seems to have kept up a lively business as a trader. Much of his pottery was sold to peddlers who perhaps paid in kind rather than in cash. Previous to 1810 he must have had a store, for he sold such articles as pins, combs, salt, tea, and rum.

For Jesse Wadhams, Hervey did the tasks usual in a pottery. May 23, 1803, he noted: "half days work at the frame" (turning); May 25 he spent digging clay; in 1809 he presented bills for "turning 8 doz Milkpans @ 9d; to a days work Glazing; to Burning the Kiln one night and day." Most of the entries, however, are itemized accounts for piece work done for Wadhams or long lists of articles made and sold, sometimes at retail and sometimes at wholesale. Often buyers were charged for loading the ware.

Already Hervey Brooks' habits of thrift, which must not be judged by present-day practice, were evident. In 1803 he got rid of six cracked milkpans and a warped jug for a little more than four shillings, to Heman Beach, a peddler. The habit of wringing the most out of every deal and of accounting faithfully for every cent was customary in that day. So it is not surprising to find a memorandum when Brooks lent a postage stamp or when a friend borrowed ten cents for the Sunday collection plate. Not even

FIG. 4 — JARS AND PORRINGER
A, light-brown glaze with dark-brown splashes; *height*, 9 inches. *C*, light-brown glaze, with yellow slip decoration in design of two roosters. *D*, chamber mug with trailing decoration in yellow slip (called "painting") and date *1854*. *E*, creamer with light reddish-brown glaze, made for Brooks' granddaughter. *F*, reverse of *C*, marked *Goshen*

cracked milkpans were wasted in economy-minded Goshen.

The last bill entered against Jesse Wadhams is dated June 22, 1810. During the following years, several transactions indicate that other potters were at work in South End. Twice during 1814 Hervey made out a bill to David Vaill to "turning" milkpans or bowls, and he also itemized finished ware. Possibly Vaill was a peddler, not a potter, but there is little doubt about George Holton, to whose account four entries are put down in 1815: "To 2 days work glazing ware." In 1822 and 1825 Isaac Wadhams is billed "To ½ day digging clay — \$.37" and "to 2 quarts sand — \$.06" and "8£. White clay — \$.25." During Jesse Wadhams' lifetime Brooks had sold sand in small quantities to Pitt Buell and a certain Norton. Since common sand was plentiful enough in South End, they presumably bought a finer material for glazing.

In 1811 Brooks worked for a time in Granville, where he was accustomed to making periodic visits in the home of his wife's father. Three years later this entry occurs: "Wednesday February 2nd 1814 we moved from Granville and arrived at our present place of residence in Goshen February 5th 1814." This marks the time, according to the South End history, when Brooks bought the house and land that had previously been owned and occupied by Nathaniel Merrills. He records that he was living there in 1858; the original building, however, had been torn down long before. The house that replaced it was the potter's home until his death (*Fig. 2*). He says:

June 17th 1829. Pulled down my old House. Thursday June 25th finished the cellar wall and underpining.
Wednesday July 1st raised the new house, (without rum).
Tuesday November 10th 1829, Moved into the new House.

In December 1813, Revellard Dutcher Jr. came to work with Brooks for a year, his wages to be \$109. He is the only person mentioned at any time as assistant. After his departure Brooks must have taken his ten-year-old boy, Isaac, into the pottery. Isaac, however, had no desire to be a potter, nor was he happy in the alternative prospect of selling clocks. Before he was twenty years old he ran away to Georgia. This was in 1823. His father dolefully figured out that Isaac owed him \$133 on his apprenticeship, \$144.76 for clocks, and \$37 on his wagon. The debt was never paid, although it was marked "settled." Several years later, when Isaac was sick and alone in New York, his father made the journey to Staten Island to bring him home. Georgia claimed Isaac eventually, while the younger son, Watts H. (both were named after the famous hymn writer), remained in South End.

Hervey Brooks left a particularly careful record in 1819 of his work and expenses. It throws a helpful light on old-time methods of production and distribution:

An acct of my expenses in & at the Shop for 1819:
March 29th & 30th To Watertown Woodbury & Washington 2 days making contracts for ware &c. Expenses \$1.50
2 days splitting wood
3 days into York State making contracts &c. Expenses \$3.50 May 20th Myself & Team 3 days to Wethersfield after sand, Expenses 4 dollars
25th Turned 6 doz. Milkpans
26th glazing & Setting 1 day
28th diging Clay 1 day; Drawing 3 loads clay
29th Burning 1 day
31st drawing the kiln & loading ware
June 2nd turned 4 doz. large pots; carried a load of ware to Washington; carried a load of ware to Mount tom
8 ½ day at the Shop painting &c.
June 18 Isaac with team drawing clay
[Loads to Woodbury, Bethlehem, Holbrook, N. Y:, Kent, Cornwall, Canaan — (Expenses 34 cents)]
Aug 22 ½ day painting platters
Aug 26 glazing & painting
Sept 19 4 doz. Bowls & 3 do. pudg bags

FIG. 5 — COVERED JARS FOR VARIOUS PURPOSES
A, almost black glaze; *height*, 8 inches

FIG. 6 — SLIP-DECORATED PLATES
Yellowish-brown glaze. *Diameter of A*, about 13 inches

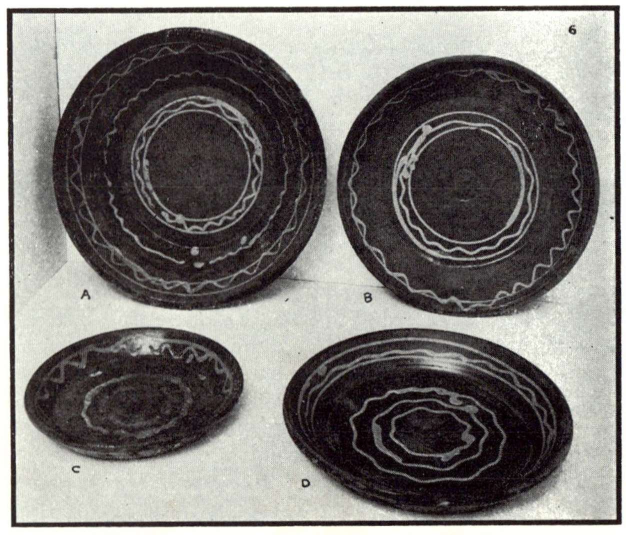

26–7–8 Sheffield & Salisbury — 40 cents
Nov. 24th 1 day after lead & painting
25th 1 day glazing
Dec. 4th 1 day setting
6th 1 day burning

The account books show that he must have followed a similar routine in succeeding years. New names appear from time to time. Usually the transactions were connected with the pottery. Once in a while Hervey made a deal in bricks or watched Samuel Buell's brick kiln. From his own land he sold many a load of clay, which he dug and hauled. Sometimes he took in exchange articles that he peddled along with his pots and pans. Amos Sanford settled an account with "six good new clocks." These doubtless came from the shop of Frederick Sanford, a clockmaker who lived in South End from 1812 to 1829 and whose brother — presumably Amos — worked with him. Another member of the Sanford family, Garwood, must have been a chairmaker: Brooks records buying from him six chairs for $8.50, two rocking chairs at $1.25 and $3.00, and other similar purchases. From 1835 to 1838 he bought seventeen clocks from Richard Ward, who is listed by Wallace Nutting as a clockmaker in Salem Bridge (now Naugatuck), Connecticut, between 1832 and 1840.

The demand for household pottery had appreciably declined before the middle of the century, but Hervey Brooks kept his business alive by turning out, in addition to his more ornamental wares, such things as safes for stove pipes, drain tiles, and flower pots. These coarser articles constituted his entire later output. Some of his most interesting offhand pieces, however, were made during this period, when he had greater leisure.

In the summer of 1847 the two oldest daughters of Isaac Brooks — Ann and Mary Candace — came from Georgia to their grandfather's home. Ann went almost immediately to Albany to learn the "mantuamaking trade," returning after a ten-months' apprenticeship to live with her grandparents. Mary Candace for a time taught school in Litchfield for the munificent sum of $1.12 ½ a week. Then, after attending a term at "Mrs. Kellogg's celebrated school for young ladies" in Great Barrington, she went back to the south.

Hervey Brooks' wife died in 1858, leaving him alone with Ann.

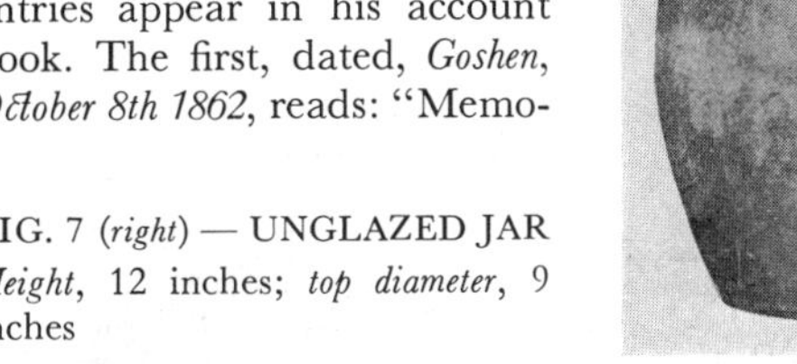

She kept his house, but rather indifferently. She left him after two years, and the old potter was cared for by a housekeeper until his death, February 17, 1873, at the age of ninety-four. In his failing years two touching entries appear in his account book. The first, dated, *Goshen, October 8th 1862*, reads: "Memorandum. It may be remembered that I have made in the course of this summer, a kiln of ware, consisting mainly of Flowerpots and Stove tubes, and have this day finished burning the same. Hervey Brooks." But his potting days were not quite over. Two years later — he was then eighty-five — he wrote: "Goshen, September 23rd, 1864. Memorandum. It may be remembered that I have made a kiln of ware this summer, consisting of Milkpans, some Pots, Pudding pans and Wash bowls, but mostly of Stove tubes and Flowerpots, and have this day finished burning the same. Hervey Brooks."

FIG. 7 (*right*) — UNGLAZED JAR
Height, 12 inches; *top diameter*, 9 inches

The feature of particular interest in the output of the Wadhams and Brooks potteries is the use of white slip for decoration. This material was ordinarily imported from England, the only local source of supply being a bed of kaolin in Monckton, Vermont. Hervey made at least one trip to Troy, New York, to buy white clay for Wadhams. It may possibly have been Monckton slip. In the same year — 1809 — he notes time spent "painting" platters. "Painting" was the potter's term for a process executed, not with a brush, but by trailing the liquid slip through a quill or spout to make the desired pattern. The red lead for glazing, which cost $9.00 per hundredweight, was purchased in New Haven.

During the period when the two potters worked together, Brooks made numerous entries that show what objects were made. Forms mentioned before 1810 include: half-pint, pint, quart, and gallon jugs, pint and quart bowls, pint and quart mugs, two- and three-quart pitchers, a small cream pot; small, "midling," and large platters; a porringer; pudding pans, milkpans, small and large pots, preserve pots, chamber pots, an earthen jar, a small churn, an inkstand, pudding "bags," and sap pans.

Churns of redware seem unusual and not very practicable. They are almost non-existent today. A churn cover with the hole and cup for the plunger may be seen in Figure 9. Pudding bags were presumably the deep open pots made by every potter for steaming or baking puddings.

The later items in the account book, entered when Brooks worked alone, are evidence of the gradual change in the type of pottery that was in demand. American redware, even in country districts, was being replaced by pictorial Staffordshire earthenware. It is more than a coincidence that Hervey's first mention of a "puncheon" for a stove pipe occurs in 1829 and that flower pots are first noted in 1831. Although pitchers, dishes, pudding pans, and churns still found a market, the potter added to his sales by making an occasional wash bowl or bed pan, and in one instance he notes a "spitting dish." Once Brooks sold for seventy-five cents a pot filled with gin. By 1845 his principal output was flower pots, safes for stove pipes, and tubes that were intended for drain pipes or water conductors. In 1850 he records making a pitcher for "emptyings," in which some of the dough was reserved and set away to create yeast for the next batch after each baking.

It is rather surprising to read of porringers made in 1855, but Brooks notes the sale of three in that year. They could have been used but rarely at so late a time.

Hervey Brooks' last bill for ware was made out in 1867. His active days were then over. For six years more he kept his household accounts with scrupulous care, but the writing grew ever more feeble; the hand that had worked so long was about to fail.

FIG. 8 (*left*) — PRESERVE JAR
It bears the impressed mark *H. Brooks*. The iron tool with which the mark was made is today in the possession of John N. Brooks

FIG. 9 (*center*) — BROOKS POTTERY
A, churn cover, with hole and cup for the plunger. *B*, shallow bowl. *C*, inkwell

FIG. 10 (*right, below*) — SMALL WARES
A, slip-cup (for pouring slip). *B*, cuspidor. *C*, mug

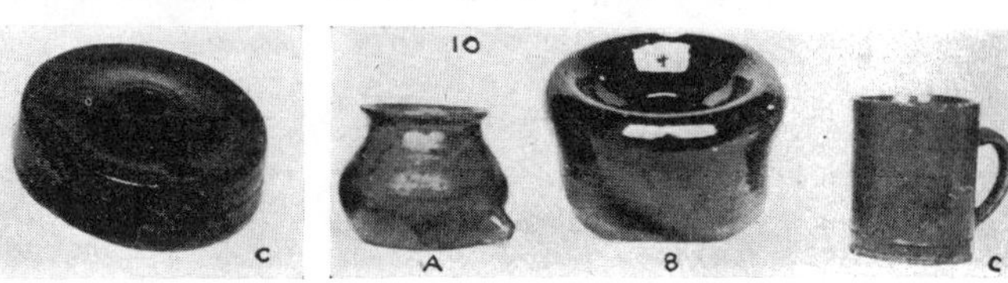

Fig. 1 — Equipment from the Lamson Pottery, Now Acquired by the Edison Institute of Technology, Dearborn, Michigan
Around wall, left to right: stone glaze mill, work bench, speed wheel, wedging table, throwing wheel. *Centre, left to right:* clay mill, glaze kettle (which, when in use, was set on a half-barrel to raise to a convenient height), screen box. The seats of the wheels are not in place, and the boards fronting the wheels are too high for actual use

The Exeter Pottery Works

By F. H. Norton

For nearly one hundred and fifty years the Exeter Pottery Works, or Lamson Pottery, was operated continuously in Exeter, New Hampshire, by four generations of the same family. Circumstances enable us today to reconstruct with considerable exactitude the methods used in Exeter for the manufacture of a type of ware that is really this nation's most representative folk pottery. This reconstruction has been accomplished with the aid of two men who were intimately connected with the enterprise in its later years, and who have generously given every assistance in recalling the details of its operation. Furthermore, the machinery has been purchased and preserved by Henry Ford. Such preservation of the early tools of our native craftsmen is of inestimable value. The pottery building is still standing at 84 Main Street, in much the same condition as it was a hundred years ago; and in its dusty loft may even yet be found many of the old tools and pieces of pottery.

History and Genealogy

The potter's craft is difficult to learn, and necessitates many years of apprenticeship. Hence it is usually handed down from father to son through several succeeding generations. In the Lamson (Lampson) and Dodge families, at least eight potters have been located through a study of early directories and of two books of genealogy — *Descendants of William Lampson of Ipswich, Mass.*, by William J. Lampson, 1917, and *Genealogy of the Dodge Family of Essex County, Mass.*, by Joseph Thompson Dodge, 1898. Since these works leave a number of points unsettled, I shall welcome corrections and additional information.

Jabesh Dodge was born in 1746 or 1747, lived in Exeter, and married Lydia Philbrick, also of Exeter. It is recorded that he worked as a potter. He is undoubtedly the originator of the Exeter concern, though in what year is not known. It must nevertheless have been long before 1819, the date when the present building was erected, because Jabesh died in 1806. Where Jabesh learned his trade is not recorded. But since his father, Benjamin, was a chairmaker in North Beverly, the son probably was an apprentice in one of the neighboring Peabody or Danvers potteries.

Jabesh had four sons. Benjamin, born 1774, moved to Portland, and possibly practiced his father's craft there; for his son Benjamin is listed as potter in the Portland directories between 1847 and 1868. It was he who established the well-known Lamson and Swasey pottery, where, about 1875, Longfellow wrote his poem *Keramos*.

The second son, Joseph, born 1776, moved to Portsmouth, where perhaps he too followed the family occupation. He had two sons, Jabez, born 1804, and Samuel J., born 1814. The former is listed in the Portsmouth directory for 1851 as potter and cordwainer. The latter moved to Exeter, where he undoubtedly worked in his grandfather's pottery. Samuel's son was Charles S. Dodge, who married Mary L. Lamson at Exeter.

The third son of Jabesh was Samuel, born 1783. He apparently had no children. Frank Lamson is of the opinion that he was trained as a potter and built the present works in 1819. The New England directory for 1849 lists him as a potter in Exeter.

The fourth son, John, was born in 1791. He also learned the trade at his grandfather's pottery. His son, John Edwin, lived in Portsmouth.

Turning now to the Lamson family, I find that Asa Brown Lamson, born 1818, was a potter in Exeter, probably in partnership with Samuel Dodge. Asa had two sons, both of whom were trained in their father's craft.

Rufus, born 1844, owned the present Paige pottery in Peabody about 1860 or 1870. Later he moved to Portland, where the Portland directory for 1879 lists him as a potter. He was at that time in partnership with Swasey, with whom he had taken over the establishment of Benjamin Dodge.

The second son, Frank Hudson, born 1859, worked in the Exeter pottery with his father, and later carried it on until its close about 1895. He was the brother-in-law of Charles S. Dodge. Thus it may be said that this pottery was operated continuously by one family for four generations over a period of some one hundred and thirty years — an illustration of the custom I have mentioned of continuing the craft in the family.

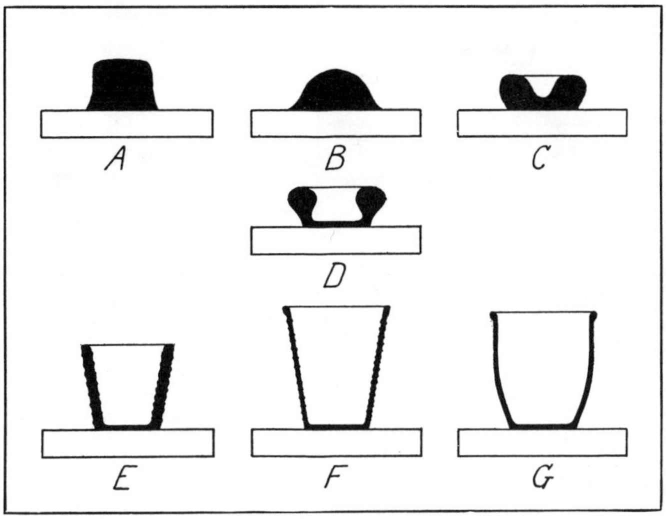

A B C D E F G

Fig. 2 — Steps in Throwing a Lard Pot

Manufacturing Methods at Exeter — *Source of the Clay*

The clay used at the Exeter works was obtained from local deposits, and no single source of supply was exclusively utilized. The material was teamed from the local brickyard or from a nearer clay bank. Like that used in other red ware, it was a red-burning glacial clay. According to an old craftsman who has worked in potteries all over New England, it was the best clay known for throwing on the wheel. The Crafts Pottery in Nashua employed it also as a glaze on their stoneware.

Preparation of the Clay

The clay as received from the bank was worked up to the proper consistency by mixing with water in what is now, except for the lack of a bottom outlet, called a vertical pug mill. This mill, still in existence, will hold six hundred pounds of wet clay. It consists of a half hogshead in the centre of which is pivoted a vertical wooden shaft. The upper end of the shaft originally turned in a socket in a ceiling beam. The shaft had blades set in the lower end and was turned by a sweep and horse, and not by hand with the capstan bar shown in Figure 1. This mill was intended for outdoor use in summer. During the winter a second mill, inside a shed, was employed. Having been mixed in the mill, the clay was shaped into balls and stored in a damp, stone-paved closet until it was needed for use on the wheel. It was not washed or purified, as in modern practice, although many of the pebbles that it harbored were removed by hand.

Just before it was used the clay was wedged, that is, thoroughly worked by hand on the wedging table to eliminate air bubbles and laminations, and to develop an even consistency. It was also roughly formed into cylinders of the proper size to make the desired pieces. Scales helped to establish this size, in accordance with a list that recorded the suitable weight of clay for all the regular articles made. Thus was ensured the same wall thickness for all pieces of a given variety.

Forming the Ware

Virtually all of the ware made in this pottery was turned on the wheel. The pottery possessed three kick wheels, that is, wheels driven by foot power. One of these is still in the possession of Mr. Lamson, and the other two are now in the Edison Institute of Technology, Dearborn, Michigan (*Fig. 1*). The mechanism is simple, consisting of a vertical shaft and crank connected to a foot treadle, with a heavy flywheel mounted on the lower end of the shaft and a disc of lignumvitæ or iron on the upper end.

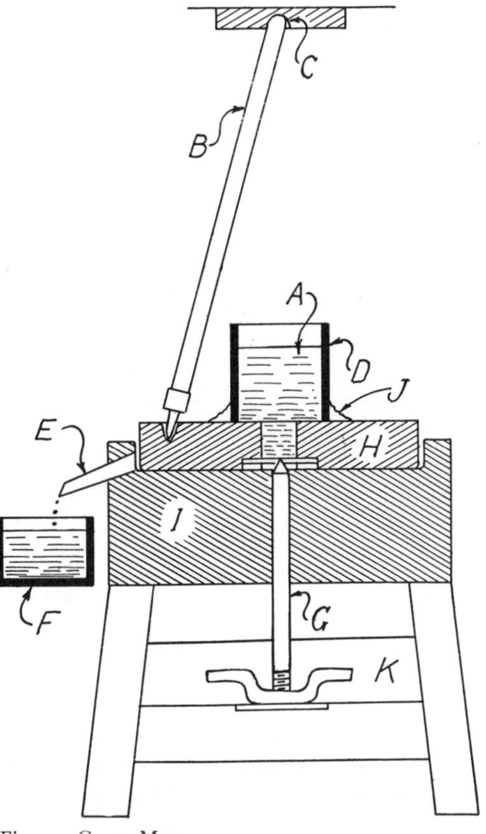

Fig. 3 — Glaze Mill
A. Red lead, loam, and water; *B.* stick for turning upper stone; *C.* socket for stick in ceiling beam; *D.* earthenware cylinder; *E.* lead spout; *F.* earthenware jar to catch finished glaze; *G.* pivot to support upper stone; *H.* upper stone; *I.* lower stone; *J.* wet clay; *K.* nut to adjust height of lower stone

One of the wheels is particularly interesting because of its belt, which gives the throwing disc about three times the speed of the crank shaft. This wheel, then known as a "speed wheel," was suitable for the throwing of smaller pieces.

The operation of throwing is most fascinating to observe; but so rapidly does a skilled potter work that the layman cannot easily grasp the definite sequence of steps followed in the process. [For an illustrated analysis of these steps, the reader may consult *Potter and Potter's Wheel*, in Antiques for January, 1931. Since every potter has methods peculiar to himself, details will differ, but essentially the process is the same wherever applied.— *Ed.*] In Figure 2 is shown a cross section of the clay during the formation of a lard pot. The rough cylinder of clay (*A*) was thrown down on the centre of the revolving wheel, sprinkled with water, and grasped firmly with the wet hands until it was centred, or made to run true (*B*). Water was used as a lubricant to prevent the clay from sticking to the hands; indeed the hands had to be kept wet throughout the whole process. Centring, in appearance a simple operation, in fact requires much skill

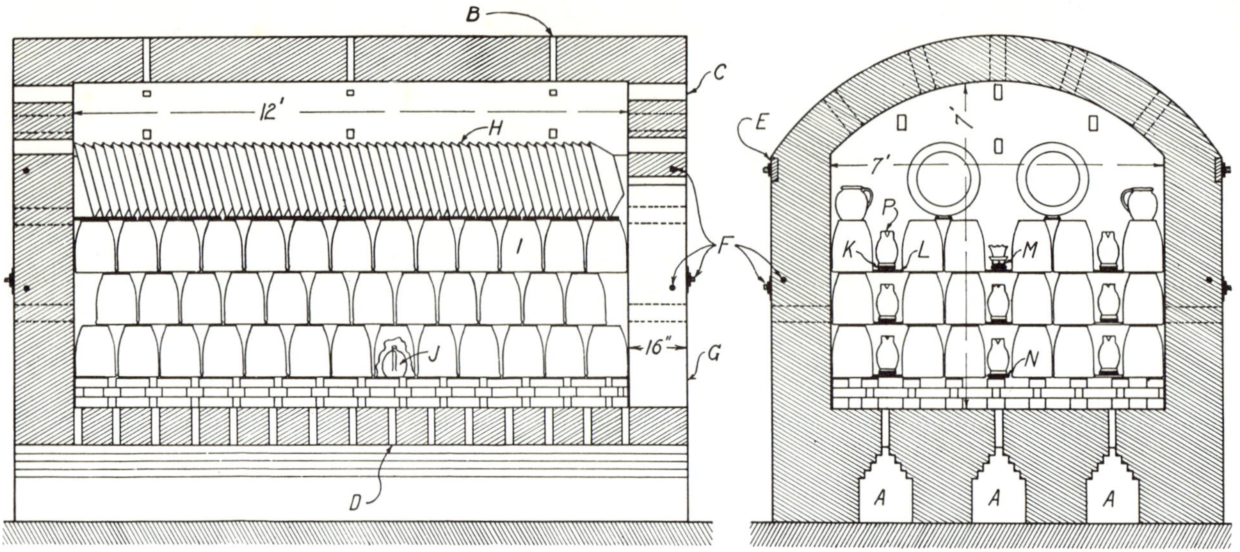

Fig. 4 — A Reconstruction of the Kiln Built by Jabesh Dodge
A. Fire holes; *B.* smoke vents in crown; *C.* sight holes; *D.* flues in the floor; *E.* iron skew back; *F.* bolts in brickwork; *G.* door; *H.* milk pans; *I.* lard pots; *J.* small jugs set under the lard pots; *K.* flat setting tile; *L.* picked setting tile; *M.* frog or stilt to set under glazed ware; *N.* round setting tile; *P.* pitchers or other thin ware

The thumbs were next forced down into the revolving clay, while the fingers guided the outside (*C*). It took experience to judge the thickness of the bottom, which was finished by pressing the thumbs outward sufficiently to furnish the correct bottom diameter (*D*). The clay was now given what is called a "draft" to form the wall (*E*): there were a number of ways to hold the hands in this operation, but the principle was, by guiding the clay inside and out, to force it upward into a cylinder. With most clay a second or third draft was needed (*F*) to bring the wall up to a little more than its finished height, and roughly to form the upper rim.

The last operation consisted in giving the correct form and a smooth exterior surface. This was accomplished by holding one or more fingers against the clay on the inside, and opposite them on the outside a "rib," which was a small piece of hard wood with a rounded edge. This operation usually increased the diameter and decreased the height of the article. The fingers formed on the inside surface the ridges that are evident on all the old thrown pieces. The work of a skilled potter is indicated by a thin wall, particularly near the bottom; by a piece that is true; and by a good finish on the outside and top.

The finished vessel was removed from the wheel by passing a wire between it and the wheel top. Then the potter, after wiping his hands, lifted the piece carefully and set it on a board. Here considerable skill was required to avoid deforming the soft clay. This operation accounts for the finger marks found on many of the old pieces. An attempt is being made by means of these marks to identify the makers of particular items. The larger pieces were often removed with paddles or special lifters to prevent deformation.

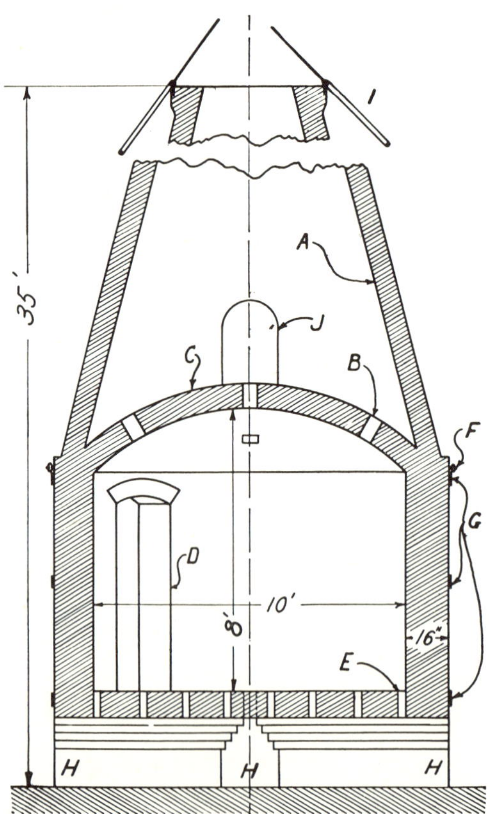

Fig. 5 — The Second Lamson Kiln
A. Conical stack; *B.* vent hole; *C.* crown; *D.* door; *E.* flues in floor; *F.* anchor chain; *G.* kiln bands; *H.* fire holes (4); *I.* stack dampers; *J.* stack door

Drying

After its removal from the wheel, the ware was set at once in rows on drying boards. In summer these boards were placed in the sun, but in winter or in rainy weather they were set around the kiln. Later a special wood-fired drying oven was built of bricks. Two or three days usually sufficed for drying.

Glazing

Practically all the ware was glazed, with a raw lead glaze that was fired at the same time as the body. It was prepared by mixing together ten pounds of red lead with about three pounds of fine loam. The latter was carefully screened through a horsehair sieve of about eighty meshes to the inch. It should be noted that loam is superior to sand, because it contains a little clay, which introduces alumina into the glaze. This ingredient increases the viscosity of the melted glaze and prevents it from flowing off the ware. The red lead, screened loam, and water were ground together in a stone mill (*Fig. 3*). The work was all done by hand, and would, at the present day, seem extremely arduous. The finished glaze was stored in tubs or kettles.

This was a clear glaze and most common on red ware. Although it had a yellowish tinge it was quite transparent and intensified the red color of the body. Green glazes were made by burning brass shavings and grinding into the clear glaze about three per cent of the oxides (copper and zinc) thus obtained. Browns and blacks were obtained with varying amounts of manganese dioxide. The mottled effects observed in many old pieces were due to imperfect mixing of the coloring oxides with the glaze. The resulting specks or blotches later flowed down to some extent.

A little flour paste was added to the glaze. This served two functions: its gummy character prevented the heavy lead oxide from settling out of the glaze solution too rapidly; likewise it made the dried glaze adhere strongly to the ware without undue danger of chipping or breaking off when handled. It is probable that only a small amount of the paste could be mixed at a time, because of its tendency to ferment on long standing. Modern glazes are made with gums of more stable character.

The ware to be glazed was filled with liquid glaze and immediately emptied with a rolling motion to coat the edge evenly. If the inside only was to be done, the top edge was wiped clean with the finger to prevent sticking when the piece was set upside down. Ware glazed on the outside was held by the bottom and immersed. The glaze was usually not applied to the bottom; any unintentional coating was at once wiped off.

Most of the ware made at the Lamson pottery had a uniform colored glaze; but some of the pieces, especially the earlier ones, had variations of yellow, brown, and green formed by the addition of copper and manganese. Fragments picked up in the kiln yard indicate the beauty of many of these Lamson glazes.

Fig. 6 — Utilitarian Ware from the Lamson Pottery
The tall piece on the right is a chimney safe, which was set in the wall for a stovepipe to pass through

Fig. 7 — Special Pieces Made by F. H. Lamson
Marked "FL *1875–1885*"

Burning

The original kiln, built by Jabesh Dodge, was constructed entirely of red bricks approximately as shown in Figure 4. Three fire holes at each end permitted introduction of the fuel, which consisted entirely of pine wood. The floor was immediately above the fire arches and contained holes for the passing of gases. The door, of the usual type, was bricked up for each burn. The crown was a sprung arch perforated with numerous small holes for the escape of the gases. Ironwork, of a simple nature, held the kiln in shape. Three trap doors in the roof of the kiln shed allowed the smoke and gases to escape. Later cast-iron doors were added to the fire mouth to protect the brick, as is now done in scove kilns.

Sometime between 1875 and 1885 this kiln was replaced by one similar to the pottery kilns in use before that time in England, and gradually adopted in this country. Even now many potteries are using kilns of this sort. The sketch in Figure 5 will make this later construction clear. There were four furnaces under the circular chamber. The heat, which passed up through the arches and floor, was regulated by adjusting the position of the fire. The kiln was bound together with three iron bands, and, as an extra precaution, an anchor chain was clamped around at the height of the crown. Unlike the earlier kiln, fire brick was used in the fire arches, which materially reduced the necessity for repairs. The tall stack gave a good draft and also kept the kiln shed free from smoke.

The method of setting the ware was quite different from the usual modern practice of employing saggers for glazed pieces. The larger pots and jars were always inverted to protect the inner glaze, and smaller pieces placed under them. After several rows had been arranged on the floor of the kiln with spaces between, setting tiles of two kinds were laid on the ware, to support additional tiers of thin ware, such as pitchers. Milk pans were set at the top of the charge on special tiles to keep them from rolling off.

The average time required to burn a kiln of ware was thirty hours. The temperature averaged 1800°F., and completion of the burn was judged by the amount the charge in the kiln settled during the firing period.

Type of Ware

The Lamson ware included all of the household types then in use — milk pans, cooking dishes, custard cups, bean pots, chimney safes, washbowls, pitchers, spittoons, chambers, jars, vases, pots, and jugs. In the later years of operation, flowerpots were the main product. Originally they were of the old-fashioned type with an integral saucer, but, about 1890, the straight, tapered flowerpot without glaze came in. The advantage of nesting was at once recognized, allowing as it did cheaper kiln setting and more compact shipments. At first it was believed that this type of pot could not be made by hand on the wheel, but John Donavon, who was then throwing for Mr. Lamson, managed, after many trials, to make the pots so accurately as readily to nest together.

Distribution of Ware

Lamson pottery was sold from carts to hardware and general stores in surrounding cities. In some seasons two teams were constantly on the road covering Newburyport, Portsmouth, Rochester, Hampton, Derry, and other neighboring towns.

I wish to acknowledge gratefully the assistance given me by Frank Lamson and John Donavon in reconstructing the processes used in this pottery. — *F. H. N.*

The Osborne Pottery at Gonic, New Hampshire

By F. H. Norton *and* V. J. Duplin, Jr.

In connection with its division of Industrial Coöperation and Research, the Massachusetts Institute of Technology has recently installed a Department of Ceramics. Collateral to his technical investigations of modern ceramic problems, F. H. Norton, Assistant Professor in this department and co-author of the following notes, has been making studies of the materials and processes employed by various early American potters. Antiques is happy to publish one of the first resultant contributions to the literature of this obscure but deeply interesting subject. — *The Editor.*

History

The chance remark of an antique shop proprietor led to our finding a hitherto obscure pottery in the New Hampshire hills. Later, business that led us to Gonic permitted a rather thorough investigation of this interesting old establishment, and enabled us to obtain well authenticated representative specimens of its red ware. At the same time, with the help of William A. Osborne, we found it possible to reconstruct, in considerable detail, the manufacturing process used at Gonic and other early earthenware potteries of its kind.

Unfortunately, the Osborne homestead burned some years ago, and all the family papers were destroyed. However, the family can be traced back by genealogical records, although several doubtful statements occur.

The great-grandfather of the present William A. Osborne is stated on page 12, volume 21, of the *Biographical Review, Strafford and Belknap Counties*, to have been a Quaker immigrant who settled somewhere in the neighborhood of Salem, Massachusetts. On page 556 of the same volume he is called John, of Pittsfield, New Hampshire. It seems probable that the first reference is the more accurate, as Salem was, at one time, quite a pottery centre. The grandfather was Elijah, who, it is stated, was probably born in Salem, and there learned the potter's trade.

Yet no trace of an Elijah Osborne can be found in Essex County records around this time. At any rate, he eventually moved to Loudon, New Hampshire, married Margaret Green, and established a pottery, where the sons born of his marriage were trained to their father's trade. At least one, James L. Osborne, was born at Loudon in 1831.

Another son, Green, carried on the Loudon pottery for a few years, and then moved to Pittsfield to take up farming. About 1839 Elijah moved to Gonic with his son James and, perhaps, with his son John C. Presumably the father at once began a pottery, and, with the help of those two sons, carried on the work. Later, James and his brother John continued the business as partners until about 1875, when they separated. Thereafter, James, with the help of his son William, maintained the ancestral pottery probably until 1885, when machine-made ware caused competition to become severe.

William A. Osborne, who still lives at the pottery on Jenness Road in Gonic, was born in 1856. Although he helped his father at the pottery, he was not trained in the potter's art; for the older man foresaw the coming of the machine product, and realized that it would soon make his own trade unprofitable.

It is worthy of note that the trade of potter almost always ran through generations of the same family. This is because few crafts require so long and specialized an apprenticeship as does pottery. It was an exceptional man who could claim to be a master of the craft in less than seven years. Hence, when a pottery is found in some isolated village, it is almost certain that the family can be traced back to some other and earlier pottery.

Fig. 1 — The Old Pottery Shed at Gonic
William A. Osborne of the old family of Gonic potters stands beside the middle door

Clay

The clay used in the Gonic pottery was taken from the deposit now worked by the New England Brick Company, and still owned by the Osborne family. Hereabouts clay is plentiful; in fact, Gonic (Squanamagonic) is the Indian name for "Land of the Clay Hills." The clay is glacial, and is similar to the brick clay widely distributed along the coast and rivers of New England. This particular deposit is composed of a brownish sandy top clay of fair plasticity, below which occurs a plastic blue clay. It was the lower clay that was generally employed for throwing.

The brickmaker's method of mining it was used. A well drained hillside deposit was plowed and harrowed and allowed to dry. The resultant clay lumps, sometimes broken up with a roller, were scraped or shoveled up and carried to the pottery. The purpose of this procedure was to drain off as much as possible of the soluble salts in the clay in order that a white scum might not form on the burned ware. While expensive, it is a method still employed by some local brickyards.

Forming the Ware

The gathered clay was now placed in a horse-driven pug mill to be kneaded into a uniform and plastic mass, which was then formed, by hand, into balls ready for the potter. A day's supply of clay was made up each morning by William and his father. It should be noted that, contrary to the popular belief, the clay for this common red ware was not screened or purified.

The balls were next set on a kick wheel and formed into the type of ware desired. When finished, each piece was cut free from the wheel with a wire, and carefully moved to a board. Objects as small as a teacup, or as large as a five-gallon jar, were formed on the same wheel by the skilful hands of the potter. It is this part of the process that requires long years of training. The lignum-vitæ wheel top used at Gonic is shown in Figure 3. The depression worn in its surface by the clay is an indication that it has had many years of use.

Drying the Ware

The Gonic pottery was run on a seasonal basis, so that the ware was usually dried by setting the soft pieces on boards in the sun and wind. In wet or cold weather they could be dried on racks around the warm kiln.

Glazing

Most of the pieces were glazed, at least on the inside, since the soft red earthenware was quite permeable to liquids. Lead glazes were employed exclusively, and were made by grinding sand and red lead together, and adding a small amount of coloring oxide. The red lead was purchased from hardware stores in both Somersworth, New Hampshire and Berwick, Maine. The sand was obtained locally. The source of the coloring oxides is not known, but was probably the same as that of the lead.

There is nothing mysterious about these old

glazes. All may be readily reproduced. The red colors were simply a clear or yellowish glaze that intensified the naturally red-colored body. The blues were produced with cobalt, the greens with copper, the yellows with iron, and the browns with manganese or iron.

Because of the cheapness of the ware the glazes were fired with the body in one burn. The glazes were prepared in the form of a thin slip, in large iron kettles, into which the dried pieces were dipped. In some cases, only the inside of a piece was glazed — a process accomplished by pouring the slip into the vessel, and quickly pouring it out again. The outside bottoms of the pieces were seldom or never glazed. Probably all of the glazes were crazed when taken from the kiln.

The mottled effects typical of Gonic ware were achieved by applying a second glaze of another color in blotches and spatters. One method of doing so, which is rather characteristic of this pottery, was to dip the ends of the fingers in the second glaze and spot it over the surface. This method of application is shown in the mug in Figure 3. After glazing, the ware was again dried before it was fired.

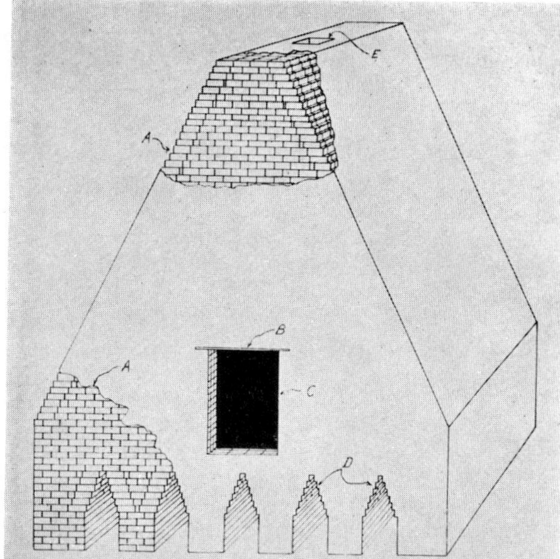

Fig. 2 — Drawing of the Osborne Pottery Kiln
a, Kiln scoving removed to show construction of brickwork
b, Iron bar to support bricks over doorway
c, Doorway for setting and drawing kiln
d, Arches for burning wood fuel
e, Exit flue for escape of smoke and hot gases

The kiln for firing the ware is evidently a development of the scove kiln (a kiln plastered over with clay), long used for burning brick. A fairly accurate drawing of the structure (*Fig. 2*) was made from measurements of the foundation and kiln shed at Gonic, and from the description supplied by Mr. Osborne. It is undoubtedly similar to the old earthenware kilns used around Peabody, and is, therefore, of interest in showing exactly how the ware was burned.

Construction of Kiln

The kiln is of the up-draft type, with wood fires under five arches. It was made entirely of common red brick. As the same clay was used for the kiln brick as for the ware, the temperature range was limited and repairs on the arches were frequently necessary. Fire brick was not generally used until later, except in stoneware kilns. It is noteworthy that the kiln crown was cobbled, not constructed as a true sprung arch.

The ware to be fired was passed through a door at one end of the kiln, and placed on a floor consisting of tiles with cracks between them to permit the circulation of heat. The ware was seldom piled more than one course high, though often small pieces were set inside larger ones. Sometimes a good-sized vessel would be inverted over several smaller objects. The normal charge would be two hundred and fifty to three hundred pieces. The ware was fired for three days and nights to a temperature of about 1800° Fahrenheit; but the temperature was estimated entirely by eye, and not always correctly, if we may judge by the overburned fragments still lying about the pottery.

Type of Ware Made

The ware made at Gonic included all the types of common household earthenware, such as jugs, jars for pickles, crocks, pitchers, cups, milk pans, pudding dishes, shaving mugs, and the like. Some of them were very graceful in shape, and had beautifully mottled glazes. Yet the glazes were so varied in character that it is impossible to assign to this particular establishment any pieces except those illustrated. They were found in the loft of the old pottery building, and were given to the authors by Mr. Osborne.

A number of very attractive items seen in this vicinity were attributed to Gonic, but could not be positively identified. If, however, there is any one characteristic that may be associated with Gonic ware, it is a mottled yellow and green glaze; for this we found on many broken fragments around the pottery.

Of the pieces illustrated, the large jug (*Fig. 3*) is glazed a beautiful golden russet with fine spottings of brown. It is twelve inches tall and has a pouring lip. A small hole near the bottom, made after burning, would indicate that it had been used to hold water for a grindstone. The mug (*Fig. 3*) is four inches in height and diameter, having a light brown glaze, finger-spotted with dark brown. The large pickle jar (*Fig. 4*), thirteen inches high, has unfortunately lost much of its glaze as a result of the vinegar seeping through the body. Nevertheless, there is enough left to show that it was variegated with flowing blotches of green, brown, and yellow. When perfect it must have been a remarkably fine piece, with its graceful contour and soft, flowing colors. A number *4* is scratched on the bottom, probably to indicate its capacity in gallons. The bean pot and water jar (*Fig. 4*) are typical household articles, both of the usual soft red clay, and glazed on the inside only.

Distribution of Wares

The Osborne family made no effort to stimulate wide sales for their wares. The only advertising attempted by the pottery was the dumping of broken scrap in the front yard to indicate to passers-by that a pottery was operating. Save for the few pieces sold on the spot, all the ware was taken in a wagon and distributed among general stores in the surrounding towns of Rochester, Dover, Farmington, Somersworth, Berwick, and Barrington. A medium-sized milk pan brought twenty cents; cups, ten cents; and large jars, forty or fifty cents each.

Fig. 3 — Products of the Gonic Pottery
Jug in golden russet glaze, with fine spottings of brown. A small hole near the bottom suggests its use for dripping water on a grindstone. *Height: 12 inches.* Mug in light brown glaze finger-spotted with darker brown. *Height: 4 inches; diameter: 4 inches.* Top view of potter's wheel, which is worn by many years of use

Fig. 4 — Products of the Gonic Pottery
Red ware jar glazed within only. Pickle jar, a pleasingly shaped piece that must once have been fine in color as well as in form. The action of vinegar has removed most of the original glaze, which seems to have been variegated with flowing blotches of green, brown, and yellow. *Height: 13 inches.* Bean pot with interior glaze

Fig. 1 — Pitcher, Covered Jar, and Jug (*Lyndeboro*)
All of these pieces show, both within and without, the same dark brown glaze, mottled with lighter brown. The jar once possessed a single handle. The pitcher is 3½ inches high; the jar, 2¼ inches; the jug, 4½ inches.

Lyndeboro Pottery

By Leonard F. Burbank

IF any collectors of pottery own a piece of Lyndeboro ware, whether pot, jug, or pan, they have something of a rarity. It will not be beautiful, in the usually accepted sense, but it will be interesting and well worth caring for. In books on the potter's art in America, Lyndeboro ware is not spoken of, for the works were small and their output crude. Lyndeboro, a little town in southern New Hampshire, was settled in 1750. A range of hills running from east to west divides the township in two. On the northern side of these hills Peter Clark became one of the early settlers.

This Peter was the first of several Clarks to carry on the potter's art in Lyndeboro. Born February 4, 1743, in Braintree, Massachusetts, he lived in his native place, operating a pottery until his removal to New Hampshire. For a long series of years he kept a diary, and in this we find many references, with the dates carefully noted, as to when he "sot" his kiln; when he "made ware;" and when he "drawed" his kiln.

Under date of January 23, 1775, in this diary, appears the entry "sot out for Lyndeboro with my family." January 25 is recorded as the date of arrival in that community. From that time on, Peter Clark continued to be a resident of the place. Under date of April 19 appears the succinct but illuminating entry "the fight began at Concord." Thereafter Clark took an active part in the War of the Revolution, during which he was commissioned as captain, and, later, as major. For some years his diary contains mixed but always brief jottings of activities with the army and of doings at home. February 26, 1776, he writes, "Moved into my house."

After he had served with the army, we find him actively engaged in affairs of the town, holding various offices within the choice of the people, and, at the same time, always busy with his own affairs. He built his kiln near his house, and for many years carried on potting; but just when he gave up his business is not known, for in 1801 he ceased maintaining his diary. He died October 14, 1826.

Several of the Clark family were potters, and for many years were actively engaged in the business. In the *History of Lyndeboro* we learn that a son, Peter, also built a pottery, which, it is said, did more business than any other in town.

The elder Clark's second son was William, born May 18, 1766; died November 11, 1855. The latter's two sons, Peter and Benjamin, were also potters. This third Peter, known as Captain Peter, was born October 12, 1797. He died September 5, 1879. Benjamin F., born September 23, 1808, learned the potter's trade; but subsequently became a minister, settled in North Chelmsford, Massachusetts, and died there May 28, 1879.

We have found no record of the dates when the various potteries belonging to the descendants of the original Peter Clark began to turn out their wares, or when they ceased; but, although none of these establishments are now in existence, it is known where they stood. Joseph A. Johnson, now, or formerly, a resident of Lyndeboro, says, "We have no means of knowing when the manufacture of brown earthenware was first established in the town, but in 1826, and a few years later, it was made by the family of William Clark of North Lyndeboro."

The clay for the ware was drawn from Amherst, New Hampshire, some ten miles to the eastward; and mugs, pots, milk pans, jugs of many sizes, bean pots, pots for baking brown bread, and other articles were made and were peddled about the neighboring towns. The methods of potting were primitive. A ball of clay having been thrown upon the wheel, the machine was set in motion by a foot treadle, and the utensil shaped by the hands. The body of the ware, when fired, became red, and showed a texture and color similar to that of brick. The glaze was characteristically, but not invariably, of a dark brown color; and from its texture, its uneven thickness, and mottled appearance, we may judge that the potters never became highly skilled in their art. Yet they made many rather pleasing pieces.

Fig. 2—Pitcher and Jug (*Lyndeboro*)
In these two pieces the glaze is of a dark yellowish cast. In the case of the jug, the color is splashed with brown. Most Lyndeboro pieces show the same glaze inside and out. In the majority of pieces, some part of the foot exposes the basic red clay. Height of pitcher, 8½ inches; of jug, 7 inches.

Although the Clarks were the best known and most active potters in the town, there were others who carried on a similar business; for we find mention of a John Southwick, who was associated with Peter Clark. In the *Farmers Cabinet*, printed at Amherst, New Hampshire, under date of September 8, 1815, occurs the following:

> The subscriber having removed his pottery from Lyndeboro, to Vermont, acquaints those indebted to him that he will be at his father's house in Lyndeboro the 15th to the 20th day of September next, when he requests they will call upon him and make payment, or they may expect costs.
> *Ebenezer Hutchinson, April 8, 1815.*

From this we may surmise that Hutchinson carried on some sort of a pottery in Lyndeboro, but there is no record of such an enterprise in the town history.

No doubt anyone, today, browsing about Lyndeboro, or the nearby towns, will be able to discover specimens of the local ware; but such pieces will be of a lowly type: jugs, pots, and pans. Such better pieces as were turned out by the local potters doubtless constituted an outlet for the creative fancy of their makers and were not intended to serve for commercial purposes.

Fig. 3 (left)—Tall Jar (*Lyndeboro*)
An interesting decorative piece, one of a pair, whose surface appears to have been banded with a comb-like device, first used while the piece stood level on the wheel, and then applied at different angles to give the recurring wave pattern. The glaze shows a soft green foundation with blendings of brown and yellow. Height, 7 inches.

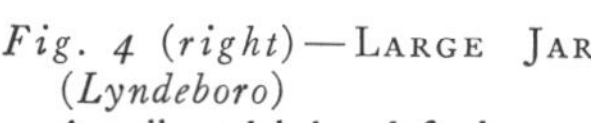

Fig. 4 (right)—Large Jar (*Lyndeboro*)
A well modeled and finely proportioned piece with integral handles and a well executed beading about the neck. The glaze is of splotched brown. Height, 8¼ inches.

Fig. 5—Two Pitchers and a Jug (*Lyndeboro*)
The two pitchers show a dark brown glaze. The jug is slightly mottled with yellow. The pitchers are, respectively, 3½ and 4¼ inches high; the jug, 5¾ inches.

EDITOR'S NOTE

For the illustrations accompanying Mr. Burbank's article on Lyndeboro and its potteries, Antiques is indebted to Mrs. J. M. Robinson of Malden, a great-great-granddaughter of Peter Clark, pioneer potter of the New Hampshire village. Since the specimens here reproduced have been carefully preserved by the family for several generations, it is reasonable to assume that they are the product of this elder Peter's kiln.

The fact that, for some years, Peter Clark conducted a potting business in the town of his birth, Braintree, Massachusetts, is worthy of emphasis; for his subsequent removal to New Hampshire offers specific exemplification of the transfer of the craft traditions of one locality to another and quite distant place. In the early days such transfers must have been frequent in all lines of home industry.

Mrs. Robinson preserves the diary, mentioned by Mr. Burbank, and it is from the many entries in this document that we derive much of our knowledge of Peter Clark's activities both before his departure from Braintree, and after.

All the entries in this diary are of the briefest. The outbreak of the Revolution and Peter's own departure to participate in the fray receive no more extended notice than do barnyard occurrences and preparations for making and firing pottery. While working in Braintree, Clark sold some, at least, of his wares in Hingham. This we learn from an entry of November 18, 1768. Another entry, that of May 13, 1772, records an excursion to Danvers for clay. The exodus to Lyndeboro was apparently under contemplation as early as 1774, though actual moving did not occur until January of the following year, and the making of pottery until nine months later.

Clark's note, quoted by Mr. Burbank, on the outbreak of hostilities at Concord seems to imply that the event was not unexpected. But if his sympathies with the patriot cause were aroused, as they undoubtedly were, he fails to express them in his diary; and whatever the family upheaval consequent upon his later determination to enlist in the Continental army, there is no indication of it in the crisp entry of August 14, 1777, "Set out for Bennington."

He memorializes the dead Washington with a line, dated January 12, 1800, "Meeting house dressed in mourning for General Washington;" and a bit of local scandal that must have kept Lyndeboro tongues joyously wagging for many a long day is dismissed with the six words "Polly Lewis ran away with Dickerman."

An unemotional man Peter Clark, but a tremendous worker, a brave and uncomplaining patriot, a useful and trusted citizen. Once, at least, in his lifetime he took his pen in hand to indite more than a five word memorandum. That was after the battle of Bennington, in which he had actively participated. Mrs. Robinson still preserves the letter which her great-great-grandfather wrote to his family in description of the memorable Vermont engagement. Devoid though it is of any expression of emotion, or of the sensations which the embattled farmer may have experienced when face to face with British regulars, it is worth reprinting. So here it is:

Bennington, August 18, 1777.

These, with my love to you and my dear Children, and Brothers and Sisters. Hoping you are as well as I am at present, except something of a cold, and much fatigued with marching, and last Saturdays action. We are now about twenty miles east of Stillwater. We came to this town last Monday from Manchester. Last Wednesday the whole Brigade was paraded to march to Stillwater, and while under arms, the General received intelligence that there was a large body of the enemy coming to destroy the stores at Bennington: whereupon the Brigade was dismissed until towards night, and then sent off. Lt. Col. Gray of Londonderry, with about two hundred men, who, early the next morning, discovered the enemy at a mill, about seven miles from this place, and finding them a large body, after firing at each other a few times, retreated, and met the Brigade about halfway between this mill and Bennington, where the Brigade made a stand: and threw up a slight breast work.

The enemy came down within about a mile and one half of us and made a stand.

Their number we could not find out, but it appears by prisoners taken there was about fifteen hundred—

The next day was Friday, and by reason of rainy weather, nothing of any consequence was done. The next day Saturday, August 16, at twenty minutes past three, in the afternoon, the Battle began in earnest, we being at this time in every part of them, and as near as I can tell, I think the battle held about one half an hour, and was equal to Bunker Hill, excepting there was not so many cannon.

The enemy had two brass field pieces, we had none. The Lord of Hosts sent them off in such haste, they left their all and fled.

However, we took many of them. But here I must not end for we had another Battle, much harder than the first, for we were about tired out, and many of our people gone off with the prisoners who had not been in the first Battle—which brought on another Battle, which continued until dark, but finally they were ordered to flee before us, and leave behind them two more brass field pieces, small arms, and other things.

So God gave us a complete victory over them.

Many think: all considered the greatest victory since the war by the Americans.

Peter Clark.

Covered Jar
Portland, Me., pottery.

Cider or Vinegar Jug
Portland, Me., pottery.

Glazed Earthenware Preserve Jar
Probably from Long Island.

Stoneware Pitcher
Bears mark of Armstrong & Wentworth, Norwich, Conn.

Stoneware Pitcher
From Hartford, Conn.

Jug from Hartford, Conn.
The name of the maker is clearly stamped upon it.

Massachusetts Pitcher
Red ware decorated with wave figures in the glaze.

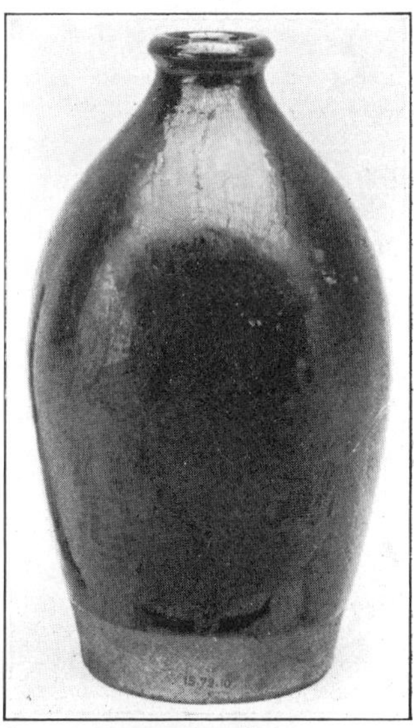

Glazed Stoneware Bottle
From New London, Conn.

Some Specimens of New England Pottery in the Metropolitan Museum, New York

35TH ANNIVERSARY ARTICLE

BY LURA WOODSIDE WATKINS

New England pottery in the Smithsonian Institution

THE CASUAL VISITOR to the Hall of Everyday Life in Early America in the United States National Museum may wonder why space is given to a collection of New England pottery intended for the most prosaic purposes. A few objects in this display will look strange to him, but the milk pans, cooking utensils, jugs, and jars may awaken vague memories of things seen in his childhood. Whatever looks familiar he saw long, long ago and cannot now remember what became of it.

Fig. 1. Early redware jug, probably about 1700; greenish color mottled with orange. Fragments of this form of vessel were found in the Kettle pottery at Danvers, Massachusetts.

The better-informed observer may ask himself, "What is the significance of this exhibit?" and "Why is it here? Was it so important a part of our early culture?"

To answer these questions one must go back to the very beginnings of New England, when Englishmen landed in the marshes and forests and began to make from the materials at hand the utensils they had been unable to bring with them on small crowded boats. Wood was the most plentiful material. That the pioneer's first dishes were wooden ware is well known. It is a less familiar fact that the colonists utilized the abundant clay along the seacoast almost immediately after they landed.

In 1629 Francis Higginson, the minister at Salem, reported that a brick kiln was being put to work to make bricks and tiles for houses, and he commented on the quality of the clay for earthen pots. Six years later, a "pot-baker," as he called himself, appeared in Salem. He was William Vincent (later Vinson). In the following year John Pride, another potter, was granted land there. In 1635 Philip Drinker and his family landed in Charlestown.

These men established what was to be a continuous tradition. Drinker's son Edward worked in Charlestown and Boston until 1700, while Vinson's grandson was still making pottery in Gloucester as late as 1749. These artisans taught apprentices, who were bound to them for seven years and thoroughly trained. The craft flourished. So great was the need for pottery containers and for plates, bowls, mugs, and pitchers for the table that there was a constant demand.

All this red earthenware, or redware, was turned on the potter's wheel without the use of molds. The glazes were compounded of red lead, sand, and water, which produced a clear glassy coating that allowed the natural body color to show through. The coloring was often varied by accidents of firing in the wood-burning kilns or by imperfections in the materials. The only intentional variations of color were obtained by the addition of manganese for brown or black, or copper oxide for green. Green was used sparingly, sometimes as an addition to decoration, although occasional pieces, like the small jug in the Watkins collection, are entirely glazed with a brilliant true green color.

My husband and I obtained much authentic information about the objects made in the colonial period in a

Fig. 2. The rather neat and careful style of early slip decoration, on a shard from the side wall of a fifteen-inch pan (called a "platter"), excavated at the site of the pottery of James Kettle (1687-1709/10) in Danvers. *All photographs are from the Smithsonian Institution.*

Fig. 3. Exceptionally fine example of apparently early redware with tooled decoration, found in Salem. The base is worn glassy smooth from continuous use.

series of digs carried on during more than fifteen years on different sites. Fragments from the pottery of James Kettle (Kettell) in Danvers are displayed with this collection and show that pottery plates, pans, and bowls were sometimes elaborately decorated with white slip. Kettle worked at his home site from about 1687 to 1709-1710. We now know that his father, John, was also a potter, who had lived in Gloucester until 1664 and later in Beverly. This knowledge assures us that the earthenware made by James represents the very beginning of the pottery tradition in New England. The Kettles were undoubtedly related to the Kettells of Charlestown, several of whom carried on the craft there in the seventeenth century. James Kettle is the earliest American potter whose name and pottery site are known.

Charlestown became an important center for the potters in the eighteenth century. There is much documentary evidence about them, but not a piece of their pottery. It is almost certain, however, that a great deal of the better-made ware of early type emanated from Charlestown. It was sold by the boatload along the coast, even in Maine and Connecticut.

Potters trained in the same ways of turning and firing were also numerous in Essex County, Massachusetts. They flourished in the South Danvers area (now Peabody), especially from the Revolutionary period to about 1812.

An excavation on the site of the potshop of Daniel Bayley in Newburyport, Massachusetts, gave us the most detailed picture of eighteenth-century potting that has been found anywhere. Bayley, and later his sons, had a shop behind their house on High Street from 1764 to about 1795. We recovered some complete utensils at this location and many others in part (ANTIQUES, January 1939, p. 22). The latter have been restored at the Smithsonian and are shown in a section devoted to Bayley's wares. Here are tall cylindrical ale mugs with bands of tooling, tea bowls used as cups, larger bowls, a decorated porringer, a sugar bowl, plates and platters with slip decoration, pitchers, and various forms for cooking in a brick oven. Some of the pieces, such as a black saucer, are not typical of a potter's traditional output. The saucer was no doubt made during the Revolution when imports were scarce.

The discoveries at the Bayley pottery show that trailing or painting with white slip was a regular procedure —a fact that we were later able to verify in the earlier Joseph Bayley and Kettle potteries and in a number of others of the pre-Revolutionary period.

Another method of decoration was effected by tooling bands of straight or wavy lines about a vessel as it was slowly turned on the wheel. There is reason to believe that this style was more often practiced in the seventeenth and eighteenth centuries, or in locations where the imported white clay was not easily obtainable. The redware crock (Fig. 3) is a noteworthy example. The persistence of the tradition in a simple way is shown in the bowl (Fig. 6) made by Peter Flanders of West Plymouth, New Hampshire, in the first half of the nineteenth century. The Gills of Plymouth, even later, tooled their wares.

The redware industry, which we are able to follow through the years, spread out in the course of time from Charlestown and Danvers to frontier settlements in western and northern New England. There was also a highly developed potting craft in southeastern Massachusetts founded about 1740 by Paul Osborn, a brother of Joseph Osborn of Danvers. The Osborns were Quakers and their relatives and descendants carried on

Fig. 4. Restored pieces from the pottery of Daniel Bayley, Newburyport, Massachusetts (1764-c. 1795). Bayley usually decorated his plates, platters, chamber pots, and porringers with white slip applied with a brush.

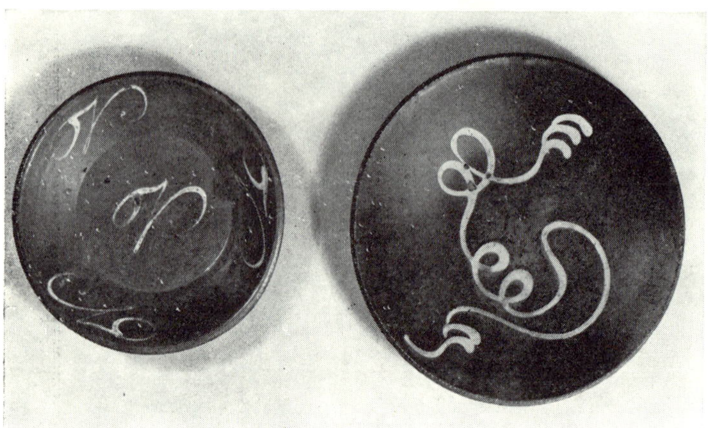

Fig. 5. Eighteenth-century redware plates were deep like milk pans, had smooth rims, and were shaped by turning without the use of molds. The pie plate shaped over a rounded mold and having a notched edge was introduced into southwestern Connecticut about 1800 by potters from New Jersey trained in the Pennsylvania style. The example (right) is from Norwalk.

the tradition in both areas for many years. Some of the handsomest redware has been found in southeastern Massachusetts. Country potteries of the kind, making redware only, persisted until the 1880's.

The only departures in style from the forms and decorations introduced by the early Massachusetts potters and bequeathed to their descendants in the craft are seen in the wares of southwestern Connecticut. In South Norwalk two traditions mingled. Potters trained in New Jersey brought certain styles characteristic of Pennsylvania rather than of New England. In Norwalk the typical Connecticut pie plate, rounded in form and with notched rim, appeared after 1800. Many of these slip-decorated plates, shaped over a mold, cannot be distinguished from those made in New Jersey and Pennsylvania.

In spite of the general use of redware utensils, the disadvantages of a pottery coated with lead glaze, which sometimes caused lead poisoning, were obvious. The matter was aired in the public press, and home manufacture of stoneware was urged. It was difficult to make this ware in New England in the early days, because there was no suitable clay in the region. There had been several attempts to produce stoneware—one in Charlestown as early as 1740—but the costs of trans-

Fig. 6. Peter Flanders, who made this unusual black bowl, began his career in Concord, New Hampshire, in 1807, with a plate ornamented by similar tooling. He worked in West Plymouth, New Hampshire, until 1856.

Fig. 7. Made as a christening present for Dorothy Melissa Ann Goodrich of East Kingston, New Hampshire, this deep pan was probably the work of an Exeter potter; banded with light slip and a wavy line of dark brown on tan ground.

Fig. 8. Brown-stained stoneware jar, perhaps made in the short-lived pottery of Jonathan Fenton in Boston, about 1795. The name of *Marshall Timson,* who probably decorated it, is inscribed on the reverse, and *Lydia Osborn* appears under the *Boston* stamp. The reverse also shows signs of a rubbed-out attempt at decoration in which the girl's name and *Charlestown* are discernible.

porting the clay from New Jersey or Pennsylvania were too great. After America became independent stoneware was attempted with varying degrees of success.

The first successful New England stoneware was made about 1750 in Greenwich, Connecticut, not far from the New York line, by Adam States, a potter of Dutch origin who utilized clay from Long Island across the Sound. A good many descendants of States and his brother Peter also became potters. The family worked in Norwich, Stonington, New London, and elsewhere. By 1800 stoneware manufacture had been established in various towns up the rivers. Connecticut potters, migrating to Vermont, introduced the ware in Dorset, Bennington, Burlington, and other places, but the clay was always shipped up the Hudson to Troy, New York, and then carried overland.

New England stoneware in itself is not of great interest. Only a few pieces dating from the 1700's have been found. The incised jar (Fig. 8) in the Smithsonian exhibit was made in the last decade of the century at Boston. In the nineteenth century, since there was no longer any demand for small pieces, the whole art of potting deteriorated to the production of thick and utilitarian wares. The stoneware forms were chiefly jugs, pots, and crocks. The appeal they have for us today

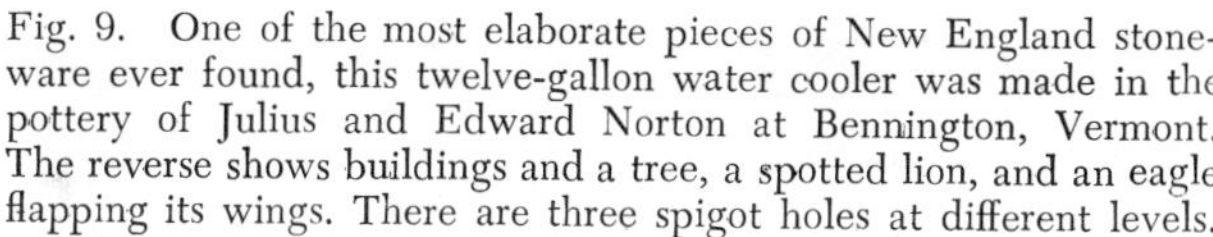

Fig. 9. One of the most elaborate pieces of New England stoneware ever found, this twelve-gallon water cooler was made in the pottery of Julius and Edward Norton at Bennington, Vermont. The reverse shows buildings and a tree, a spotted lion, and an eagle flapping its wings. There are three spigot holes at different levels.

Fig. 10, The robin was a favorite subject with stoneware potters. Loammi Kendall, who worked in Chelsea, Massachusetts, from 1836 until after 1870, produced this crock and may have done the decoration.

comes more from their decoration than from the objects.

In the early 1800's the potters satisfied their urge for embellishment by impressing on their vessels such simple motifs as a sequence of hearts, crosses, or tassels (as on Charlestown ware), sometimes enlivened with a dash of blue. Men of more imagination incised with sharp-pointed sticks a spray of flowers, a bird, or a fish. But this was done with the greatest restraint, adding just a note of style to the curvilinear forms of the earlier stoneware.

In the late period—from 1850 to 1880—decoration became much more elaborate: in fact, a wholly new traditional art developed. Using cobalt blue or sometimes brown slip, the potter trailed or brushed on his prosaic pots designs inspired by his everyday surroundings. Sprays of flowers, foliage, birds, deer, chickens, figures of people, houses, trees and various simple conventional motifs glorify the sturdy ware in an original manner.

The outstanding example of New England stoneware is without doubt the twelve-gallon water cooler in Figure 9. The deer on one side are apparently stalked by a lion on the other who never quite springs upon them in spite of encouragement by the eagle. The composition is obviously the handiwork of the same decorator who painted a deer on a small crock in the collection, marked *Edmands & Co.* (Charlestown), and another of identical form and decoration made at Bennington. Water coolers, with their large surfaces, offered excellent background for embellishment. One of the two or three known examples of New England stoneware with relief decoration is of this form and may be seen in this exhibit. It was made by Hastings and Belding of Ashfield, Massachusetts, in the 1850's, and displays a figure of George Washington between floral sprays in cobalt blue.

Stoneware is more easily understood than the traditional and skillfully turned redware. It is usually marked with the name of the manufacturer, so that its source and date may be determined. Although unrelated to the ware itself, the folk art of its decoration has an esthetic appeal even for those who have no interest in ceramics. Redware, especially in its earlier manifestations when it was the output of skilled craftsmen, is not so readily appreciated. Its charm is due not only to its often luscious coloring, but also to the restraint and ease with which common clay was so suitably fashioned for its purpose.

Redware from the Collection at Old Sturbridge Village

Slip decoration was frequently and attractively used by many New England potters. These forms with reddish brown glaze were shaped over a mold, not turned on the wheel.

IV Stoneware—New England

Between New England redware and New England stoneware and, indeed, between two articles by Lura Woodside Watkins, is a suitable place for a few words about this remarkable lady.

Wife of the late Charles H. Watkins, who often assisted with her digging of early pottery sites, she is the daughter of Charles L. Woodside, who wrote some of the first authoritative studies on American lighting devices.

Her first article on pottery in *The Magazine* ANTIQUES, was "The Stoneware of South Ashfield, Massachusetts," in September, 1934 (pp. 102–105). Her latest article, "New Light on Boston Stoneware and Frederick Carpenter" (pp. 81–86), was in the issue for June, 1972. So for almost forty years, she utilized the pages of ANTIQUES to make an unparalleled contribution to our knowledge of American ceramics—at the same time submitting important articles on other subjects, including American glass.

Only with difficulty did we avoid letting this book become *The Lura Woodside Watkins Anthology*. Without her work, we not only would have had little to edit, but we would have had nothing to consult as a guide to the accuracy of other authors in the field. Her book, *Early New England Potters and Their Wares* (Harvard University Press, 1950), is one of the few we are able to recommend without qualification to anyone seeking accurate information about the activities of our early potters. Important examples from her collection of New England pottery may be seen, on exhibit, at the Smithsonian Institution's Museum of History and Technology, where her son, C. Malcolm Watkins is Senior Curator of Cultural History.

Mrs. Watkins combined consultation of land deeds, wills and probate records, newspapers, directories and the like, with digging at the site for discards and wasters left behind, laboriously cross-checking references until she had pieced together concrete evidence of what was made where. Her studies served to dispell the myth that colonial potteries were located only in large communities and to push back the working dates of our pioneer potters well before 1750, a date that had been accepted for years as a starting point for earthenware production in New England. Mrs. Watkins also devoted portions of *Early New England Potters and Their Wares* to correcting and expanding on articles that appeared in ANTIQUES, including her own. Her checklist of New England stoneware potters, as reprinted here (pp. 77–80), was revised and enlarged, with the "Chase" family of Somerset listed under the more usually accepted spelling, "Chace." So precise a scholar is she, in fact, that she once filled the better part of two pages correcting a two-page article by Charles D. Cook on Rhode Island pottery that had appeared in the magazine in January, 1931, but is not reprinted here. We quote from pp. 118 and 119 of her book to clarify the history of the Crafts pottery, which is described on pp. 97–98 of this anthology:

> The Crafts pottery was an offshoot of the stoneware business begun by Thomas Crafts in Whately in 1833. His son James M. was the first manager of the Nashua works when he was only twenty-one years of age, and while Martin, his brother, was still running a stoneware pottery in Portland, Maine. Martin went to Nashua in 1839 and bought out the business two years later. For ten years the Nashua shop was operated by Martin Crafts, and it is known as his pottery. In 1843 his uncle, Caleb Crafts, who had tried to make a success of the Portland business after Martin had abandoned it, was also in Nashua. His name appears in 1843 and 1845 directories. He then returned to Whately, leaving Martin in charge of the works. In 1849 James M. Crafts was again in Nashua, and he was soon followed by another brother, Thomas Spencer Crafts. Martin left the management to them in 1851, while he went to Boston to conduct a wholesale stoneware agency for the sale of their products. The pottery closed in 1852, James going back to Whately to take up farming, while the younger brother set out for California.

Mrs. Watkins' book details the early history of Jonathan Fenton, between his activities in Boston, as described in her article in the following section, and his work in Vermont, as outlined in an article by John Spargo (pp. 87–90). Mrs. Watkins tells how she discovered the site of a pottery in Dorset Hollow, Vermont, operated by Fenton from 1801 until 1810, when he purchased his land and homestead in East Dorset. She notes finding fragments of redware *and* stoneware, indicating that both were made at the site.

John Spargo's research on the Fentons and Nortons was exhaustive and has, for all intents and purposes, withstood the test of time. His best book, *The Potters and Potteries of Bennington,* was published by Antiques, Inc., in 1926. One does not have to read much of what Spargo has written, however, to gather that he found it difficult to suffer the mistakes—or what he was convinced were the mistakes—of other authors. One wishes he had spent less effort flailing away at Barber, Pitkin and others, and more in establishing solid bases for his own conclusions. Nonetheless, now that the books of Barber, Spargo and Lura Woodside Watkins have been reprinted and are available to a new group of readers, it is perhaps just as well that the old arguments be aired once again.

As the Editor, Homer Eaton Keyes, notes above the article on the Nortons, Spargo spearheaded the movement to create an historical museum in Bennington. On its establishment in 1927, he was named the first Director-Curator. Anyone genuinely interested in the history of American ceramics or glass will find it rewarding to visit the Bennington Museum.

It is of tangential interest that original pencil drawings of the old Norwich pottery, similar to the one illustrating the article by Henry R. Armstrong (pp. 99–101), turn up from time to time. The duplication was cause for mystification until we encountered the source in *A New Drawing Book of American Scenery, Containing Thirty-Four Views From Nature, With Instructions for Beginners in Landscape,* by Benjamin H. Coe, Teacher of Drawing, published by E. B. & E. C. Kellogg, Hartford in 1845.

Note, too, that the water cooler illustrated in the Armstrong article had to have been manufactured after 1881 for, insofar as is known, the Risleys did not use the mark, "Norwich Pottery Works."

Mrs. J. H. W., Maine, has supplied photographs of a small gray stoneware jug stamped THOS. DANEY, ELLSWORTH. This simple piece, only 5½ inches high, adds the name of a previously unknown potter to the roster of New England makers of stoneware listed by Lura Woodside Watkins in ANTIQUES for August 1942. Since the jug was found in Maine it is safe to assume that Daney's pottery was in the town of Ellsworth in that state. Collectors of stoneware will welcome any information about Thomas Daney.

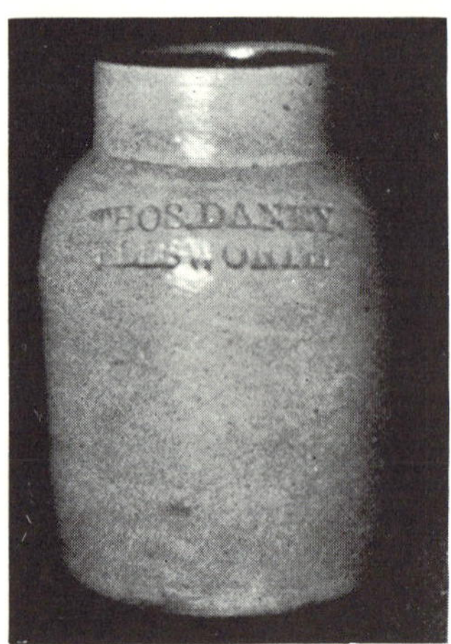

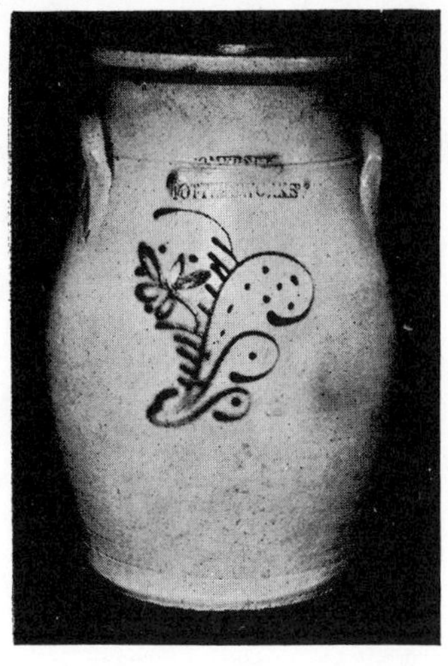

A CHECK LIST OF NEW ENGLAND STONEWARE POTTERS

By LURA WOODSIDE WATKINS

With the exception of Figures 2 and 3, all illustrations from the Wells Historical Museum.

FIG. 1—CHURN. Marked *Somerset Potters Works.*

STONEWARE crocks and jars are a familiar reminder of the past in many parts of New England. Their vigorous contours and naïve decorations appeal to all who appreciate beauty in utilitarian objects. In fact, they represent the last remnants of a folk expression in ordinary American handcraft. Stoneware is hardly a collectible in quantity, but it will always be prized by those who have gathered a few pieces for use in home or garden.

This list of stoneware potters and their marks has been prepared as a convenient guide for the collector who wants to ascertain the age of his pottery or to learn more about the men who made it. As far as the locations of the potteries are concerned, the record is approximately complete, although much could be added to the other data presented. There are undoubtedly many other marks besides those given here. In recording marks I have confined myself (with the exception of the Bennington marks, for which I am indebted to John Spargo) to those I have actually seen and that I have entered in my notebook at the time. A few additional marks I have found on fragments dug on pottery sites.

The custom of stamping a place name on stoneware did not become general until after 1800. Indeed, I have never seen a piece made in New England before that time bearing a mark of any sort. The *Boston 1804* mark seems to be the earliest example of identification by stamping. The potter who thus advertised the city where he worked is himself lost to view – temporarily, we hope, for he did some excellent potting. The mark of Peter Cross of Hartford is perhaps the first to include the maker's name.

The dates given do not always represent the exact duration of a pottery: in some instances, they stand for the period of stoneware manufacture. Thomas Crafts, for example, made pottery from 1802 to 1861, but he did not operate a stoneware kiln until 1833. His mark on stoneware, therefore, was used after that date. Where the entire period of stoneware production is unknown, I have given a date found in a directory or other record to indicate the approximate time when the pottery was running.

In the brackets are grouped either the different individuals or the firms

FIG. 2—PRESERVE JAR (*after 1856*). Four-gallon. Marked *M. Crafts/Whately.* Work of Martin Crafts. *From the collection of Frederick A. Adams.*

FIG. 3 (*above, right*)—WATER COOLER. Four-gallon. Marked *Hastings & Belding: Ashfield, Mass.* Unusual applied relief decoration. Probably by Franklin Wight, son of John Wight, a potter of Marlborough, New Hampshire. Wight was employed at Ashfield in 1852-53. He signed his initials on another remarkable cooler with same type of decoration, now at the Wadsworth Atheneum, Hartford, Connecticut (see Spargo, *Early American Pottery and China*). Wight also worked at St. Johnsbury, Vermont, where he made coolers closely resembling the Atheneum example. *From the author's collection.*

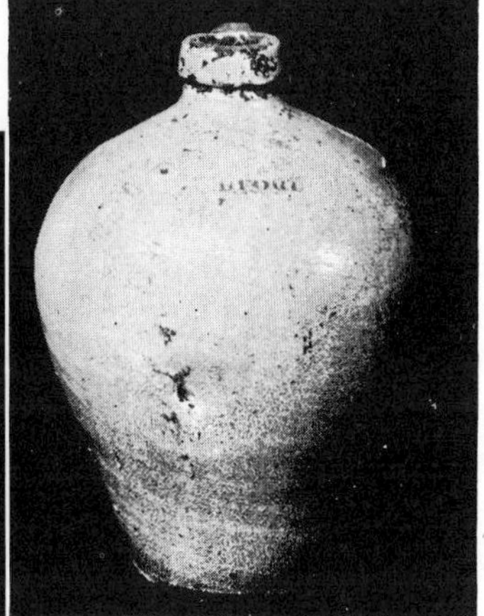

FIG. 4 (*below, left*)—CROCK. One and one-half gallon. Marked *F. B. Norton & Co./Worcester, Mass.*

FIG. 5 (*below, right*)—JUG. Marked *Medford.* Rare product of T. Sables & Co.

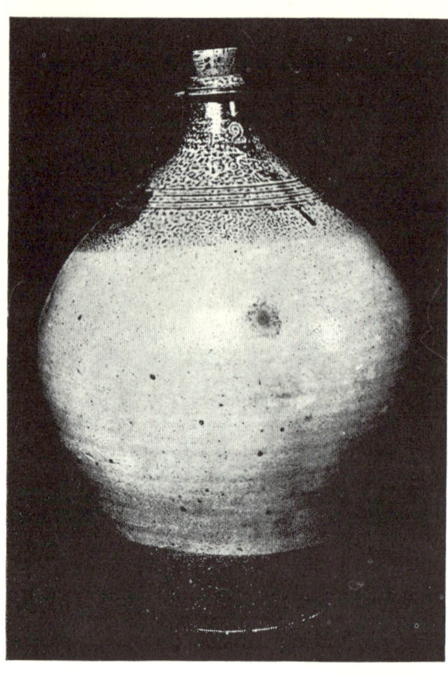

FIG. 6 (*left*)—JUG. Two-gallon. Marked *Boston.* Resemblance to pieces marked *Boston/1804* places this jug in first decade of nineteenth century.

FIG. 7 (*below*)—JUG (*c. 1850-1861*). Two-gallon. Marked *J. & E. Norton/ Bennington, Vt.*

FIG. 8 (*below, right*)—JUG. Marked *F. B. Norton & Co./Worcester, Mass.* Shape and decoration typical of period from 1850-1880.

FIG. 9 (*extreme right*)—CIDER PITCHER. Marked *F. B. Norton & Co./Worcester, Mass.* Typical Norton decoration frequently seen on crocks and other articles bearing various firm names of users.

that worked successively in one pottery. In some places, more than one stoneware concern was in operation at the same time.

In this listing, a few changes from similar charts made heretofore may be found. These changes I have made with reason. It will be noted that Boscawen, New Hampshire, is not included. For a long time it has been accepted that highly glazed brown stoneware ornamented with bands of incised decoration was a Boscawen product. Investigation of the Burpee dumps and conversations with some of the town's very old inhabitants, who could well remember the pottery and who had early examples of its ware, have convinced me that the Burpee family never made anything but ordinary redware. It is more than likely that the stoneware which has been given the Boscawen tag came from Nottingham, England, and was conveyed up the Merrimac River to the little New Hampshire settlement. Certainly nothing in the history of New England stoneware potting would lead us to believe that so sophisticated a ware could have been produced in a remote country village. Furthermore, it bears the closest resemblance to known specimens of Nottingham pottery and is found all along the New England coast, as well as in New Hampshire.

The reason for including the mark *R. & C. Fenton Dorset, Vt.* under East Dorset needs explanation. Jonathan Fenton was a resident of Dorset for nine years before he owned property. During that time, according to local tradition, he worked in Dorset, later moving to East Dorset. Upon examining the pottery dump in Dorset Hollow, I found confirming fragments of form and type peculiar to the opening years of the century. In 1810 Fenton bought land and built a pottery at East Dorset. His son Richard was then thirteen and Christopher four. Richard bought a half interest in his father's pottery in 1827, but there is no record as to whether he had worked continuously with him up to that time. There is a possibility that he may have gone back to Dorset in the 1820's, with his young brother as apprentice, to run the Dorset Hollow pottery, but it does not seem probable. After 1827 his whereabouts are known. Recorded deeds give proof positive that the brothers were in business together in East Dorset from 1830 to 1833. Unless contradictory evidence concerning the Fentons' early activities comes to light, it seems reasonable to attribute this mark to the period of their partnership in East Dorset. The only example of this mark I have seen occurs on a jug in the Dorset Public Library.

There is a question as to whether the mark *Boynton* should be credited to Boynton at Burlington or at St.-Albans. Were it known whether the same Boynton worked at both places, this might be determined. The *Nichols & Alford* mark noted here was used on Rockingham ware. The firm also made stoneware and must have had a regular stamp for it.

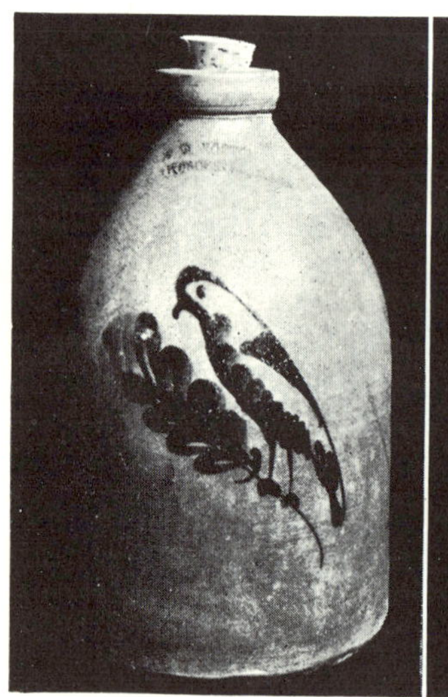

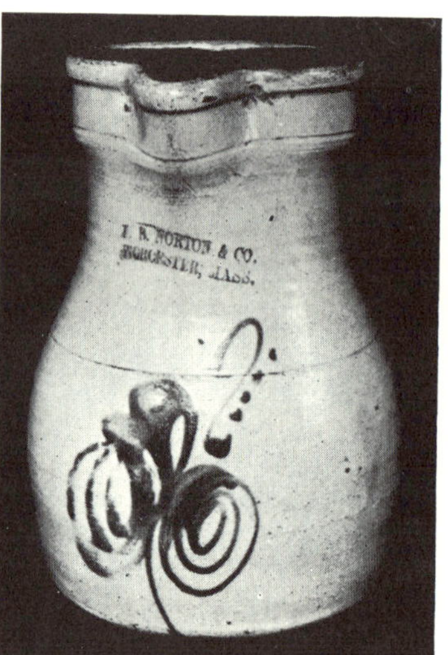

CHECK LIST

MAINE

Bangor

Bangor Stoneware Co. Late pottery
Marks:
Bangor Stoneware Co. Bangor/Maine

Gardiner

Lyman & Clark (Alanson Potter Lyman and probably Decius W. Clark), 1837-1841
Mark: *Lyman & Clark*
Thompson & Co.
F. A. Plaisted & Co., 1860's
Note: Census of 1850 lists one pottery

Portland

Portland Stone Ware Co., 1846 to present time
John T. Winslow, 1846-?
Marks:
J. T. Winslow/Portland, Me.
Portland Stone Ware Co. in circle with firm name.

Crafts pottery, 1834-1841
Martin Crafts, 1834-1838
Caleb Crafts, 1837-1841
Mark:
M. Crafts & Co. / Portland
Eleazer Orcutt, 1837
Mark:
Orcutt & Crafts / Portland
Caleb Crafts & Co., 1841

NEW HAMPSHIRE

Keene

Keene Stone & Earthen Ware Manufactory, 1871-?
J. S. Taft & Co.
Marks:
J. S. Taft & Co./Keene, N. H.
J. S. Taft & Company/Keene, N. H.

Nashua

Martin Crafts and James M. Crafts, 1838-1841
Martin Crafts and Caleb Crafts, 1841-1845
Martin Crafts, 1845-1851
Marks:
T Crafts & Co. / Nashua
Martin Crafts / Nashua
Martin Crafts / Nashua, N. H.

VERMONT

Bennington

Norton pottery, *c.*1800-1894
John Norton, *c.*1800-1823
John Norton & Sons (Luman, John Jr., and Norman), *c.*1812-1823
L. Norton & Co. (Luman and Julius Norton), 1823-1827
L. Norton, 1828-1833
Julius Norton, 1841-1844 and 1847-1850
Norton & Fenton (Julius Norton and Christopher Webber Fenton), 1844-1847
J. & E. Norton (Julius and Edward Norton), 1850-1859
J. & E. Norton & Co. (Julius, Edward, and Luman P. Norton), 1859-1861
E. & L. P. Norton (Edward and Luman P. Norton), 1861-1881
E. Norton, 1881-1883
Edward Norton & Co., 1883-1894
Marks:
L. Norton & Co.
L. Norton & Co./Bennington, Vt.
L. Norton & Son/Bennington, Vt.
L. Norton & Son/East Bennington, Vt.
L. Norton/Bennington, Vt.
Julius Norton/East Bennington, Vt.
J. Norton/East Bennington, Vt.
Julius Norton/Bennington, Vt.
J. Norton/Bennington, Vt.
Norton & Fenton/Bennington, Vt.
Norton & Fenton/East Bennington, Vt.
J. & E. Norton/Bennington, Vt.
J. Norton & Co./Bennington, Vt.
J. & E. Norton & Co./Bennington, Vt.
E. & L. P. Norton & Co. / Bennington, Vt.
E. Norton/Bennington, Vt.
Edward Norton/Bennington, Vt.
Edward Norton & Co./Bennington, Vt.
Edward Norton Co./Bennington, Vt.
E. Norton & Co./Bennington, Vt.
The Edw'd Norton Co./Bennington, Vt.
Bennington Factory (Late mark)
I. Judd, Jr./Bennington (Probably presentation piece)

The marks *L. Norton & Son, Norton & Fenton,* and *E. Norton & Co.* sometimes appear without the word *Vt.* It is possible that other Bennington signatures so abbreviated will come to light. This list includes only the marks on common stoneware.

Burlington

E. L. Farrar & Co., 1854
Nichols & Alford, 1854-1856
Nichols & Boynton, 1856-?
O. L. & A. K. Ballard, 1850's and 1860's
A. K. Ballard, 1868
Ballard & Brothers
F. Woodworth, 1870's.
H. E. Smith, ?-1895
Marks:
E. L. Farrar & Co./Burlington, Vt.
Nichols & Alford / Manufacturers/1854/Burlington, Vt.
Nichols & Boynton/Burlington, Vt.
Boynton
J. Boynton
O. L. & A. K. Ballard
A. K. Ballard
Ballard & Brothers/Burlington, Vt.
F. Woodworth/Burlington, Vt.

Dorset (Dorset Hollow)

Jonathan Fenton, 1801-1810

East Dorset

Jonathan Fenton, 1810-after 1835
Richard L. Fenton, 1827-1833
Jonathan Fenton, Richard L. Fenton, and Seth Curtis, 1827-1830
Richard L. Fenton and Christopher W. Fenton, 1830-1833
Jonathan Fenton and Job Cleaveland, 1833/after 1835
Marks:
J. Fenton/East Dorset
J. Fenton & Co./East Dorset
R. L. Fenton/East Dorset
R. L. Fenton & Co./East Dorset
R. & C. Fenton/Dorset, Vt.

Fairfax

George W. & J. H. Farrar (*Vermont Stone Ware,* billhead), 1840
Farrar & Stearns, 1852
A. S. Stearns, 1852
E. L. & C. W. Farrar, 1856
Mark:
E. L. & C. W. Farrar/Fairfax, Vt.
Lewis & Cady, 1856
Lewis, Bostwick & Cady, 1856
Mark:
Lewis & Cady/Fairfax, Vt.

Poultney (possibly stoneware)

Samuel Woodman (or son John), 1800-*c.*1820

St. Albans

Boynton & Farrar, 1860

St. Johnsbury

St. Johnsbury Stoneware Pottery, 1804-1859
Richard Webber Fenton
Leander W. Fenton
Fenton & Hancock (L. W. Fenton and — Hancock; probably Frederick Hancock, who married Charlotte Anne Fenton, grandniece of Richard Webber Fenton and granddaughter of Jonathan)
Marks:
L. W. Fenton/St. Johnsbury, Vt.
Fenton & Hancock/St. Johnsbury, Vt.

MASSACHUSETTS

Ashfield

Orcutt, Guilford & Co. (Walter Orcutt and John Guilford), 1848-1850
Hastings & Belding (Wellington Hastings and David Belding), 1850-1854
Van Loon & Boyden (Staats Van Loon and George W. Boyden), 1854-1856
Marks:
Ashfield, Mass.
Orcutt, Guilford & Co./Ashfield, Mass.
Orcutt, Belding & Co./Ashfield, Mass.
Walter Orcutt & Co./Ashfield, Mass.
Hastings & Belding/Ashfield, Mass.
Van Loon & Boyden / Ashfield, Mass.

Ballardvale

Late pottery, running in 1890
Weston & Willard
Willard & Sullivan
L. Willard & Sons
Marks:
Ballardvale
L. Willard & Sons/Ballardvale

Boston

Jonathan Fenton, 1794-1796
Maker unknown, *c.*1804
Marks:
Boston
Boston/1804

Cambridgeport

Bullard & Scott, after 1870
Mark:
Bullard & Scott/Cambridgeport, Mass.

Charlestown

Thomas Symmes & Co. (Grace Parker and Thomas Symmes), 1742-1747
Edmands pottery, 1812-1905
Barnabas Edmands, 1812-1850
Edmands & Co. (Edward T. Edmands, Thomas R. B. Edmands, and Charles Collier), 1850-*c.*1865
Powers & Edmands, 1868
Marks:
Charlestown
Barnabas Edmands/Charlestown
Barnabas Edmunds / & Co. / Charlestown
Edmands & Co./Charlestown

Chelsea

Loammi Kendall, 1836-after 1870
Marks:
Chelsea
Loammi Kendle/Chelsea

Dorchester

William Seaver and Ebenezer Baker, c. 1769-1772

Medford

T. Sables & Co. (Thomas and John Sables, and Job Clapp), 1838-1844
Marks:
Medford
T. Sables & Co./Medford

Somerset

Chase pottery, 1847-1882
B. G. & C. Chase, *c.*1856
L. & B. G. Chase
Marks:
L. & B. G. Chase/Somerset
Somerset Potters Works

Taunton

Seaver pottery, 1772-*c.*1830
William Seaver, 1772
John Seaver
John and William Seaver
Wright pottery
A. Standish
Standish, Wright & Co., 1849
Franklin T. Wright, 1860 and 1865
Franklin T. Wright & Son, 1868
Marks:
A. Standish/Taunton, Mass.
Standish & Wright
F. T. Wright & Co./stoneware/Taunton
F. T. Wright & Son/Taunton, Mass.

Whately

Stephen Orcutt, after 1802
Orcutt & Wait (Stephen Orcutt, Luke and Obadiah Wait), before 1830
Mark:
Orcutt & Wait/Whately
Crafts pottery
Thomas Crafts, 1833-1861
Mark: *T. Crafts & Co/Whately*
Caleb Crafts, 1845-1854
Mark: *C. Crafts & Co./Whately, Mass.*
Martin Crafts, after 1856
Marks:
M. Crafts/Whately
Martin: Crafts: Whately
Wells, Crafts & Wells (Edward A. Crafts, David D., and Isaac N. Wells), *c.*1855
D. D. & I. N. Wells, *c.*1855
Marks:
Wells, Crafts & Wells/Whately, Mass.
D. D. & I. N. Wells/Whately, Mass.
David Belding, 1840's
Mark:
D. Belding/Whately

Worcester

Norton pottery
Frank B. Norton and Frederick Hancock, 1858
F. B. Norton, 1865
F. B. Norton & Co., 1868
F. B. Norton Sons
Marks:
F. B. Norton & Co./Worcester, Mass.
F. B. Norton Sons/Worcester, Mass.

CONNECTICUT

Bridgeport

Bridgeport Potteries, *c.*1814-after 1840

Greenwich

Dutch potter, before 1742

Abraham Mead, 1742-1791

Hartford

Isaac Hanford, 1796-after 1800

J. C. Fisher, 1805

Peter Cross, 1805-*c.*1815

Mark:

P. Cross/Hartford

Benton & Stewart (George Benton and Levi Stewart), *c.*1810-1818

Mark:

G. Benton & L. Stewart/Hartford

Daniel Goodale, 1818-1830

Marks:

D. Goodale

D. Goodale/Hartford

Goodale & Stedman/Hartford/1822

T. Harrington, 1825

Goodwin & Webster (Horace Goodwin and McCloud Webster), *c.*1810-1850

M. C. Webster & Son (McCloud Webster and Charles T. Webster), before 1840-1857

Webster & Seymour (C. T. Webster and O. H. Seymour), 1857-1873

Seymour & Bosworth (O. H. Seymour and S. B. Bosworth), 1873-

Marks:

Goodwin & Webster

M. C. Webster & Son/Hartford

Webster & Seymour/Hartford

Seymour & Bosworth/Hartford

S. B. Bosworth/Hartford, Ct.

Thomas O. Goodwin, 1820-1870

Harvey Goodwin, 1820-1870

Mark:

T. O. Goodwin/Hartford

Orson S. Cadwell, 1856

Mark:

O. S. Cadwell & Co./Hartford

New Haven

Jonathan Fenton, 1792-1793

Jacob Fenton, before 1800

Absalom Stedman, *c.*1831

Stedman & Seymour

Marks:

Stedman/New Haven

Stedman & Seymour/New Haven

John McPherson, 1865

New London

Stephen T. Brewer, 1826-*c.*1830 (or later)

Marks:

S. T. Breuer/New London

S. T.* Brewer/New London*

Norwalk

Smith pottery, 1825-*c.*1890

Asa E. Smith, 1825-1837

Selleck & Smith (A. E. Smith and Noah Selleck), 1837-1843

Smith & Day (A. E. Smith and Noah S. Day), 1843-*c.*1847

A. E. Smith & Son (Theodore), 1848

A. E. Smith & Sons (Theodore, Asa, Howard Hobart), 1849-

A. E. Smith's Sons (same), between 1860 and 1874

A. E. Smith's Sons Pottery Co. (also E. W. Smith), 1874-1887

Wilfred Smith, 1887

Norwalk Pottery Co., 1888-1890

Marks:

Smith & Day Manufacturers/Norwalk, Con. (within an oval)

Same mark with each change of firm name

Norwich

Bean Hill pottery, 1766-after 1828

Christopher Leffingwell, *c.* 1766-1796

Charles Lathrop, 1792-1796

Tracy & Huntington (Andrew Tracy), 1796-1800

Joseph Hosmer, 1800-1805

William Cleveland, 1805-1814

Armstrong & Wentworth (Peleg Armstrong and Erastus Wentworth), 1814-1828

Marks:

E. Wentworth/Norwich

Armstrong & Wentworth/Norwich

Risley pottery, *c.*1836-1895

Sidney Risley, *c.*1836-1875

George L. Risley, 1865-1881

Joseph F. Winship, 1846-*c.*1875

Norwich Pottery Works (B. C. Chace), 1882-1885

George B. Chamberlain, 1885-1887

Otto N. Suderberg, 1887-1895

Marks:

S. Risley/Norwich

The Norwich Pottery Works/Norwich, Conn.

Stonington

Adam States, 1798

William States, 1811-1824

Swan & States (Joshua Swan and Ichabod States), 1824-1835

Marks:

W. States

Swan & States/Stonington

From the Collection of the S.P.N.E.A.

Stoneware churn, lacking cover and dash; brown salt glaze; maker's mark D. GOODALE. HARTFORD. By Daniel Goodale Jr., made probably between 1825, when he acquired sole rights to the business, and 1830, when he ceased production. Height 18¾ inches.

New England pottery. *Left:* stoneware birdhouse with brown salt glaze, from the pottery of Asa Smith, Norwalk, Connecticut; made probably in the 1860's; height 7¾ inches. *Center:* redware mantel ornament in the form of a cabin; made by Daniel Clark (d. 1828) who founded the Millville Pottery near Concord, New Hampshire, about 1791; height 3¾ inches. These two pieces were presented to the Society by descendants of their makers. *Right:* stoneware jar with gray salt glaze, lacking cover; bears the distinctive swag decoration in blue used by the unidentified "Boston 1804" maker; height 5½ inches.

New light on Boston stoneware and Frederick Carpenter

BY LURA WOODSIDE WATKINS

The Lynn Street works

SOME EXTREMELY fine stoneware was made in the Boston area in the last decade of the eighteenth century and the first quarter of the nineteenth. But the origin and in certain cases the maker of some of the surviving pots have remained a mystery. Especially puzzling have been the circumstances surrounding the brief Boston potting career of Jonathan Fenton (the father of Richard and Christopher Webber Fenton of Bennington fame) and the origin of the handsome stoneware marked BOSTON/1804.

Fenton is mentioned in the often-repeated note about the first Boston stoneware that appeared in Thomas Pemberton's 1794 "Description of Boston" (*Collections of the Massachusetts Historical Society for the Year 1794*, Vol. III): "At the Stone Pottery lately set up in Lynn street by Mr. Fenton from New Haven, all kinds of stone vessels are made after the manner of the imported Liverpool ware and sold at a lower rate. The clay for this manufacture is brought from Perth Amboy in New Jersey."

Jonathan Fenton was born in Mansfield, Connecticut, on July 18, 1766, and he worked in Boston only from 1793 or 1794 until 1796. (In January 1797 he went to Walpole, New Hampshire, and later to Dorset, Vermont, where he started a pottery in 1801.) Fenton had as his co-worker in the Lynn Street pottery Frederick Carpenter, who was born not far from Fenton in Lebanon, Connecticut, on November 13, 1771. Both Carpenter and Fenton were probably trained in the stoneware pottery of Jonathan's brother Jacob at New Haven. It is also recorded that Carpenter was married in Boston in December 1796 and was still in that city when his first child was born on October 17, 1797.

For a long time it has puzzled me that two such young and inexperienced men without any considerable funds should have attempted such an expensive venture as setting up a pottery in a strange city. Because there was no suitable stoneware clay in New England, it had to be freighted around Cape Cod from New Jersey at what must have been tremendous expense.

The answer to this problem now appears to be that the two potters had the backing of William Little, a prominent merchant and like Carpenter a native of Lebanon, Connecticut. It is not known when Little moved to Boston, but in 1790 he was married there to Frances Boyd, the daughter of General James Boyd of Newburyport, and in

Thomas Hutchinson house, built in the latter part of the seventeenth century by Colonel John Foster. *Stark's Antique Views of ye Towne of Boston*, c. 1901.

HUTCHINSON HOUSE.

Fig. 2. *Left.* Jar with monogram cartouche *J. F.* Attributed to Jonathan Fenton at the Lynn Street pottery in Boston, c. 1793-1796. Mark and decoration painted with blue slip. Height 14 inches. *Collection of John P. Remensnyder; photograph by Ronald B. Johnstone.*

Fig. 3. Monogram cartouche of Fig. 2.

Fig. 4. *Right.* Jar of same shape as Fig. 2 with a floral decoration that appears on several other forms. Marked BOSTON; attributed to Jonathan Fenton. Height 14⅜ inches. *Remensnyder collection; Johnstone photograph.*

1792, when he was forty-three, he acquired one of the most notable mansions in Boston, on Garden Court Street in the North End (Fig. 1).

That William Little was the moving spirit behind the pottery venture in Boston is strongly suggested by the following facts. On November 15, 1792, he purchased a small house on Greenough Lane, which ran between Charter and Lynn Streets. The lot was only fifteen feet wide and the dwelling small and narrow. In the light of later developments we may surmise that this was to provide a lodging place for the two potters, neither of whom had a street address listed in the Boston directories. This assumption is strengthened by the fact that Little sold the house in 1798, a couple of years after the pottery had closed.

Little held a number of civic offices—at one time he was a state representative and in 1793 he was on the Boston board of selectmen. At a meeting of the board in March of that year, he was on a committee of three "to consider the application of Jonathan Fenton asking leave to erect a stone pottery." This application was granted on April 10 "for carrying on a Stone pottery at the North end."

The pot shop was built during that spring. On August 14, 1793, the *Columbian Centinel* carried an advertisement which read:

STONE POTTERY

STONE WARE, of all kinds that is usually made, consisting principally of jugs of different sizes, Butter and Pickle Pots, Mugs, Pitchers, and Gallipots. To be sold at the Manufactory in Lynn-Street, North-end, or at store No. 46 State-street.

Number 46 State Street is the address listed for William Little's business in the Boston directory of 1789. It may be wondered why the manufacture of stoneware would seem important to a wealthy merchant. The answer may be that Little, whose wholesale firm dealt in Jamaica rum, tea, coffee, molasses, ginger, wines, corn and rye meal, ship bread, and a host of other things in large quantities, including "Liverpool ware," had foreseen that there would be a good profit in homemade stoneware, even when sold at a modest price. Liverpool ware, as the term was then used, was stoneware imported at great expense from Germany and Belgium via Liverpool. The principal forms were those for the storage of acid foods such as vinegar and pickles. Acids could not be kept in American redware vessels with their lead glaze, which sometimes caused lead poisoning. The inventories of lost possessions after the Boston fire in 1760 show that imported stoneware jugs and jars were then valued at several dollars apiece.

The *Columbian Centinel* advertisement adds somewhat to our knowledge of the first Boston stoneware. Marked jugs and pots have been preserved in various collections, but, so far as I have learned, mugs, pitchers, and gallipots have not. The mark generally used was the word BOSTON in letters of uniform size. Occasional pieces with a mark of letters separately stamped may antedate this more common style. Mugs and pitchers without marks may be in existence, but are so far unrecognized. Gallipots (tiny bowls used by doctors and druggists for mixing pills) would not have been marked. These are mentioned in the account book of the one earlier stoneware potter in Massachusetts, William Seaver of Taunton, who may have offered serious competition to the new Boston works. Seaver's gallipots sold for one shilling a dozen.

Since Fenton is the only stoneware potter definitely known to have been working in Boston at this time, we must assume that the BOSTON pieces were made in his pottery in Lynn Street. Pieces so marked have survived in sufficient quantity to enable us to distinguish two definitive styles, one assumed to be that of Fenton, the other that of Carpenter. Differences in form are especially notable. The pot in Figure 2, owned by John P. Remensnyder, bears a cartouche with the initials *J F* (Fig. 3)—thus the work of Jonathan Fenton. By analogy the jar in Figure 4 may be

Fig. 5. Jug with incised bird and vine touched with blue. Marked BOSTON. Height 11⅝ inches. *Henry Francis du Pont Winterthur Museum.*

Fig. 6. Jug with impressed fish tinted blue. Marked BOSTON. Height 11⅝ inches. *Collection of Mr. and Mrs. C. Malcolm Watkins.*

Fig 7 The "Timson" jar. This elaborate pot was probably the work of Frederick Carpenter. Below the impressed BOSTON mark, across flower and leaf, is the name *Lydia Osborn* in script; on one side the name *Marshall Timson* is inscribed; on the reverse the word *Charlestown* has been rubbed out. Height 10½ inches. *Smithsonian Institution, Watkins Collection; photograph by Russell B. Harding.*

assumed to be from his hand. Both have handles projecting outward from the shoulder. By analogy also, Mr. Remensnyder has attributed to Fenton a chamber pot and two jars bearing the same floral decoration. Another pot similar to the one with Fenton's initials, decorated with a blue-tinted bird on each side, is in the Watkins Collection at the Smithsonian Institution and may be attributed to him on the same basis.

A photograph sent by Albert H. Gilbert of Dorset, Vermont, shows a series of marked pieces made by Fenton in Dorset and now in the rooms of the historical society there. None of them have handles close to the neck, like those we see in work attributed to Carpenter. Fenton apparently favored a shoulder attachment of handles and incised work tinted blue, and pieces with these characteristics were probably shaped as well as decorated by him.

The jug from the Winterthur Museum (Fig. 5) may have been made by Fenton. This and one in the Brooklyn Museum showing a full-rigged ship and bearing a monogram cartouche like that in Figure 3 are the most elaborate examples of this kind so far discovered. Jugs ornamented with a sizable blue codfish (Fig. 6) may also be attributed to Fenton. They have been found both with and without the BOSTON stamp. Fenton continued to use this fish decoration on his Dorset pottery. A well-known example formerly in the Barrows House at Dorset was spirited away some years ago by a collector who could not resist it.

The famous "Timson" jar (Fig. 7), a presentation piece ornamented with untinted incised work, corresponds in contour and handle placement to other pieces attributed to Frederick Carpenter. This jar originally had the word *Charlestown* on the reverse, but it was rubbed out so that it can barely be detected. The jar is also inscribed with the names *Marshall Timson* and *Lydia Osborn*. The significance of all these inscriptions has so far eluded all my efforts to discover it.

Carpenter was a master of form rather than of decoration, but I believe he had a sense of color and was probably responsible for the use of Albany slip (red ocher) applied not only as a lining but also on the entire surface of some pieces. The pots were dipped top and bottom before burning, and the resultant color is a warm reddish brown, almost mahogany, that nearly covers the surface. The basic body color of early Boston pieces is a warm gray, not the cold bluish gray of ordinary stoneware. This may be due to a slight admixture of a different clay.

The year 1796 saw the close of the Lynn Street pottery. By January of the following year Fenton had moved to New Hampshire, and within a few years he was established in Dorset Hollow, Vermont, in a pottery of his own. As I said before, Carpenter remained in Boston through his marriage in 1796 and the birth of his first child in October 1797. Soon thereafter the Carpenters returned to New Haven, where Frederick seems to have worked in Jacob Fenton's pottery until its close in 1801. Then in March of that year he was back in Massachusetts—not in Boston, but in Charlestown.

Boston/1804

As the Lynn Street pottery closed in 1796, the mysterious stoneware marked BOSTON/1804 could not have been made there. But where? More than twenty years ago, when working on *Early New England Potters and Their Wares* (Cambridge, Massachusetts, 1950), I made a diligent search of directories, vital records, and even the census records, but failed to discover a potter who could have been working in Boston at that date. The explanation now appears to lie in the history of a hitherto unknown pottery in Charlestown and in the fact that Carpenter was living in that town when his third child was born, in 1801. A study of land records reveals the whole story.

Fig. 8. Jug entirely coated with brown stain and stamped with the only decorative motif so far found on the 1804 pieces. The impressed swag and tassels and the mark BOSTON/1804 are touched with cobalt blue. Note the characteristic reeded lines below the neck. Height 14½ inches. *Peabody (Massachusetts) Historical Society; Harding photograph.*

Fig. 9. Butter pot with cover, attributed to Carpenter on the basis of the same swag and tassels that appear on Fig. 8. Height 9½ inches. *Author's collection.*

On July 4, 1800, John Little, the younger brother of William, paid one Ebenezer Wait $250 for a rectangular piece of land running to low-water mark on the Mystic River in Charlestown. A later document shows that it contained seven acres. It was located at approximately the present corner of Medford and Lexington Streets. On January 6, 1803, John Little conveyed to Frederick Carpenter, stone potter, for $100 a house lot of one acre, which was part of the land he had purchased from Wait. In the deed Little says, "On my part of this land I have erected a stoneware manufactory."

John Little was not a potter, however. His name appears in the Boston directory only once—in 1800. His business address was that of his brother's warehouse and salesroom at 46 State Street and his home was on Middle Street.

Shortly after selling the lot to Carpenter, John Little got from his brother a mortgage on the remaining land and one-half of the buildings—a mortgage that was never paid off. Thus the pottery was virtually owned by William Little, the presumed patron of the earlier Lynn Street pottery.

The new stoneware was advertised in the *Boston Gazette* as early as July 11, 1803. At that time the ware could have been unmarked. Specifically mentioned were "Stone butter pots, excellent for preserving butter in the warm season of the year. Also an assortment of stone jugs for sale at No. 46 State Street." Three days later an advertisement offered "a few crates stoneware—containing jugs, butter pots, pickle jars, from one quart to three gallons."

On September 12, 1803, an advertisement appeared in the *Gazette* under William Little's own name, mentioning stone pickle and butter pots—"stone jugs assorted sizes with a great assortment of stone ware." A similar notice ten days later called attention to "pickle pots with covers, with a great variety of stoneware."

In these advertisements the reader is referred not to the pottery but to Little's business address, where the merchandise was offered for sale. This usually appeared as 46 State Street or neighboring numbers that were probably in the same building.

Little did not advertise pottery again until August 20, 1804, when he listed "beef, butter, and pickle pots, and jugs," along with looking-glass plates, starch, gin, and olives. A second notice in November tells us nothing further about the product. Although prices are never mentioned, we may infer that the ware he was advertising was not imported, but was made at the Mystic River works by Frederick Carpenter, master potter. No other potters are recorded in connection with this venture. The BOSTON/1804 mark must have had the effect of advertising this stoneware as of local manufacture and of indicating that it was something new.

Carpenter's style of potting was characteristic, often making a signature unnecessary. Whatever the reason for dating the ware, the pots are identifiable as the work of one man. So far I have learned of only ten examples with the 1804 mark; the whereabouts of three of these is not known. The mark appears impressed in two lines on neck or shoulder, often with a numeral to indicate capacity. The most beautiful of the plain examples are stained a true mahogany color. The mark is found more rarely with a swag and tassels colored blue (Fig. 8). Several pieces with this embellishment, but without BOSTON/1804, were also presumably the work of Frederick Carpenter (Fig. 9). As previously noted, the word BOSTON is printed with a large capital B followed by smaller capitals. A few pieces with this mark but lacking the date may also be attributed to the Mystic River works. I have such a piece in my own collection—a small jug of luscious color and rounded form.

The few examples that can be ascribed to this Charlestown works are as fine as anything ever turned in an American pottery: only a true artist could have formed the perfectly symmetrical jars with handles close to the neck. All this stoneware was curved; in 1804 both pickle pots and butter pots were ovoid. The straight-sided pickle pot did not appear until later.

The pottery on the Mystic River must have been a financial failure but it was still going in 1810, when John Little conveyed to Daniel Tufts the use of a well near the pottery workshop. The deed reserved "the free use of sd well for two families and the stoneware manufactory."

Charlestown

In 1812 Carpenter joined forces with Barnabas Edmands in a new venture—some historians say as "foreman," others as "partner." Edmands was not a potter, but the owner of a Charlestown brass foundry which produced fireplace implements. The pottery land, which was near

Fig. 10. Two-gallon jug marked BOSTON.
An identical jug has been found by Mr. Remensnyder with an elaborate Charlestown mark with an eagle perched on a gun carriage over a pile of cannon balls. Height 14¾ inches.
Collection of Mr. and Mrs. C. Malcolm Watkins.

Fig. 11. Covered pot marked CHARLESTOWN, stamped with three hearts. Height 14½ inches. *Collection of Mrs. Walter Cullity.*

Fig. 12. Plain pitcher. Tooled line below neck. Height 10 inches. *Collection of Mrs. Lawrence S. Cooke.*

the state prison, was purchased by Edmands and his brother-in-law William Burroughs on February 12, 1812. A late advertisement of the company asserts that the pottery was established in that year.

Carpenter sold his Mystic River house two years later and at that time (or perhaps earlier) moved to a house on Austin Street near the Edmands pottery, where he remained until his death on June 20, 1827. He and his wife had eleven children, the youngest only a year old when Carpenter died. By 1832 all but five of this brood had died, most of them in early youth.

This family could not have been well-to-do, but the probate records of Carpenter's estate show that it enjoyed certain amenities not always found in a workingman's home. There were an illustrated family Bible valued at $10 and a nine-volume set of Shakespeare, besides forty other books and pamphlets. Also, Carpenter subscribed to a lending library—the Union Library. His status in the town is evident from his ownership of Pew Number 2 in the Universalist Church, his half share in a tomb in the "old berring ground," and a share in the Bunker Hill bank. The house held some good mahogany furniture, chairs listed as windsor, fancy, and fanback, and two easy chairs. Also listed were brass andirons and fire set, a pair of glass lamps, looking glasses, china, silver, glass, and a good supply of household linens, blankets, and coverlets.

When Carpenter died he left more than three thousand unfinished pieces (including 263 pots that were damaged in the making and consequently of little value) for which the estate was paid $584.92. The objects mentioned in the inventory were pots and jugs in capacities of from one pint to three gallons, beer bottles, covers for butter and pickle pots, and plates. It is evident that during Carpenter's lifetime the output of the Edmands pottery varied but little from that of the Mystic River pottery.

In the period before 1820 New England stoneware was customarily identified by place name only. Since Carpenter and several young apprentices, members of the Edmands family, were the only potters who appear to have worked there in the early period, it is safe to assume that he alone turned the very handsome pots that are marked CHARLESTOWN but carry no firm name. Identical jugs attributed to Carpenter have been found, some with the BOSTON mark and some with the word CHARLESTOWN. The plain jug in Figure 10 has the Boston stamp while a duplicate in shape and size, owned by Mr. Remensnyder, is impressed with a very elaborate Charlestown mark showing an eagle perched on a gun carriage over a pile of cannon balls. Even the tooled lines below the necks of these two jugs are the same.

There are many distinctive stoneware pots attributable to Charlestown, all of a warm gray tone, dipped top and bottom in ocher stain. Even without a mark these could be identified by their modest ornament, which usually consists of small stamped motifs such as eagles, crosses, and hearts (Fig. 11). The stamped number apparently indicates capacity. The pitcher in Figure 12, although its only ornamentation is a tooled line below the neck, is as handsome as anything ever turned out by a potting artist.

My thanks to Mrs. Richard Creaser, Ruth Tyler, and Richard Muzzrole for their help in research, and to all those who have so generously permitted the use of their photographs.

The Fentons—Pioneer American Potters

By John Spargo

Illustrations, except as noted, from the author's collection

EVERY collector of American pottery, and every student of its history, is familiar with the name of Christopher Webber Fenton and with some, at least, of the interesting products of the Bennington potteries with which he was associated. Surprisingly little is known about Fenton, however. The meagre accounts given by Barber and Pitkin, upon which all other writers have relied, are at least ninety per cent wrong—a mere hodgepodge of misinformation, guesswork and mistaken inference. Correction of this must be left to some future occasion.

What has not been made known heretofore, and is here published for the first time, is the fact that Christopher Webber Fenton, the Bennington potter, was one of a family of pioneer American potters, identified with some potteries established in Vermont in the first decade of the nineteenth century and long ago forgotten. The brief account here given of these men will measurably fill a gap in our ceramic history.

On the tax-list of the town of Woburn, Massachusetts, for the years 1688 to 1691, both inclusive, appears the name of one Robert Fenton. It does not appear after 1691, either on the tax-list or in any other public record that I have been able to discover. In 1694 a Robert Fenton appears in Windham (later called Mansfield), Connecticut. Presumably this is the same man who had resided at Woburn some years previously. Of this Robert Fenton of Windham (Mansfield), Connecticut, we know that he was a carpenter by trade, that he was evidently a man highly respected, though of no considerable property, and that he held several important town offices. We know also that he had eight children. His seventh child, a son, was born at Windham (Mansfield), in 1710, and was named Ebenezer. This Ebenezer Fenton had fifteen children by two wives. His eldest son by his first wife was Jonathan, born in 1740.

This Jonathan Fenton married, in 1762, Mary Cary, a young widow. In 1779, at Mansfield, he enlisted for a term of two years' service in the Revolutionary War. Jonathan and Mary Cary Fenton had six children—three sons and three daughters. The second son, born July 18, 1766, was named Jonathan after his father; the third son, who was the fourth child, born September 4, 1771, was named Richard Webber. Both these sons became potters, pioneers in the industry of Vermont.

I do not know where Jonathan Fenton, Junior, learned the potter's trade. What I do know is that he was a practical potter, and a good one; that he established a small stoneware pottery at East Dorset, Vermont, quite early in the nineteenth century; that marked specimens of his work have survived to bear witness to his excellent craftsmanship (*Fig. 1*); that he was the father of at least two potters, one of them being Christopher Webber Fenton, of United States pottery fame. After much research and investigation, I have been able—thanks to the assistance of Mr. Herbert Williams Denio, Librarian of the Vermont Historical Society, to get the dates of the birth of his eight children, with the place of their registration. This list enables me to trace the wanderings of this early Connecticut potter, and also to fix the approximate time of his arrival and settlement at East Dorset, Vermont.

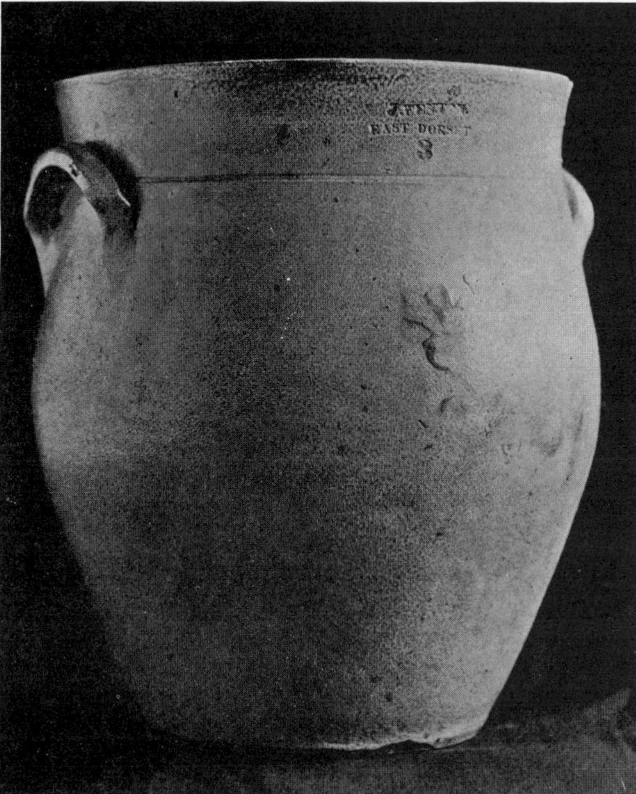

Fig. 1 — Stoneware Jar (*first quarter nineteenth century*)
Marked *J. Fenton, East Dorset. Owned by Harold G. Rugg.*

One child was born at New Haven, Connecticut, in 1793; a second at Boston, Massachusetts, in 1794; another at Boston, in 1796; a fourth at Walpole, New Hampshire, in 1797; a fifth at Windsor, Connecticut, in 1799. The sixth child was born at Dorset, Vermont, November 1, 1801; the seventh in 1804, and the eighth—Christopher Webber Fenton—in 1806. Now, the United States Census for Vermont, taken in 1800, shows that there was no head of a family named Fenton in Dorset when that census was taken. Jonathan Fenton and his family must, therefore, have settled there either toward the end of 1800 or some time in 1801 prior to the birth of the sixth child, which event took place on November 1, as above noted.

Referring to Christopher Webber Fenton, Pitkin* says that he learned his trade "at a red earthenware pottery at Dorset, Vermont." As a matter of fact, this pottery pro-

**Early American Folk Pottery*, Albert H. Pitkin, Hartford, 1917.

Fig. 2 — Stoneware Jar (*1826–1834*)
Roughly decorated with cobalt blue. Salt glazed, and marked *R. L. Fenton & Co., East Dorset.*

duced stoneware of a good quality as well as red earthenware. From the records of deeds in the office of the Town Clerk of Dorset I have been able to identify the site of the pottery with absolute certainty, but not to determine when the industry was started.

Upon this site, at East Dorset, I have dug up many fragments of red earthenware, "slip" covered on the inside; red earthenware, lead glazed; light stoneware, salt glazed; stoneware of the same quality, slip covered; and some with colored ornamentation. Some excellent stoneware jars of good color and shape bear the impressed mark "J. Fenton, East Dorset, Vt.," showing that Pitkin was (as usual) in error.

Richard L. Fenton, fourth child and eldest son of Jonathan, was also a potter. We may assume that he learned his trade under his father at East Dorset. That, however, is conjecture. We know that he was working as a potter at Bennington in 1828, when he was thirty-one years old. He was then employed by Judge Luman Norton, who, at that time, was carrying on the pottery established in 1793 by his father, Captain John Norton. Richard L. Fenton, it is interesting to note, was one of those summoned for assistance when Captain Norton was stricken. From the diary of one of the neighbors, now in possession of the Bennington Battle Monument and Historical Association, we learn that he was one of those who assisted in "laying out the corpse" of the old Captain. In the records of the time there are references to this R. L. Fenton as a delinquent taxpayer, and the *Vermont Gazette*, of September 16, 1828, contains an advertisement signed by him relating to a strayed bull. From the diary above referred to, we find that he moved his family back to Dorset in March, 1830.

In the land records of the town of Dorset, there is a deed from Jonathan Fenton to Richard L. Fenton, dated December 9, 1826, conveying to the latter "one-half acre more or less," one-half of a water privilege "together with one-half of a potter's factory." It would be interesting to know whether the pieces of stoneware impressed with the marks: "R. L. Fenton, East Dorset," and "R. L. Fenton & Co., East Dorset" (*Fig. 2*), were made before 1828, when we find him at Bennington in the employ of Luman Norton. That would indicate that he had given up the pottery at East Dorset before 1828. It is not clear why, owning a ha'f interest in a pottery at East Dorset, he should have been working as a journeyman potter for Norton at Bennington. There are, however, various possible explanations. He may have been held in Bennington by a lease entered into before he had acquired the half share of his father's pottery. It may be that his brother, Christopher Webber Fenton, was working with his father and that the little pottery could not support more. Or it may have been profitable for him to work at Bennington for a few years in order to obtain additional capital. I have not been able to find out when the East Dorset pottery stopped. Richard L. Fenton moved his family back to Dorset in 1830, continued to work for Luman Norton as journeyman until some time in 1831, and died in July, 1834. The pieces of stoneware bearing his name may have been made between 1826, when he acquired the half interest of the pottery, and 1828, when we find him working in the Bennington pottery for Luman Norton. Certainly they must have been made before July, 1834. I am inc ined to think that, for some time after 1826, Jonathan Fenton and his son acted as partners, and that the mark "Fenton & Son," or "J. Fenton & Son" was used for a while. I have not yet found pieces so marked, but have heard of such. Pieces marked "R. L. Fenton & Co., East Dorset," raise the question of the partnership covered by the "Co." While positive evidence is lacking, I am inclined

Fig. 3 — Bennington Stoneware (*1845–1847*)
The jug is marked *Norton & Fenton, Bennington*. The jar, undecorated, is marked *Norton and Fenton, East Bennington, Vt.* The difference in nomenclature means nothing. Both names were in simultaneous use for the same village.

Fig. 4 — Rockinghamware Pitchers (*1845–1847*)
Made by Norton and Fenton in Bennington. "Rockingham," it will be remembered, is a term rather widely applied to mottled brown glazes.

to believe that these pieces were made between 1831 and 1834—that is, between the time when R. L. Fenton returned to Dorset from Bennington and his death; and that the "Co." refers to his younger brother, Christopher Webber Fenton. To the mark, "R. L. Fenton, East Dorset," I should ascribe a somewhat earlier date. That Richard L. Fenton was a competent potter the surviving specimens of his work prove.

Christopher Webber Fenton, the youngest of the eight children of Jonathan Fenton, was born at Dorset, January 30, 1806. Pitkin suggests the possibility that he may have worked for Captain John Norton at Bennington, but intimates his doubt of it. He says that, "From the dates and ages given in the Norton Family Records, it is safe to assume that Mr. Fenton first associated himself with Mr. Luman Norton." Unpleasant as it is to criticise Pitkin's book, knowing as I do the circumstances in which it was written and published, it is necessary to state that there are no known "Norton Family Records" which give the least foundation for the belief that Christopher Webber Fenton "first associated himself with Mr. Luman Norton"; nor is there any other scrap of evidence to support that assumption. On the contrary, the "Norton Family Records"—in so far as they bear upon the matter at all—indicate that there was no such association. The first business association of C. W. Fenton with the Norton pottery began in January, 1845 (after Luman Norton had retired from the business), when Fenton joined his brother-in-law, Julius Norton, son of Luman, in a partnership which lasted only to June, 1847. It is not unlikely that Fenton had been employed at the Norton pottery for some years before he became a member of the firm.

Christopher Webber Fenton married, on October 29, 1832, Louisa, eldest daughter of Luman Norton. He was described in the records as a "Merchant," which would seem to show that he was not at that time following the potter's trade. In 1842 we find him residing at Bennington and petitioning for the benefit of the Bankrupt Act, asking to be declared a bankrupt. In his petition he describes himself as a "laborer." His connection with the Bennington potteries as member of the firm could not have existed then. There is positive evidence that it began in 1845 with the partnership between him and Julius Norton.

Although Pitkin makes him out to have been "a practical potter, of extraordinary skill, well-nigh a genius at his trade, artistic in his tastes, a naturalist, something of a chemist, a profound student," the simple truth is that he was in nowise distinguished as a practical potter. Neither is there the slightest evidence that he was "a naturalist," a "profound student," or anything of a chemist. All that Pitkin evolved from his own imagination. Not one of the old potters who worked with Fenton with whom I have talked could recall a single piece of his work which attracted the notice of his fellow workmen. This is quite remarkable, for stories concerning the work of craftsmen of skill abound in the reminiscences of old potters. Not a solitary piece of Fenton's work has been preserved to show his skill; not a single story of special skill at his trade survives. Many are the stories told of his habits, his manners, his business experiences, but none of his skill as a potter. As a matter of fact, men who worked with him agree that he was quite an ordinary workman, so far as his technical skill went. Such evidence as we have shows him as a man of rather more education than the average mechanic of his day, but not noted for exceptional learning or for intellectual pursuits. Not much given to reading, possessing something of a natural talent for drawing, being ready at making pencil sketches of designs and patterns to illustrate his ideas; rather good at figures, somewhat irritable and uncertain in temper; and given to drinking overmuch: such are the main characteristics of the man as he

Fig. 5 — Stoneware Jar (*mid-nineteenth century*)
Marked *L. W. Fenton, St. Johnsbury, Vt.*

is remembered. His ability and energy as a business promoter, rather than as a practical potter, give him the important place he holds in the history of American pottery.

This is not the time nor the place to trace Fenton's connection with the Bennington potteries nor to tell in detail the story of his career. The brief account here given is intended simply to establish his place in the record of a rather remarkable family of American potters. Incidentally, it adds to our interest in the little pottery at East Dorset about which so little is known.

Mention must be made of another Fenton, who was also a potter; though we know little about him. He worked in New Haven, Connecticut, in 1800, and in 1801 moved to Burlington, N. Y., and established a pottery there. That he was a member of the same family hardly admits of any doubt. Dr. S. R. Wilcox, who as a young man worked in the United States Pottery at Bennington, and in 1858 went with Christopher Webber Fenton and Decius W. Clark to Kaolin, S. C., tells me, that at that time there was a potter at Bennington who also went to Kaolin, named Jacob Fenton. Dr. Wilcox says that, as he remembers, this Jacob Fenton was "a man not out of the thirties," and he thinks he was a nephew of Christopher Webber Fenton. While positive evidence is lacking, I suspect that he was the son of Jacob Fenton of Burlington, N. Y.

Now we must retrace our steps and go back to the opening of the nineteenth century in order that we may take note of that other son of Jonathan and Mary Cary Fenton, of Mansfield, Connecticut, Richard Webber Fenton. Like Jonathan, his brother, Richard Webber became a potter. He appears in St. Johnsbury, Vermont, in 1804. We find his name in the records of the Town Meeting as one of a committee elected "to Expel dogs from the Meeting House on Sundays." This is the earliest reference that I have been able to find of a man who was long honored as one of the best-known citizens of the northern Vermont town. General R. W. Fenton established a stoneware pottery at St. Johnsbury in 1808. From Fairbanks' *History of St. Johnsbury*,* I quote the following:

"POTTERY: An old-time landmark, with low red buildings west of the river half a mile south of the Center Village, was the Pottery established in 1808 by General R. W. Fenton, somewhile known as the St. Johnsbury Stoneware Pottery. Its products were in constant demand until the introduction of tinware. The business was successfully carried on by General Fenton and by his son Leander until the entire establishment went down in flames, November, 1859. All sorts of domestic ware were turned out on those potters' wheels, from jugs, jars, bowls, bottles, and milkpans, at a dollar a dozen, to fancy flower pots at sixty cents each, and St. Johnsbury pottery gained high repute; occasionally surviving specimens of it may still be seen. The power was supplied by a merry little brook that came tumbling down the hillside."

*Page 144.

Fig. 6 — STONEWARE JAR (*mid-nineteenth century*)
Marked *Fenton & Hancock, St. Johnsbury, Vt.* The St. Johnsbury pottery was founded by General R. W. Fenton, in 1808. It was carried on later by his son Leander, who eventually formed a partnership with one Hancock, until 1859 when it was destroyed by fire. The labels and the uncompromising forms of these jars, Figures 5 and 6, seem to justify mid-century attribution.

From the same authority* we learn that there was another pottery at St. Johnsbury, conducted by one William Hutchinson; but with that I am not at present concerned. The younger of the two Fentons of St. Johnsbury marked his ware, "L. W. Fenton, St. Johnsbury, Vt." I have an excellent jar bearing that mark. (*Fig. 5.*) This Leander W. Fenton seems to have been in partnership with a man named Hancock, and pieces marked "Fenton & Hancock, St. Johnsbury, Vt.," are still to be found in northern Vermont. In my own collection there is a stoneware jar so marked (*Fig. 6*). While I have heard of jugs and jars marked "Fenton, St. Johnsbury, Vt.," and "Fenton & Son, St. Johnsbury, Vt.," I have not personally seen anything bearing either mark. I have, however, seen a good many unmarked pieces said to have been made at the Fenton pottery at St. Johnsbury and apparently well authenticated. Further research may add to our knowledge of these early Vermont potters and their works.

NOTE.—The hitherto recognised authorities on early American pottery have been Albert H. Pitkin, whose *Early American Folk Pottery*, published at Hartford, in 1917, devoted considerable space to Bennington and its wares, and Edwin Atlee Barber, who wrote extensively on both glass and pottery. Barber's major work is probably *The Pottery and Porcelain of the United States*, published in New York in 1893. In this, eleven pages are devoted to the United States Pottery at Bennington. Barber's *Anglo-American Pottery*, published in Indianapolis in 1899, has been the most widely known of his writings, due to the extensive and long-standing interest in historical blue china.—ED.

*Page 152.

PORTRAIT OF A POTTER-MUSICIAN

By HELEN C. NELSON

JULIUS NORTON needs no introduction to students of American ceramics. He was a gifted member of the well-known family which made pottery in Bennington, Vermont, for one hundred and one years. His grandfather, Captain John Norton, was Vermont's first potter, starting the business in 1793. John's son, Judge Luman Norton, followed his father's calling, and *his* son, Julius, also carried on the family tradition. Father and son, Luman and Julius, worked together at first, and then independently. From 1844 to 1847 Julius was in partnership with his brother-in-law and former employee, Christopher Webber Fenton, son of another early Vermont potter. After this partnership was dissolved Julius continued operating a business which remained active until 1894 interrupted only by a fire in 1845.

Both Norton and Fenton were deeply interested in the manufacture of porcelain, and it was started at Bennington during their partnership. Except during the brief period of his association with Fenton, Julius Norton's production was chiefly stoneware, yet to him goes the credit for certain innovations that helped to build Bennington's fame for other types of ware. The most notable of these was introduction of the so-called Rockingham ware which became one of Bennington's major products. The use of similar mottled brown glazes on yellow ware and of similarly fashioned forms had, of course, long been common in England, and they were not new even in the United States, though at that time they were made only in places other than Vermont.

But while Julius Norton's name is well known, his face is probably unfamiliar to American collectors. Here reproduced is a limner's portrait of him as a young man. It reveals Julius not as a potter or business man, but as a musician. He had a passion for music, played both violin and piano, and was reputed to be the best flutist in Bennington County. Aside from its subject interest, the canvas is a most delightful American primitive portrait.

A LIMNER'S PORTRAYAL OF JULIUS NORTON, POTTER. Music was the avocation of this prominent business man of Bennington, Vermont, who flourished about a hundred years ago. *Privately owned.*

The painter of this picture is anonymous, as are most of the nineteenth-century itinerant limners whose works now enhance our growing gallery of American primitives. Probably he was a head-hunter, and, like other limners, superimposed the faces of sitters on bodies they selected from those he had previously painted to peddle from town to town. But this canvas was obviously painted from the subject. The fingers are possessed of but one joint apiece, but the flute, dear to the heart of the potter-musician, is painted with notable skill, and the accurate detail shows complete knowledge of the subject. Painting musical instruments was perhaps a new venture for the artist, and since the flute was a highly prized possession of the sitter, we may imagine that it called for special attention and heroic effort. So, too, did the early upright piano, so conscientiously represented with realistically rendered mahogany graining, and the sheet of music, any note of which may be read as clearly as from the printed page. The handling of these accessories tells of thorough training in the shop of a sign and carriage painter.

Studying the face we do not find such precision. It is the work of a plugger in portraiture who patched things up laboriously. Glaring evidence of bungling over-painting is apparent around the ear, which the "artist" first put in the wrong place. But, none the less, this self-taught delineator of human faces has given us a convincing likeness of a sensitive young man of the 1830's and an interesting, decorative bit of Americana as well.

One may well imagine that an artist of today, happily reveling in colors galore, would feel quite lost with nothing more at hand than the typical palette of an American limner of a hundred years ago; for, aside from red, black, yellow (orpiment was this early yellow), and greens made with black and yellow, he used virtually none but the earth colors, so called — burnt and raw sienna and the ochres. Blue is rarely in evidence, though cobalt was discovered in 1802, and ultramarine also was in use. The synthetic ultramarine which replaced that made from powdered lapis lazuli became known in 1814.

Evidently there was available plenty of very fine linen canvas, imported from France and the British Isles, though panels of wood were often used. Some of the thin, closely woven French canvases popular among limners and their sitters are in a remarkable state of preservation; but that upon which the Norton portrait is painted deteriorated rather badly, and expert relining became necessary about a dozen years ago. The painter's method, like that of many others of his breed, obviously was sound; his pigment holds up beautifully. One feels that in rising above his fellows — to the art of catching a convincing likeness — he still carried his trade psychology, developing his new-found talent to no greater extent than he deemed absolutely necessary. Hence he did not experiment with his medium as did some of the more artistic, well-tutored contemporary wielders of the paint brush.

Certainly the output of our limners mirrors a period, and a very interesting period at that; straightforward, naïve, truly homegrown, their characterizations filled a need, and now are peculiarly eloquent. Those of us whose ancestors were portrayed by sophisticated painters of the Old World and of America; and those deprived, by loss, family disagreements, or otherwise, of any ancestral portraits at all, are likely to thrill to such paintings far more than people brought up with them. But this revealing immortalization of Julius is deservedly cherished still by members of the Norton family, through whose courtesy it was photographed.

Fig. 1 — INKSTAND
Grey stoneware, salt-glazed with blue decoration. Made at the pottery of Julius Norton, 1841. *Owned by Mrs. Edward Norton.*

The Facts About Bennington Pottery

I. *The Stoneware of the Norton Potteries*

By JOHN SPARGO

Illustrations, except as noted, from the author's collection

[INTRODUCTORY NOTE:—The writer of this series of articles is widely known as a successful collector of Bennington ware. His collection is one of the largest in existence and contains many rare and unique specimens. Mr. Spargo is president of the Bennington Battle Monument and Historical Association, and is at the head of a movement to establish an historical museum in Bennington. He has just completed an exhaustive historical and descriptive work dealing with the Bennington potteries, and unquestionably knows more about the subject, in all its phases, than any other living person.]

THE first pottery in Vermont was established in 1793, two years after the State had been admitted into the Union as the first to be added to the original thirteen. The little pottery was situated in the town of Bennington, a mile or so south of the Meeting House, near the foot of Mount Anthony, on the main highway from Canada to Massachusetts. Its founder was Captain John Norton, a native of Goshen, Connecticut, a revolutionary patriot who, as captain in the eighteenth Connecticut Regiment, had seen much active military service under Washington. It is interesting to know that he was one of the guards in charge of Major André and was present at the execution of that unfortunate man.

Barber* and other writers have observed that Captain John Norton's brother, William, was associated with him in the establishment and operation of this pottery, but there is no foundation for the statement. William Norton was not in any manner connected with the pottery.

Captain John Norton had settled in Bennington in 1785, when Vermont was an independent republic. He was the owner of one of the large farms of the town and was also a large-scale distiller. At the time of the establishment of his pottery he was already a man of some substance, highly respected by his neighbors. He was active in Masonic circles. A practical potter—he had learned the trade in Connecticut—the need for a local supply of such domestic utensils as milk pans and cider jugs led him to erect a shop and a single kiln upon his farm, at the foot of Mount Anthony. This eminence derived its name from the fact that one Peter Anthony, ancestor of the famous Susan B. Anthony, had his farm on its slopes.

Within a year or two, Captain Norton erected a second kiln.

Upon the authority of Pitkin,* the statement has often been made and has commonly been accepted as true that, during the first years, "only salt-glazed stoneware was produced." This, however, is contrary to all available evidence, and may be dismissed as mere guesswork—and erroneous guesswork at that. The small jug here illustrated (*Fig. 2*) was probably made as early as 1796 and certainly not later than 1798. Its history is unimpeachable and is supported by documentary evidence. It was made by a potter named Abel Wadsworth—at Captain Norton's pottery—for a little girl named Armstrong, who was born in 1788. She was at the time, according to her own story—oft repeated in later years—little more than eight years old. She lived a long life, her death taking place in 1880, when she was ninety-two years old. She had lived in Bennington

*Edwin A. Barber, *Pottery and Porcelain of the U. S.*, New York, 1893, p. 104.

*Albert H. Pitkin, *Early American Folk Pottery*, Hartford, 1918.

Fig. 2 — "Slip" Covered Jug
Of red ware and made at Capt. John Norton's pottery about 1796.

all the time, and, some ten years before her death, she caused to be prepared a written history of the little jug.

This jug is of red earthenware, fired very hard, and covered with dark brown "slip." The body is of local clay, presumably dug on the farm, and the "slip" is probably of clay from the vicinity of Albany, N. Y. This inference is drawn from two sources: first, from local diaries of a slightly later period we learn that clay was brought to Captain Norton's from Albany and Troy for use at the pottery; second, the color is exactly that of the well-known "Albany slip." Upon each side of the jug, which is about six inches high, there appears a crude decoration in the shape of a spray of leaves, brushed into the "slip" with clay of a lighter color. The piece is excellently potted, showing that Abel Wadsworth must have been a competent workman. I count myself fortunate in the possession of this well attested product of the first Vermont pottery.

Another specimen of mine is equally well authenticated. It was probably made about the year 1800. It was owned for many years by Mrs. Peter Ostrander, one of Captain Norton's neighbors, who died in 1827. She charged her daughter to preserve it, because it was made at the first Norton pottery. Until it came into my possession, it had remained always in the Ostrander family. It is a graceful jar, ten inches in height, and is of red ware, lead glazed. Dark smoke smudges in the glaze, from the wood fires, add to its charm. The glaze is exceedingly brilliant and reflects the light so brightly that it has baffled most excellent photographers who have tried to make a good picture of it.

This piece is referred to by Pitkin.* How, in the face of the evidence of the piece itself, he could say that "only salt glaze ware was produced" I am unable to say or even to guess. But facts are facts and possess a compelling eloquence of their own. It is perhaps well to add that, in addition to the evidence of these two pieces, from the diaries of Captain Norton's nearest neighbor Pitkin might have learned that both salt glazing and lead glazing were practised at the same time. It is my opinion that the use of "slip" was first in order of time, and that, in a few years, the use of salt glaze and lead glaze was introduced, simultaneously, or nearly so. Not one of the early Bennington pieces is marked in any manner. Identification is possible only as a result of direct inheritance and documentary evidence. Marking was not introduced until later.

Some time between 1812 and 1815, Captain John Norton took his two sons, Luman and John, into partnership with him. The firm name became *John Norton and Sons*. Although there are milk pans and other pieces, in my own collection and elsewhere, known to have been made at or near this time, no pieces have been found bearing the mark. There is, however, a receipt for ware (*Fig. 3*) which gives the name of the firm and is interesting for other reasons as well. This document shows that William Henry, Esq.—who was a well-known citizen—bought wares to the value of $20.51, as follows:

12	Doz.	Milk Pans @ 9/–	$18.00
1	"	Large Platter @ 6/–	1.00
1	"	Second size Platter @ 5/–	0.84
1	"	Third size Platter @ 4/–	0.67
			$20.51

Captain Norton retired from the pottery in 1823 and the business was, for a time, carried on by the two sons, Luman and John, under the firm name of *L. Norton & Co.* So far as known, this is the first mark used at the Norton pottery, and it is found upon stoneware (*Fig. 4*). At this time, however, the firm produced stoneware, salt glazed, and red ware, both salt glazed and lead glazed. A fine jar (*Fig. 4*) of salt glazed stoneware belongs to this period, 1823–1827.

In 1827 John Norton left the firm; and, from 1828 to 1833, Luman Norton carried on the pottery as sole proprietor. Stoneware crocks and jars made at this time and marked *L. Norton, Bennington, Vt.*, are not at all uncommon. Although only twelve workmen were employed, the output was considerable. Indeed, as I have delved among old local records and noted the references to large loads of ware being sent to various places, I have wondered that such a small force could turn out so much. While some of the jugs and jars made at this time have a certain decorative value, some of the designs being quaint and pleasing, pieces marked *L. Norton, Bennington, Vt.*, are too common to have any scarcity value worth mentioning.

In 1833 Luman Norton took into

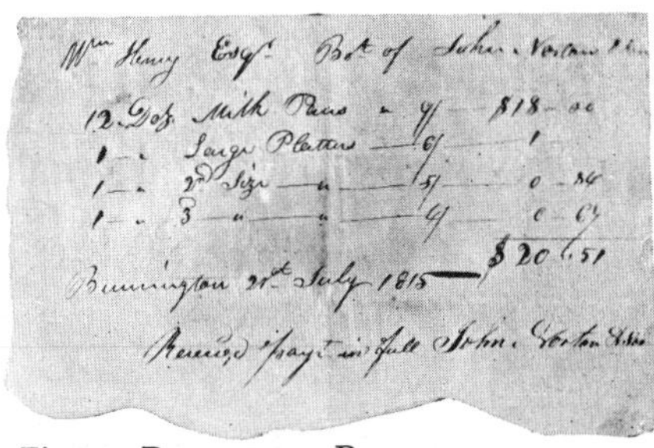

Bennington 21st July 1815

Fig. 3 — Receipt for Pottery
Signed by *John Norton & Sons*, 1815.

*Albert H. Pitkin, *Early American Folk Pottery*, Hartford, 1918, p. 22.

Fig. 4 — Decorated Stoneware Jar
Bears earliest known Bennington mark, that of *L. Norton & Co.*, 1823–1827.

partnership with him his son, Julius Norton, who, like his father and his grandfather, was an excellent potter. The pottery was then removed to the "Lower Village," where water power was available. Prior to that time horse power was used. From 1833 to 1840 two marks were used upon the stoneware — *L. Norton & Son, East Bennington, Vt.*, and *L. Norton & Son, Bennington, Vt.* (*Fig. 5*). It is important to remember that the two forms were used simultaneously and interchangeably. Because the term "East Bennington" as applied to the lower village became obsolete many years ago, it is common for Benningtonians even, to ascribe an earlier date to the East Bennington mark. Pitkin was misled by this and, in turn, has misled numerous collectors into a faulty chronological classification. Both forms of designation were in use at the same time, and, even in the date lines of the local newspapers of the period, one finds one form used one week and the other the next, or the two forms in the same issue on different pages. It is utterly baseless to ascribe an earlier date to the "East Bennington" mark.

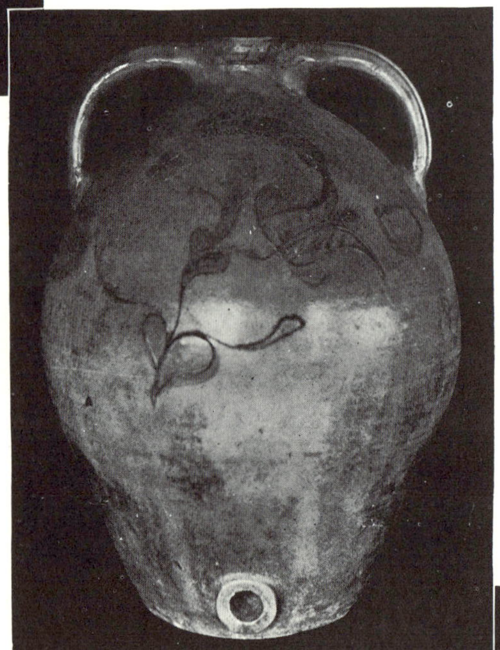

Fig. 5 — Cider Jar
Cobalt blue design — Made by *L. Norton & Son*, 1833.

This is not the time or place for any attempt to describe, or to evaluate, the personal characteristics of Judge Luman Norton and his son Julius. That I hope to do in a more extensive study of the Bennington potteries. Suffice it to say that both were remarkable men in many respects. They were men of culture, and stood foremost in the citizenship of the historic town.

At the end of 1840 Luman Norton retired from the business in order that he might devote himself to his beloved books. From the beginning of 1841 to the end of 1844, the pottery was carried on by Julius Norton alone. He was a most progressive business man as well as a thoroughly competent potter, and he introduced many new articles and greatly extended the business. In an advertisement, dated February 27, 1841, he mentions "Patented Fire-brick" and the following articles in stoneware: "Butter, Cake, Pickle, Preserve and Oyster Pots, Jugs, Churns, Beer and Blacking Bottles, Jars, Plain and Fancy Pitchers, Ink Stands, Earthen Milkpans, Stove Tubes, Kegs, Mugs, Flower Pots, &c., &c." One of the inkstands referred to is in the possession of Mrs. Edward Norton, of Bennington, and is illustrated herewith (*Fig. 1*). It is gray stoneware with cobalt blue decorations. During this period — 1841–1845 — the following marks were used:

Julius Norton, East Bennington, Vt.
J. Norton, East Bennington, Vt.
Julius Norton, Bennington, Vt.
J. Norton, Bennington, Vt.

At the beginning of 1845 Julius Norton took his brother-in-law, Christopher Webber Fenton, into partnership with him. I have pointed out, in an earlier article,* that Pitkin is in error when he says that Fenton was in partnership with Luman Norton at an earlier date, and that he is equally wrong in describing Fenton as a potter of extraordinary ability and talent. It is not necessary to enlarge here upon these errors. It is sufficient to warn the serious students of our ceramic history, and collectors of Bennington pottery likewise, that the accounts of the Norton-Fenton partnership given by both Barber and Pitkin are so contrary to the known facts, and so misleading, that they should be utterly disregarded.

*See Antiques for October, 1928 (Vol. IV, p. 166).

Fig. 6

Fig. 6 — Twenty-Gallon Jar
Height, 2 feet, 4 inches. Incised inscription. Made in 1864 by *E. & L. P. Norton* to celebrate the election of a local celebrity to the State Legislature. The inscription reads:

Calvin Park
1864
Hic Jacet
The animating spirit and divine afflatus of the owner.

Were it the last drop in the Jug
And you gasped upon the spout
Ere your fainting spirit fell
I'd advise — to draw it out.

Fig. 7 — Rockingham Pitchers (*1845–1847*)
Made by *Norton & Fenton, Bennington.* See Antiques for October, 1923 (Vol. IV, p. 168).

The firm name was *Norton & Fenton* and was impressed in the wares. Sometimes the legend *East Bennington* was used and at other times *Bennington.* Here, again, it is idle to attempt to ascribe an earlier date to one of the two forms than to the other. Norton and Fenton made stoneware, yellow ware, white ware, and Rockingham—the latter being the brown glazed ware, frequently mottled, in which manganese was the coloring material. They also experimented with hard paste porcelain and contemplated going into its manufacture upon an extensive scale. A disastrous fire which took place in June, 1845, led to the rebuilding of the pottery upon the old site, on a much larger scale. The talent of Fenton found expression, at this time, in the introduction of several novel features in the construction of the kilns and in the arrangement of the works in general. The partnership of Julius Norton and Christopher Webber Fenton lasted only until June, 1847, when it was formally dissolved.

Neither Julius Norton nor any other member of the Norton family had any connection with the famous United States pottery with which Fenton was identified for more than a decade. Judge Luman Norton, whose daughter Fenton had married, furnished his son-in-law with a large part of the capital with which he started manufacturing upon his own account, in 1847, after the dissolution of the partnership between himself and Julius Norton. Other than that, there was never any connection on the part of any member of the Norton family with the business enterprise of Fenton.

The story told by Pitkin of the two young men, Julius Norton and C. W. Fenton, being in partnership with Judge Luman Norton and anxious to go into the manufacture of finer, ornamental wares; of the unwillingness of the Judge, and the launching out into the new enterprise by the two young men, on their own account, is entirely apocryphal. Baseless, too, is the story told by the same writer of the partnership of these two young men with Henry Hall. The elder Norton was never in partnership with Fenton; there never was such a separation; there never was a partnership of Julius Norton, C. W. Fenton and Henry Hall. In the proper place and time the evidence upon which these corrections are based will be published.

From the foregoing it will be perceived that the Norton-Fenton partnership was a brief episode in the history of the Norton potteries. Pieces marked *Norton & Fenton*, therefore, properly belong to the classification of wares produced at the Norton potteries. They have, however, an associational interest with the Fenton enterprises which are conveniently lumped under the single designation of the United States Pottery. That is to say, while none of the other Norton pottery products have any connection or association with the Bennington wares sought after by collectors, those of the Norton-Fenton period have, and hence definitely belong to any collection of "Bennington pottery" as that term is understood by collectors.

In discussing the *Norton & Fenton*, *East Bennington*, mark, Pitkin calls it "extremely rare" and says that a brown glazed pitcher and a stoneware jug are the only pieces he ever saw so marked. This statement is utterly incomprehensible to me. There can hardly be a dealer in antiques in all New England who has not had some pieces so marked. Not only are there several in my own collection, but I know of scores of others. At one time and another I have seen hundreds of pieces so marked. Such statements mislead honest dealers and collectors and cannot be permitted to go unchallenged. Several Norton and Fenton pieces are herewith illustrated (*Figs. 7 and 8*).

From 1847 to 1850 Julius Norton again carried on the business alone, manufacturing stoneware and some Rockingham. Meanwhile Fenton had gone into business on his own account, making some of the wares not so much sought after. I shall deal with his enterprises separately. At this time the Norton wares were marked, *Julius Norton, Bennington, Vt.*, and *J. Norton, Bennington, Vt.* From 1850 to 1859 Julius Norton was in partnership with his uncle, Edward Norton, and wares made at that time were marked with the firm name, *J. & E. Norton, Bennington, Vt.* In 1859 Julius Norton's son, Luman Preston Norton, was taken into the firm, the name of which was changed to *J. & E. Norton & Co.*, which name, with the addition of the words *Bennington, Vt.*, was impressed into the ware produced. This mark was used from 1859 to 1861, in the latter of which years Julius Norton died. In the same period the mark, *J. Norton & Co., Bennington, Vt.*, was occasionally used.

From 1861 to 1881 Edward Norton and Luman Preston Norton carried on the business. Jugs, jars, pots, churns, and other articles, marked *E. & L. P. Norton, Bennington, Vt.*, belong to this period and are exceedingly common (*Fig. 6*). From 1881 to 1883 Edward Norton carried on the business alone, Luman P. Norton having withdrawn. The marks used during this period were *E. Norton, Bennington,*

Fig. 8 — Stoneware
Made by *Norton & Fenton*, 1845–47. The jug on the left is marked *Bennington;* the jar on the right, *East Bennington.* The terms are synonymous

Vt., and *Edward Norton, Bennington, Vt.* From 1883 to 1894 the business was carried on by *Edward Norton & Co.* Mr. C. W. Thatcher having joined Edward Norton in 1883, a partnership continued to the death of Edward Norton, in 1885, and was then maintained by the latter's son, Edward Lincoln Norton, to 1894, under the same firm name.

Thus, for one year more than a century, the Norton potteries were carried on without a break. With the exception of C. W. Fenton (who was connected with the family by marriage) and C. W. Thatcher, no person other than members of the Norton family had ever been associated with the ownership or management of the business. Thus the first pottery in Vermont had a longer continuous history than any other pottery in the State, or indeed than any other Vermont industrial enterprise of any kind. It is pleasing to know that during all those years the factory never experienced a strike, a lockout, or any other labor trouble.

Speaking generally, it may be said that the value of specimens of pottery bearing the mark of any of the Norton firms, other than *Norton & Fenton*, is entirely independent of the standards set by the Bennington wares that are sought after by collectors—products of the Fenton enterprises—and is determined principally by their desirability for decorative purposes. Thus, a good specimen marked *L. Norton & Co.*—the earliest known mark—has a certain historical value which would give it rank above specimens bearing the later marks. Pieces marked *E. & L. P. Norton* are so numerous that they are of comparatively little value, except as their desirability for decorative purposes may determine. From this point of view—decorative quality quite regardless of relative scarcity—a late example, bearing one of the commonest marks, may excel an earlier specimen bearing a relatively scarce mark. Some of the quaintest and most interesting designs are shown in the accompanying photographs.

CHRONOLOGICAL LIST OF ALL MARKS USED BY THE NORTON POTTERIES

In the following chronology the second member of each pair of dates usually represents the year at the beginning of which a new mark came into use and an old one was discarded. But since this is not invariably the case the subjoined list should be checked by reference to the main text of the article.

L. Norton & Co., Bennington, Vt.	*1823–1827*
L. Norton, Bennington, Vt.	*1828–1833*
L. Norton & Son, East Bennington, Vt. *L. Norton & Son, Bennington, Vt.*	*1833–1840*
Julius Norton, East Bennington, Vt. *J. Norton, East Bennington, Vt.* *Julius Norton, Bennington, Vt.* *J. Norton, Bennington, Vt.*	*1841–1845*
Norton & Fenton, East Bennington, Vt. *Norton & Fenton, Bennington, Vt.*	*1845–1847*
Julius Norton, Bennington, Vt. *J. Norton, Bennington, Vt.*	*1847–1850*
J. & E. Norton, Bennington, Vt.	*1850–1859*
J. Norton & Co., Bennington, Vt. *J. & E. Norton & Co., Bennington, Vt.*	*1859–1861*
E. & L. P. Norton, Bennington, Vt.	*1861–1881*
E. Norton, Bennington, Vt. *Edward Norton, Bennington, Vt.*	*1881–1883*
Edward Norton & Co., Bennington, Vt. *E. Norton & Co., Bennington, Vt.*	*1883–1894*
Edward Norton Company, Bennington, Vt.	*1886–1894*

Bennington Factory—An unusual mark, date of use unknown, but probably after 1885. I have not been able as yet to determine, with certainty, whether the one piece that I have seen so marked was made at the Norton potteries at all or at a smaller pottery in Bennington, owned and operated by Enos Adams. The quality of the ware, however, leads me, in the absence of anything more definite, to believe it to be a Norton product of relatively late date.

A Strange Face from Whately

An extraordinary outburst of creative enthusiasm on the part of a potter—indeed, the only outburst of the kind attributable to the individual in this instance responsible—is a curious jug belonging to Mrs. Helen M. Merrill of Longmeadow, Massachusetts, who has favored the Attic with photographs and various particulars.

Slightly more than seven inches in height and fashioned like a toby jug, with a huge, crude face, gaping mouth and protruding, bat-like ears, this jug offers something of a mystery; for its broad countenance is pockmarked with inscriptions. Across the forehead runs the legend *A Friend. To. My. Countrey.* On the left cheek appears *E. G. Crafts, Whately Mass.* On the right cheek, is *O The. Dimocratick. Press.*, and across the lower lip *United Wee Stand, Divided, Wee, Fall.* Beneath the handle is lettered in faded gilt the date 1833.

The piece is in perfect condition, except that the lobe of the right ear is missing. An ear-ring hole is drilled in the lobe of the left ear, and it is not improbable that a similar hole originally perforated the other ear, and that the lobe was broken off when someone endeavored to hang the pitcher up by its ears.

As to the precise significance of the various inscriptions, no one is able to offer enlightenment. The members of the Crafts family are said to have been Massachusetts Democrats. They were, therefore, supporters of that irascible hero of the party, Andrew Jackson, who, in 1832, had for the second time been elected President of the United States. The fact may account for the display of patriotic enthusiasm. But it in no wise explains the curious mixture of symbols which appear in relief on the jug: six stars, three on each side; and two sprays of rose, thistle and shamrock, well modeled and charmingly disposed, flanking the handle.

STONEWARE FROM THE NASHUA POTTERY
Left to right: Small jug with blue decoration and the inscription MARTIN CRAFTS, NASHUA. Four-gallon jug with blue decoration; somewhat warped in firing; marked MARTIN CRAFTS. NASHUA, N. H. Small jug of an older pattern, probably made in the first years of operation; marked T, CRAFTS & CO. NASHUA.
From the author's collection

The Crafts Pottery in Nashua, New Hampshire

By F. H. NORTON

Assistant Professor of Ceramics, Massachusetts Institute of Technology

IT IS well known that the Crafts family operated a pottery in Whately, Massachusetts. Information concerning another pottery run by the same family in Nashua, New Hampshire, is, on the contrary, less easily available. The purpose of these notes is to record the facts that my investigations have brought to light, and of eliciting further information from readers who may have additional data concerning the pottery, its owners, or its products.

Thomas Crafts was born at Whately, Massachusetts, September 10, 1781 (*Crafts Family*, Gazette Printing Company, 1893, pages 305 and 306). About 1802 he developed a pottery in that town for the manufacture of earthenware. Black teapots were made a little later, and by 1833 stoneware was the chief product of the pottery.

The first son of Thomas, Martin, born in 1805, lived only a few months. The second son, also named Martin, was born April 4, 1809. Evidently he went into business with his father and his younger brother, Elbridge Gerry Crafts. Most of the stoneware from the Whately pottery bore the mark T, Crafts and Co. Whately. According to Spargo, the establishment closed either in 1847 or in 1848.

Since there were only a few stoneware potteries operating in New England in the first half of the nineteenth century, the Whately stoneware was retailed over a wide area. That a regular trade was carried on with Nashua, New Hampshire, is proved by two inscriptions on jugs found in Nashua, and now in my possession.

The first reads:

T. Crafts & Co.
Whately

SOLD BY
BOUTWELL & M, KEAN, NASHUA, N. H.
DEALERS IN ENGLISH & W. I. GOODS,
HARD AND HOLLOW
WARE & C. & C.

Without question Boutwell and McKean regularly ordered stoneware from Whately. Their names do not appear in the earliest available Nashua Directory (1841), but W. A. & N. McKean, their probable successors, are listed as owning the boathouse store on the north side of the Main Street bridge. In the same year the latter firm advertised as hardware dealers, and included hollow ware among its goods. It continued to at least 1850.

The other jug is marked:

Isaac Spaulding
Nashua

T, Crafts & Co.
Whately.

Isaac Spaulding appears in the 1841 directory as operating a counting room on Main and Factory Streets; but he is not listed in 1843. He probably was a hardware dealer or wholesale merchant, since a retail store would hardly be a "counting room." At any rate, he had stoneware made for him at Whately.

What is more natural than that the eldest son of Thomas Crafts, trained as a potter, should wish to establish a pottery of his own? It would not have been wise to choose a region too close to Whately. Accordingly, as he cast about for a suitable location, the excellent trade with far-off Nashua undoubtedly strongly suggested a site in that neighborhood. Wood was plentiful and the river navigable for bringing up the New Jersey clay that was used for nearly all New England stoneware at that time.

Parker's *History of Nashua* (page 464) states: "The pottery of Martin Crafts was located on the eastern side of Main St., north of the Acton railroad, and Crafts lived in the cottage standing in that location. Crafts began his works in 1838 and continued some six years. He brought his clay from Boston by boat." The evidence of the Nashua directories would lead us to believe that the pottery continued somewhat longer than six years.

INKWELL, UNMARKED
Probably from the Nashua Pottery.
Height: 3 inches.
From the collection of Mrs. C. H. Watkins

Probably Martin began, at first, with his father's money and name, for one old-style jug bears the mark T, Crafts & Co. Nashua. Later on the ware was all marked Martin Crafts Nashua or Martin Crafts Nashua, N. H.

The Nashua Directory for 1841 lists as a potter not only Martin, but also James M., his brother, who was born in Whately in 1817. When twenty-one years of age James went to Nashua, and, it is stated in the *Springfield Republican* for September 19, 1903, took charge of the pottery owned by his father. It is probable that the pottery was owned by Thomas, but it is certain that Martin and not James was really in charge. The latter returned to Whately in 1841, where he worked in his father's pottery until he went into business for himself. Thus James either was working with Martin from the beginning of the Nashua pottery, or was taken in soon afterward.

In 1843 and 1845 James is not listed, but Caleb Crafts, Martin's uncle, appears in his place. Colonel Caleb Crafts (*Crafts Family*, page 309) was born in Whately in 1800. He was a potter, and for a few years followed his trade in Troy, New York. In 1837 he went to Portland, Maine, where he was engaged in the pottery business for himself. A small stoneware jug in the author's collection bears the inscription C. Crafts & Co. Portland.

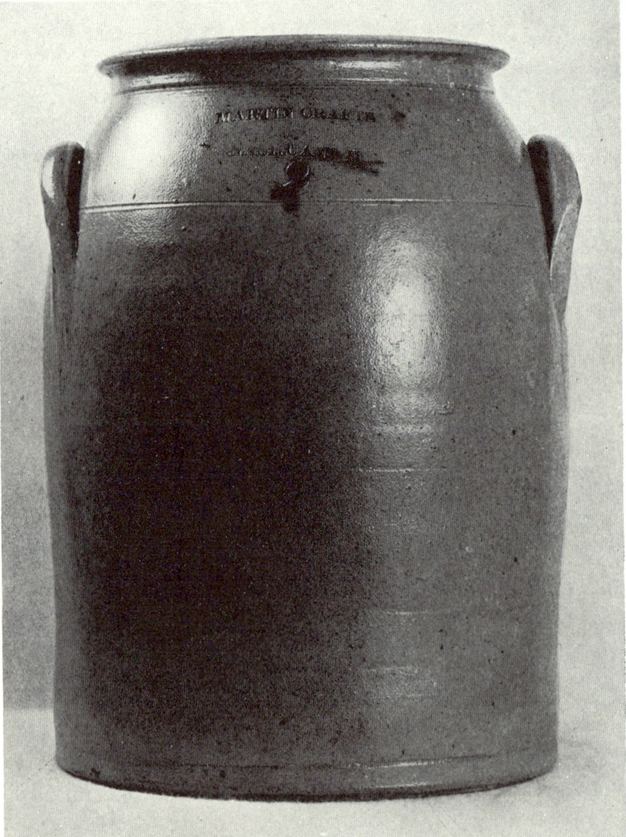

STONEWARE FROM THE NASHUA POTTERY
Marked MARTIN CRAFTS NASHUA, N. H.
Height: 12 inches.
From the collection of H. L. Hall

About 1841 Caleb moved to Nashua, where he joined his nephew in the pottery. After a few years, however, he returned to Whately. The residence for all three Crafts in Nashua is given as Kinsley Street, which was not far from the pottery.

The 1850 directory lists:

Stoneware Factory
Commenced 1838
Martin Crafts, Proprietor
Amount of business annually $16,000
Employed 9 hands

This gives a good idea of the size of the factory and the amount of ware made. At an assumed average price of thirty cents, the total for a year would be over 53,000 pieces. An average weight of five pounds would give a tonnage of over 130 per annum. Hence three or four hundred tons of clay must have been shipped up the river to Nashua each year.

We know very little about the technical details of the pottery. There is no reason, however, to believe that the ware was unlike that of other potteries. The clay may have been used raw or washed. Probably only one kiln was needed, and three or four wheels. Apparently all the ware was thrown on the wheel and salt glazed. The type of ware made is known to include various sizes of jugs and jars, of which the former are much the more plentiful. A few have blue decorations, but generally they are plain. Although I have seen no marked examples of the type, it is believed by residents that stoneware inkwells and flasks were made in Nashua. Small pieces of this character are plentiful in the vicinity.

The reason for the closing of the Nashua pottery almost synchronously with that of the Whately enterprise is not known. Possibly manufacturing costs were so high as to preclude competition with the large establishments in Portland and Charlestown, which were able to obtain clay and coal directly from coasting vessels. The closing of the Middlesex canal in 1843 may also have been a contributing cause.

Fig. 1 — The Norwich Pottery (*erected 1835-1840*)
Located originally on Cove Street in Norwich, Connecticut, this pottery has completely disappeared.

The Norwich Pottery Works

By Henry R. Armstrong

In Antiques for January, 1922,* Walter A. Dyer discusses the early pottery of New England. In any such general treatment, however, there are certain to be gaps. One, in particular, I wish here to point out, and, in a measure, to fill. In speaking of Norwich, Connecticut, Mr. Dyer mentions only one pottery—that of "Bean Hill." He makes no mention of another, which was operated under the name of "The Norwich Pottery Works."

According to the Land Records of the town of Norwich this pottery was established about 1836 by Sidney Risley, and for forty-four years the name of the Risleys—Sidney and his son, George L.—was associated with the concern. Upon the death of George L. Risley in 1881 the pottery passed into other hands and was conducted by various persons until 1895, when the business was abandoned. Today all vestige of the old works has disappeared. The grain and feed warehouses of Charles Slosburg completely cover the site.

Originally the pottery was located on the edge of Yantic Cove, which at one time extended to this point and gave the street where the pottery was located its name. This cove was filled in when the New London, Willimantic and Palmer Railroad was built. Its successor, The New London Northern Railroad, bought the pottery property from Mrs. George L. Risley, May 6, 1882, the year after her husband's death.

*Vol. I, p. 19.

The name of Sidney Risley, a potter, appears in the first Norwich voting list, published in 1840. According to the best information obtainable, it is believed that he came here from East Hartford a few years before 1840 and established the pottery. It was on land belonging to Elijah A. Bill, who was a grocer and was also engaged in various other business enterprises during his lifetime. The first mention of a pottery on the Cove Street site appears in the deed to Elijah A. Bill from Cushing Eells, September 4, 1845, which speaks of a "building now improved as a pottery." Bill and Eells bought the land from Richard Adams, September 4, 1835, this deed containing no mention of a pottery but describing "a trimmer's or painter's shop" and a "chaise maker's shop" on the land conveyed, which bordered on the cove.

"Sidney Risley, stoneware, pottery, Cove Street, W. S." was listed in the first Norwich directory, published in 1846, and in the next City Directory, 1857, he was an advertiser, as follows:

Sidney Risley
No. 4 Cove Street, W. S. Norwich, Conn.,
Manufacturer of Stoneware
In every variety. The trade supplied with all kinds of stoneware at the lowest market prices.
N.B.—All orders thankfully received and promptly attended to.

Fig. 2 — Stoneware Water Cooler (*Norwich Pottery*)
An interesting piece of gray stoneware, which exemplifies some excellent traditions of pottery. *Owned by the author.*

Sidney Risley lived on High Street, at first in a house south of West Main Street, but he later moved nearer the pottery into a brick house, which is Number 13 on the easterly side of what is now North High Street. In the early days of the pottery, the West Side, so-called, where the pottery was located, was all undeveloped territory as far as buildings went, with just a few clustering along the river. Beyond this all was open country.

On April 2, 1856, Sidney Risley, who had hitherto leased his pottery, bought the buildings and the land on which they were situated from Elijah A. Bill and continued to operate the works until his death, at the age of 61, on April 26, 1875. His son, George L. Risley, continued the business until his death, December 24, 1881. About a year later the property was again opened as the Norwich Pottery Works, B. C. Chace, proprietor. Mr. Chace was succeeded in 1885 by George B. Chamberlain, and after he had run it for about two years, the business was continued by Otto N. Suderberg until its discontinuance, in 1895.

Stoneware crocks, pitchers, jugs and bottles were the product of the old Risley pottery, which got its clay in schooner loads from New Jersey and Long Island and converted the raw material into the required shapes on lathes run by foot treadles. When enough had been manufactured and dried out, ready for baking, the kiln was loaded up and fires were started. All the "West Side" knew when the pottery was firing, for the black smoke from the wood fire of three-foot chestnut sticks swirled out from the top of the kiln in dense volumes, while the fires were kept going for thirty-six, or forty-eight, or fifty hours, according to the time required.

The stoneware was distributed to the country stores by wagon all through eastern Connecticut, and westward beyond the Connecticut river. One of the old drivers was the late Alvin T. Davis, whose pottery wagon with a pair of fine Newfoundland dogs hitched ahead of the horses is still remembered by some of the older residents. In later years some glazed and decorated ware* was added to the lines which the pottery made. I am the fortunate possessor of a handsome stoneware water cooler manufactured probably in the early days of the concern. It is light gray in color, one and one-half feet in height, thirteen inches in diameter at the top and ten inches across the

Fig. 3 — Side View of Figure 2
It seems not unreasonable to believe that the man who modelled this applied grape leaf handle was trained in England.

*Rockingham

Fig. 4 — Stoneware Jug
The Norwich ware appears for the most part to have been such commonplace stuff as this.

bottom, with the words, "The Norwich Pottery Works," printed across the face, in blue. The American eagle, which decorates the front, and the leaves adorning the handles are raised about a quarter of an inch from the surface

Norwich men who grew up as boys on the West Side retain vivid memories of the old pottery yard as their playground. When they played soldier, the crates that stood around were used as guard houses for their prisoners; and in winter, when they were sliding down the High Street Hill, their favorite fun was to end their slide with a dash through the pottery doorway to knock down as many pots as possible. The older Risley would build barricades of snow against the doorway to keep them out, but sled after sled would be sent against the barricade until it would finally be overcome and some urchin would work havoc among the accumulated pottery. Close by, on the banks of the cove, was Sheepskin Hollow, so named because of the sheepskins which were tanned there for the tannery at the end of Cove Street. Mummychug chowder, cooked at the pottery fire and made from fish caught in the nearby cove, a delight to vigorous imaginations and appetites, is another boyhood memory still fresh in the minds of a number of Norwich men, once "West Side" boys.

In the later years, the original kiln was increased by the addition of another, and extensions were made to the building used for storage and manufacturing. Located on such low ground and near to the river, the pottery was frequently threatened by high water; and once, in the second year of the management of Mr. Suderberg, a complete baking was lost when the freshet put the fires out 15 hours after they had been started, leaving a half baked lot of pottery that was a total loss.

The tragedy that brought to an end the connection of the Risley family with the business came on a Saturday morning, the day before Christmas, 1881. George L. Risley had gone to the pottery to light the fire under an upright boiler at the rear of the building. The boiler blew up, went through the roof of the building and landed about one hundred and twenty feet away, sinking deep into the mud of the cove. So great was the force of the explosion that the fifteen-hundred-pound boiler passed completely over a fifty-foot elm tree at the rear of the pottery in its flight. Mr. Risley was so badly injured that he died that evening.

Fig. 5 — Stoneware Jug
Interesting mainly in comparison with Figure 4, as illustrating the slight variations which may occur in closely similar examples.

The Stoneware of South Ashfield, Massachusetts

By Lura Woodside Watkins

IN ORDER to understand the significance of the South Ashfield venture — a small pottery, indeed, and short-lived — it is necessary to know something of the conditions that inspired it. Why should so remote a village have attracted men acquainted with the potter's craft? Where did these men get their training? And what were the reasons for the abandonment of the business after it had survived for more than eight years? A study of local history reveals the answer to these questions.

In the decade between 1840 and 1850 Ashfield was a town of about fifteen hundred inhabitants. Situated in the Berkshires, halfway between Shelburne Falls and South Deerfield, it embraced several separate communities. Its central village, then known as Ashfield Plains, stood on high land near the mill pond. Another settlement of nearly equal importance — South Ashfield, locally called "Tin-Pot" — was situated a mile and a half to the south of Ashfield Plains.

Fig. 1 — Remains of the Ashfield Pottery Works
The upper part of the shed at the left is all that remains of the original building

The appellation *Tin-Pot* was suggestively chosen, for South Ashfield was a centre of small industries and a starting point for peddler's activities of the kind that flourished throughout the New England states in the middle of the last century. Here were a tinware factory and a pottery. Ashfield Plains boasted a turning mill for wooden wares; and the whole township was noted for its production of essences distilled from native plants. Its manufacture of peppermint oil alone, carried on in seven places, at one time yielded no less than forty thousand dollars a year. Combs for peddlers' outfits were also locally manufactured, in a small way and in his own house, by one Richard Cook; while the making of palm-leaf hats and shirt bosoms provided pin money for many a housewife.

Every season hundreds of young men took to the road, driving peddlers' carts or traveling by stage and afoot with tin trunks filled with Ashfield products. Nathaniel Hawthorne in his *American Notes* describes such a peddler, whom he saw when he was journeying by stage through the Berkshires.

"Towards night," he writes, "took up an essence vendor for a short distance. He was returning home, after having been out on a tour two or three weeks, and nearly exhausted his stock. He was not exclusively an essence-pedlar, having a large tin box, which had been filled with dry goods, combs, jewelry, etc., now mostly sold out. His essences were of aniseseed, cloves, red-cedar, wormwood, together with opodeldoc, and an oil for the hair. These matters are concocted at Ashfield, and the pedlars are sent about with vast quantities. Cologne-water is among the essences manufactured, though the bottles have foreign labels on them. . . . This man was a pedlar in quite a small way, making but a narrow circuit, and carrying no more than an open basket full of essences; but some go out with wagonloads. He himself contemplated a trip westward, in which case he would send on quantities of his wares ahead to different stations."

An old bill made out by G. C. Goodwin of Boston to Cook and Ranney of Ashfield shows that the drug business flourished to such an extent that it could not be wholly supplied from local sources, and that importations were necessary. This document mentions, among other things, *Mitchell Bitters*, *Indian Vegetable Sassafras Bitters*, and *Wild Cherry and Sarsarparilla Bitters*. The last was recommended in a note from the wholesaler as "a new article in great style for Peddlers." Since its wholesale price was three dollars and a quarter a dozen, while it retailed for one dollar a bottle, it must have well merited the description.

Thus, in the year 1848, when pottery was added to the list of merchandise sent out from the little Berkshire town, we see Ashfield as a well-established manufacturing and trading post. It is more than coincidence that the making of stoneware was almost wholly abandoned in Whately in that same year, or the year before. The Ashfield pottery was an attempt to continue the craft in a location considered more favorable on account of opportunities for distributing the product. The pottery firm did, in fact, carry on its own retail business.

Although there are no less than five firm names to be found on Ashfield stoneware, only three successive organizations actually operated the pottery. The other two marks were used for selling purposes. With this in mind, a clearly defined history of the business may be traced.

Orcutt, Guilford & Co.

The Ashfield pottery building was erected by Walter Orcutt, of the neighboring town of Conway, on land owned by the Guilford family. John Luther Guilford, son of John Guilford of Ashfield, although he appears not to have been himself a potter, retained a one-third interest in the business throughout its duration. Walter Orcutt was his uncle, as was also Eleazer Orcutt, a potter, who may, or may not, have been a member of the firm. Pitkin says some of the ware is marked *W. & E. Orcutt & Co.*, but I have found no firm of this name in the town records; neither have I seen a piece of pottery so marked. Orcutt, Guilford & Co. is first taxed in 1848 for "1 ½ acre & the Potery," valued at six hundred dollars. In the following year the names are given in full as "Walter Orcutt & John Guilford & Co." Their unpretentious little building was placed on the east side of the road from Ashfield, a short distance above the South Ashfield four corners and just south of the Mill Pond Brook, which crossed the road at that point and again wound southward back of the pottery land. Today the spot may be found diagonally across from the South Ashfield post office and a little north of a deserted blacksmith's shop with some tumbledown sheds in the meadow behind it.

Walter and Eleazer Orcutt were sons of the Stephen Orcutt

who, in 1777, was Whately's first potter. Their mother was Miriam Frary. Eleazer, born at Whately December 7, 1796, married Jane Giles of Troy, New York. The *History of Whately* (James M. Crafts, *1899*. On Whately pottery see ANTIQUES for August 1925, *p. 77*) records that he was "a potter by trade" and a resident of Troy, New York. His connection with the Ashfield concern must have been an interlude between his days at Whately and at Troy. According to Pitkin, Eleazer Orcutt attended to the firing of the kiln. Walter was born at Whately May 7, 1799, and is recorded as a resident of Whately, Troy, and Conway. During his ownership of the pottery he lived in Conway, where he died March 1, 1854. His wife was Ann Eliza Blatchford. Little is known concerning the other workmen who were associated with the Orcutt family, except for David Belding, another Whately man, who became their successor. A brother of Guilford, William Frank, sold the pottery goods from a peddler's cart, traveling the country over. That the ware was distributed both by peddling and by local sales is indicated by the marks *Orcutt, Belding & Co.* and *Walter Orcutt & Co.*, which appear on sundry examples. Neither of these firm marks signifies a change in organization. In 1849 Orcutt, Belding & Co. was taxed for three horses and stock in trade, worth three hundred and seventy-five dollars. This was obviously a peddling outfit, distinct from the pottery concern, but allied with it. In 1850 Walter Orcutt & Co. was assessed for a house, barn, store, half an acre of land, and stock in trade. Orcutt was running the general store and post office of South Ashfield at that time. Pottery marks indicating the name of the distributor rather than that of the maker are not uncommon, but they do add to the confusion of the collector. In this case they explain the next step in the destinies of the Ashfield enterprise.

Fig. 2 — SALT-GLAZED STONEWARE
a. Churn, marked *Hastings & Belding/Ashfield, Mass. b.* Lipped crock, marked *Orcutt, Guilford & Co./Ashfield, Mass. c.* Covered jar, marked *Walter Orcutt & Co./Ashfield, Mass.*
From the collection of Austin G. Packard

Hastings & Belding

In 1850 Walter Orcutt sold his share of the "stone-ware factory" to Wellington Hastings and David Belding, while John Luther Guilford still retained his one-third interest. Belding, as we have seen, was already connected with the pottery and was probably the prime mover in taking over its management. The son of Elisha Belding, he was born in Whately, Massachusetts, March 7, 1813. His daughter, still living in Deerfield, and other members of the family have always spelled the name *Belden*. Local history shows that the two spellings are interchangeable, one being a corruption of the other; but the original Whately family was *Belding*, and the Ashfield potter so stamped his name on his jugs. Hence I use the latter spelling here. David was brought up among potters in the days when Whately had twenty-one native master workmen, besides journeymen potters, at work. He probably received his training in the art from Thomas Crafts, whose daughter Triphena he married, November 10, 1842. A mute record of his Whately days survives in the form of a small gray stoneware churn marked *D. Belding/Whately*, now in the possession of Doctor Francis George Curtis of Boston and Ashfield. When David Belding left Whately is not known. He had bought a piece of land in South Ashfield in 1837, but he may not have settled in the town until after the death of his young wife only six weeks after their marriage. Three years later, on October 12, 1845, Belding married Sybil Maria (Hastings) Stanley, the widow of Rufus Allen Stanley and the mother of two young children.

Wellington Hastings was the brother of Belding's second wife. He and his brother Chauncey came to Ashfield from Wilmington, Vermont. The family, descended from the Earl of Huntington, had settled originally in Salem, Massachusetts, and had subsequently moved to Vermont by way of Hardwick. Wellington, the son of Gardner and Hannah Axtell Hastings, was born in Wilmington November 6, 1812.

Belding had gone into insolvency in 1847. What was his business at that time, the court records do not show. Three years later he had recovered sufficiently to join with his brother-in-law in the potting venture. The Hastings and Belding partnership lasted four years, and the majority of the jugs, crocks, and churns found around Ashfield bear their mark. We are permitted to know rather more about the pottery in this period than in its beginnings or its ending. In 1908 Albert H. Pitkin went to Ashfield, where he gleaned some valuable bits of information from the step-daughter of David Belding. These I have since confirmed with the aid of the family. At the time, this step-daughter was living in South Ashfield, the wife of John Luther Guilford of the pottery. She was thus doubly connected with the firm.

Fig. 3 — TWO-GALLON SLIP-GLAZED CIDER PITCHER
Marked *Orcutt, Guilford & Co./Ashfield, Mass.*
From the collection of Dr. Francis George Curtis

From the Guilfords, Pitkin learned that the pottery employed only seven men, of whom three worked at the wheel, and that it had only one kiln. One of the turners was named Wight. He was exceedingly skilful in making offhand pieces and was considered the best workman. Another was Staats D. Van Loon, who first appears in the Ashfield tax list in 1851, and who remained to become a member of the third firm. Ashfield tradition says that some of the potters came from Pennsylvania. It seems likely that Van Loon, at least, had migrated from the Pennsylvania region, or from New York.

Van Loon & Boyden

In 1854, the Hastings and Belding firm went into receivership. Thereupon the business was taken over by Van Loon and George Washington Boyden, with Guilford still holding his one-third share. The pair struggled on for two years more without great success, and in 1856 abandoned the undertaking. I have been able to learn almost nothing about these closing years. Jugs bearing the Van Loon & Boyden mark are exceedingly scarce, so that little tangible evidence of the period remains. Family history discloses no information of value. The Boyden *Genealogy* states that George Boyden was born in 1830, and died April 16, 1858. He married Minerva D. Graves of Conway, who died in Ashfield three days after the birth of a son, Frank Dickinson. In 1856 George Boyden owned a house, grist mill, and other property in Ashfield, but that was after the pottery had closed. It is probable that his connection with the business was purely financial, Van Loon attending to the potting. After the industry failed, Van Loon disappeared from Ashfield, perhaps to drift to Bennington or to some other of the Vermont potteries.

Fig. 4 — Slip-Glazed Pieces
Quart measure marked *Vinegar.*
a and b, from the collection of Mrs. Harold Flower; c, from the collection of Mrs. Arthur J. Chapin

The Wares

The wares made by Orcutt, Guilford & Co., Hastings & Belding, and Van Loon & Boyden are not distinguished one from another by any points of difference. They are all stoneware of rather ordinary quality made of clay brought from Perth Amboy, New Jersey. Some pieces have a dense gray body; others — and they represent by far the greater number — have a buff or light brown body of porous consistency. The former were well fired at a high temperature; the latter either were not burned to a proper degree of hardness, or may have contained an admixture of native red clay. Between the two extremes are various gradations of color and quality. Thus the completed article may be light brown, buff, or a bluish gray, or may be so imperfectly burned as to exhibit a variety of tones. Stoneware of this description was salt-glazed in the usual manner and almost always decorated with a spray, or other design, in cobalt blue, with a blue swash over the impressed firm mark and sometimes around the handles. Less frequently a dash of brown was used. The colored slip was applied either by trailing it through a quill or by means of a brush. The interiors of pots and crocks were lined with slip glaze, black, dark reddish brown, or light brown in color.

In addition to their blue-decorated gray stoneware, the Ashfield potters produced a good deal of ware covered with a dark slip glaze inside and out. The pitcher in Figure 3, marked *Orcutt, Guilford & Co.*, is an example of this type. The bowl with ear handles and the jelly mold in Figure 4 belonged to Mrs. John Luther Guilford, and may also have been made during the first period.

All Ashfield stoneware chips easily, especially when it has been allowed to stand in a damp place. This is a serious defect, and, in itself, affords sufficient explanation for the failure of the works and the inability of its output to compete with the hard, durable products of Bennington.

In September 1933 I discovered, near the bank of the brook, the site of the pottery's waste pile. On the surface of the ground, where they had been thrown eighty-five years ago, lay fragments of all types, including a piece with the Orcutt, Guilford & Co. mark. Shards buried in the moist soil had partly disintegrated. Among the pieces was half a crock cover, warped in the making and discarded. Its upper face was embossed by molding into a conventional leaf pattern. These recovered fragments, although their number was limited, proved of great assistance in studying the pottery. Most of the pottery débris was buried by a minor catastrophe years ago. In 1878 the Mill Pond dam at Ashfield Plains, during a freshet after heavy snows and a sudden thaw, burst, flooding the valley below and the village of South Ashfield. The old pottery building, then in use as a blacksmith's shop, was swept away, only part of a shed remaining at some distance from its original location, while tons of sand and débris were washed into the meadow on the pottery land. This flood effectively removed much of the evidence that might be so instructive today.

Enough of the old factory handiwork has been saved in Ashfield homes to afford an adequate idea of its character. There are the usual common articles, such as egg and butter crocks, churns, pickle and preserve jars of different sizes, molasses jugs up to four-gallon capacity, one- and two-gallon cider pitchers, bean pots, and bowls. One of the largest utilitarian pieces is a five-gallon churn with the Hastings & Belding mark, owned by Miss Alice Turnbull. In addition to these useful pots I have seen a number of offhand things that are far more interesting. In the latter category is the dog illustrated in Figure 8. This animal was fashioned by Staats Van Loon for one of Belding's children. It was obviously made in a mold devised from one of those bisected iron dogs that were used to embellish the side rails of parlor stoves, or were mounted on marble plinths to serve as door stops. Photographs of an original iron dog of the type and of its duplicate in glass appeared in the October 1929 issue of Antiques. Van Loon's pottery canine is entirely covered on the outer surface with a rich cobalt blue.

The potter Wight made, as a gift for Belding's stepdaughter, a toy bank with the inscription running twice across it, *Harriet Sophia Stanley, 1850. Aug. 17th.* This was presented on the child's tenth birthday.

Fig. 5 — Salt-Glazed Stoneware
a. Marked *Orcutt, Belding & Co./Ashfield, Mass. b and c.* Marked *Hastings & Belding/Ashfield, Mass.*
a and b, from the collection of Dr. Francis George Curtis; c, from the collection of Austin G. Packard

A miniature churn, made by Wight for the same little girl, was bought by Pitkin and may now be seen in his collection in the Wadsworth Atheneum, Hartford, Connecticut. A perfect copy of the larger churns, even to the mark — *Hastings & Belding/Ashfield, Mass.* — it is inscribed with the date *August, 1852*, in cobalt blue. A moustache cup and a sand shaker from the Ashfield pottery are other offhand pieces recalled by descendants of the Belding family. The shaker is now owned by John Tomlinson, Jr.

More important from a ceramic point of view than any of these trifling objects is the water cooler illustrated opposite page 237 of Spargo's *Early American Pottery and China*. Not only is this a good piece of potting of graceful shape and fine proportions, but it is also elaborated with ornamental handles and a figure of Diana in relief. That it is an Ashfield product there can be no doubt, for it bears the Hastings & Belding mark, although its sophisticated style points to craftsmanship of the English school. Even without the initials FW, which may be faintly discerned on the band under the figure, it would be safely ascribed to the same Wight who delighted in making presentation pieces. Examination of the Ashfield town records reveals the fact that in 1852 and 1853 a poll tax was paid by one Franklin Wight. Here then, we may assume, is the full name of the man whose work must give him an important place among New England potters. As John Ramsay has pointed out in his excellent article *Early American Pottery* in ANTIQUES (October 1931), the Ashfield water cooler is one of the few examples of native stoneware that have departed from "unimaginative plainness." It is now preserved in the Wadsworth Atheneum collection.

Fig. 6 (left) — TWO-GALLON CIDER PITCHER
Marked *Ashfield, Mass.*
From the collection of Mrs. Arthur J. Chapin

Fig. 7 (right) — STONEWARE JAR
Marked *Van Loon & Boyden/Ashfield, Mass.* The word *Hope!* indicates that this is one of the first pieces made by this firm.
From the collection of John Tomlinson, Jr.

Whether the idea for this monumental cooler originated in the fancy of Franklin Wight is a question that will be raised by comparing the picture of the Ashfield piece with another serving as the frontispiece of Mr. Spargo's book. The latter is a cooler, slightly different in proportion, but in decoration the same, marked *L. W. Fenton/St. Johnsbury, Vt.* The potter's personal initials are, however, missing. Did Wight make this jar, too? Did he copy Fenton's work? Or are both coolers adaptations from some English original? The date of Fenton's works — 1808 to 1859 — would admit of Wight's having been employed at St. Johnsbury either before or after his stay at Ashfield. Further investigation into the history of the Fenton pottery may illumine this point. [The St. Johnsbury potters were Richard Webber Fenton and his son, Leander W. Fenton. Richard was the brother of Jonathan, the Dorset potter.]

Fig. 8 — MOLDED DOG
Rich underglaze blue.
From the author's collection

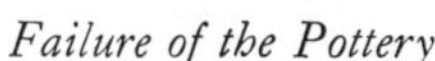

Failure of the Pottery

More than one factor contributed to the failure of the struggling enterprise in Ashfield, as well as to that of many other small potteries scattered through the New England states. The year 1857 was a time of financial panic. The closing of the Ohio Life and Trust Company in August undermined the stability of the country's entire banking system. In New England conditions were much the same as in our recent crisis, and a period of inactivity and unemployment ensued. Van Loon & Boyden must have succumbed in the general business collapse.

Inability to compete with the larger and better established works at Bennington and to produce an equally durable ware were also important elements of weakness. A third reason, too, probably doomed the pottery to failure from the outset: the westward movement had begun to be felt in Ashfield. It was found that peppermint oil and other essences could be manufactured more cheaply and on a larger scale in Michigan than in Massachusetts, and ambitious young men were leaving town. Between 1840 and 1850 Ashfield's population dropped from 1,610 to 1,394 — the greatest decrease in any ten-year period of the town's history.

Ashfield Marks

The regular custom in marking Ashfield pottery was to impress the firm name over *Ashfield, Mass.*, but this rule was not invariably followed. Much of the stoneware is stamped *Ashfield, Mass.* without the maker's name. Occasionally the firm name was used alone, as on a brown stoneware Hastings & Belding molasses jug owned by Austin G. Packard; but the omission of the town mark was probably an oversight. It is interesting to note that the firm signature and the Ashfield mark were applied separately by hand; for the Orcutt, Guilford & Co. fragment that I picked up has the first line of lettering upside down. It is impossible to estimate how large a proportion of Ashfield pottery was unmarked. We do know that the slip-glazed ware was unsigned, and some of the stoneware may also have been left without marking.

The marks in chronological order are as follows:

Mark	Date
Orcutt, Guilford & Co.	1848 to 1850
Orcutt, Belding & Co.	Distributors
Walter Orcutt & Co.	Distributors
Hastings & Belding	1850 to 1854
Van Loon & Boyden	1854 to 1856

(The author acknowledges with grateful appreciation the kind assistance of Mrs. Harold Flower and Austin G. Packard in assembling information for these notes.)

V Stoneware—New York and West

Information on stoneware from New York and west is scarce. With the exception of *Early Potters and Potteries of New York State,* by William C. Ketchum, Jr., there have been few ambitious studies published recently, so the cross-checking of facts in this section against up-to-date material is practically impossible.

The account of the pottery at Huntington, Long Island, by Romanah Sammis (pp. 108-112), is the best we have, and although we suspect inaccuracies, it is difficult to prove them. We can say that Adam States never lived in Lloyd's Neck or anywhere else on Long Island. John Spargo, in one of his books, placed him in Huntington, but Lura Woodside Watkins accurately observed that he was a resident of Horse Neck, an old name for the western part of Greenwich, Connecticut.

We can also wonder why Mrs. Sammis was so impressed with the free-standing handles or "pulled ears" of the jar she illustrated in Figure 5 (p. 109), handles relatively common to the early stoneware of Boston or New York City and familiar to most collectors.

Then we have to ask whether the marked examples are similar enough to the unmarked ones to warrant attributing the latter to the Huntington pottery. Given neither provenance nor marks we would like to know why all but the "art pottery" in Figures 1, 3 and 4 (pp. 108–109) should not be attributed to Connecticut, New Jersey or Pennsylvania. The same question arises in terms of the slipware dishes; and the stoneware shown in Figures 7 and 8 (p. 110) could, from its shapes and decoration, be attributed to potteries in Manhattan or South Amboy, New Jersey.

In serving somewhat as devil's advocates, we do not want to cast aspersions on Mrs. Sammis's scholarship in documenting the ownership of the potworks at Huntington, but we feel we must look to the future for a definitive analysis of its wares.

It may be of interest to collectors that Ketchum, in the book mentioned above, refers to four stencils, "an eagle, grapes, a cow and a rose," that were used by the Huntington pottery late in the nineteenth century. Collectors should also be warned against confusing the "Brown Brothers" mark with that of the "Brown Pottery" which operated in the South around the turn of the century.

Those interested in the Greenport Pottery will find it fully explored in Ketchum's book.

While we remain puzzled about the pottery of Huntington, Long Island, we are on firmer ground in dealing with the pottery of the Remmey family, which is why we eliminated two of the four articles written about them by W. Oakley Raymond. While Part I (pp. 114–115) was fairly accurate, Part II (pp. 116–118) was flawed by a mistaken assumption at the beginning that called into question his other conclusions. In Part III, Raymond launched into a speculative and attributive frenzy, based on a fragment of Remmey family history reported 60 years after the fact. In Part IV, having acquired a geneology of the Warne family, prepared by a local divine, he altered the facts to fit the pots and wound up with the potters of Cheesequake hopelessly confused. Anyone wishing to read the latter two articles can do so in the March and July, 1938 issues of *The Magazine* ANTIQUES. In this volume, you will find instead a more carefully researched article by Robert J. Sim and Arthur W. Clement (pp. 119–122), but we have tried to include some of the pictures from the Raymond articles.

In terms of the two accounts which are reprinted in this volume, more research is needed before we can be sure how many Crolius and Remmey potteries there were in Manhattan and exactly where they were located and when, but Raymond's conclusion that the last Remmey failed in New York City around 1820 has been refuted by Ketchum. On page 18 of his book, Ketchum reveals that the city directories continued to list John Remmey, 3rd, on Cross Street until 1826. "Then until 1831," he adds, "he is noted as pursuing the same occupation and residing on Thomas Street. So it appears that this pottery operated longer than has been recognized."

Because of interest today in the pottery of Richard C. Remmey, Raymond's second article is included. His statements on the first page must be weighed against the fact that there is no conclusive evidence that the Remmeys were potting in Philadelphia as early as 1810. The inconsistencies in this part of Raymond's account are currently under investigation and hopefully will be clarified in the near future by Susan H. Myers of the Smithsonian Institution's Division of Pre-Industrial Cultural History.

James R. Mitchell, Director of the William Penn Memorial Museum in Harrisburg, Pennsylvania, has reminded us that the towns of Old Bridge, Cheesequake, and South River were only three to five miles apart. He has also determined that Branch Green started a pottery in Philadelphia around 1809. Since this was the same manufactory purchased a number of years later by Burnett & Remmey, it might provide us with a clue as to how a piece of stoneware dated 1810 might have been thought to be a product of the family pottery there.

Recently, a redware jar of the bulbous form known to have been made in New Jersey was discovered having the same border design as No. 4 in Figure 8 (p. 121) of the article by Sim and Clement. This is the first piece of redware to turn up decorated with a coggle wheel design associated with Warne & Letts. It is now in the collection of the Newark Museum.

There isn't much to say about "The Potters of Poughkeepsie" except to point out that its author, John P. Remensnyder, was one of the first and is perhaps the best-known collector of American stoneware. Examples from the Remensnyder collection have figured prominently in every important book or catalogue written on the subject. The Orcutt he mentions, of the firm of Orcutt & Thompson, is presumably Eleazer Orcutt, the same potter mentioned by Lura Woodside Watkins as having worked at South Ashfield, Massachusetts. It is almost easier to believe that there were several Eleazer Orcutts than that one man could have been at all the potteries associated with his name—from Poughkeepsie to Portland, Maine—but maybe he just couldn't stand still. At any rate, Ketchum indicates that on August 1, 1831, the association of Orcutt & Thompson was dissolved.

There is little information to go on in assessing the articles on pottery from Ohio and Illinois at the end of the following section.

We can safely assume, however, that the covered "sugar crock" at the lower right-hand corner of page 139 is dated some fifty years too early and might just as well be a butter tub. The application of large leaves and branches is a technique normally associated with the last quarter of the nineteenth century or even later. The relief eagle design on the jar at the center of the same page was produced by making a mold from the side of a lacy-glass salt dish of the sort pressed at Sandwich, Massachusetts. Both the jar and a salt of the type mentioned are now on display at the Henry Francis du Pont Winterthur Museum in Winterthur, Delaware.

General books on stoneware that the reader may wish to consult include *Decorated Stoneware Pottery of North America* by Donald Blake Webster and *Early American Folk Pottery* by Harold F. Guilland. An interesting book on a specific area of stoneware is *The Jug and Related Stoneware of Bennington* by Cornelius Osgood.

WARNE & LETTS STONEWARE JUG (*1806*) AND CROCK (*1807*)

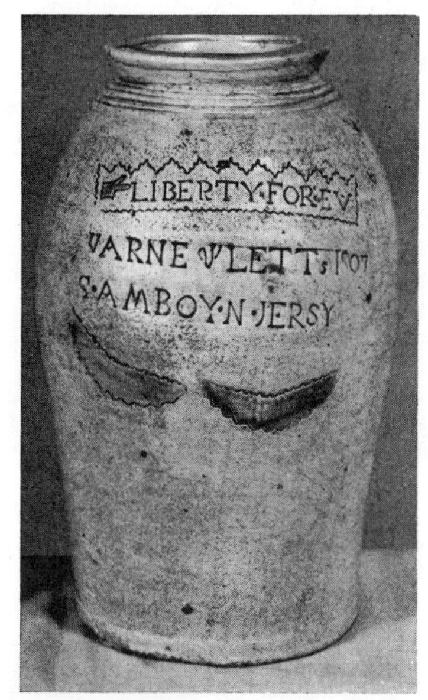

STONEWARE CROCK (*dated 1807*)

Characteristic Warne & Letts inscription with motto in serrate border and holly leaves below.
From the collection of George S. McKearin; all other illustrations from the author's collection

WARNE & LETTS STONEWARE CROCKS

The first exhibits a neatly impressed decoration about the neck. The third is unmarked, but characteristic

The Pottery at Huntington, Long Island

By Mrs. Irving S. Sammis

[*The illustrations, after photographs made especially for this article by Mr. Roger Whitman, show specimens in the collection of the Huntington Historical Society, unless other ownership is indicated*]

A GENTLE slope to the water's edge, with the warmth of a westering sun upon it and with sheltering hills rising abruptly beyond it to the east—this, in a far-off day, a man of vision looked upon, and, finding it very good for his purpose, founded there the Huntington Pottery. And the name of this man? I do not know it, nor can I tell you the date of his coming, but he came to supply the needs of a people.

He was by no means the first maker of pottery in Huntington town. When the Museum of the American Indian* recently opened its doors to the public it included in its collections Indian relics gathered within a few miles of this spot, and, among them, fragments of vessels wrought from the native clay by the red men and decorated with designs picked out in the soft clay with pointed sticks.

But from 1653 there came drifting into this region from New England, and from settlements both east and west on Long Island, people of the stock of England, that land so rich in adaptable clays that the supply still seems inexhaustible after the drain of centuries. And it was natural that in new and virgin conditions these settlers should begin to look about for signs of the clays with whose uses they had long been familiar. Search as he would, the English settler never found clays of the quality of those of the homeland. But such as he found were put to use. That, in time, the trustees of the town recognized a value in its clay beds, is shown by an agreement, under date of October 22, 1751, by which Adam States of Horse (Lloyd's) Neck might take white clay at one shilling per cord for five years from East Neck, the bounds being "from a walnut sapling on ye side of ye bank to the eastward of Jehiel Seamer's northerly to a rock near low water mark to carry away as much as he can gitt to ye west of said bounds he not to make practice of selling to any other man." Probably Adam States needed clay for making bricks for building purposes at Horse Neck.

*155th Street and Broadway, New York City.

If clays could not be mixed to produce porcelain, they must be made to do what they could for the supply of household needs; and it was then that our man of vision appeared. Perhaps he had been a potter in England; perhaps a workman who had helped to turn New England clays into acceptable utensils. At any rate, on that acre of ground at Huntington Harbor the huge hewn timbers were set up for the building that remained the heart of the pottery through all the years of its existence. Later it was added to at either end; the original kiln gave way to two new ones, both of which were, in turn, rebuilt. The main building was two stories in height, and that, with the two kilns, finally covered a tract fifty by one hundred feet in extent.

The years of disturbed relations with England, prior to and during the Revolution, saw so little of household wares brought here that the potter of that period even successfully attempted cups and saucers, but none has survived, and I must believe that, as table ware, such pieces were rather sorry specimens, something about "grapes of thorns" and "figs of thistles" being applicable in the case.

Fig. 1 — Owned by Mrs. John F. Wood.

Fig. 2 — Owned by the Huntington Historical Society.

Fig. 3 — No. 1 owned by Mrs. John F. Wood; No. 3 by the author.

Fig 4

We reach the time of existing deeds to that pottery acre in 1805, when Jonathan Titus and Sarah, his wife, on the 27th day of February of that year, transferred land, messuage, and everything pertaining thereto for the sum of $250.93 to four men, who evidently felt that there was opportunity for prosperity for more than one in the pottery business. These men were Timothy Williams, Scudder Sammis, Samuel Fleet, and Samuel Wetmore. During the spring of the same year (1805) Timothy Williams deeded his quarter interest to Moses Scudder for $65.25—an advance of $2.51—and for some time these men did business as Samuel J. Wetmore & Co.

After twenty years, in 1825, we find Moses Scudder, who presumably had bought out the other three owners, deeding the property to Benjamin Keeler, who, with his wife, Sarah C., in 1827 deeded it to Henry Lewis and Nathan H. Gardiner.

There is pottery extant bearing the marks "Lewis and Gardiner," "Lewis and Lewis," and "Lewis" only, which show the variations in proprietorship during twenty-seven years to 1854, when Henry Lewis deeded to I. Scudder Ketcham and Francis Hoyt. These men were not potters, but owned the property while it was operated by Ketcham's son-in-law, Frederick J. Caire of a Poughkeepsie pottery, whose name appears on the ware made during their period of nine years

In 1863 Ketcham and Hoyt deeded to the three Brown brothers—George, Thomas, and Stephen, who also had come to Huntington from Hudson River potteries. Later, Stephen and Thomas left the firm, and George W., son of George, entered it with his father. The name, however, continued to the end as Brown Brothers.

Work in the Huntington Pottery finally ceased in 1904; and in 1918 the last of the pottery buildings was removed.

All of these owners had to secure leases from the town trustees for dock privilege against their property. Those of 1805 and 1825 are especially interesting as showing us that the only road to the north from the head of the harbor in those days was the sandy right-of-way at the water's edge.

The earliest wares of the Huntington Pottery were made from the common, local, red, brick clay,* which, after being mixed and ground and worked to the required smoothness, was turned into shapes of many sorts and sizes. Smudges of darker colorings, brown or black, were applied irregularly for decoration. Later, the dried forms were dipped into a wash of fluid clay, which usually contained red lead, and these, after successful firing, came out in rich red shades, sometimes a veritable mahogany in tone, the decorative splashings adding, by contrast, to the richness of appearance. This ware was thick, rather soft, and easily broken; yet, fortunately, choice examples of it still exist.

When we find in our Court Records as early as 1658 disputes as to ownership in "a but of rum and a pip or 2 of windes" which Mark Megs was called upon to help unload when he "ware a weding of indian corn," and when we further study the daily and "occasional"—social, business, political, and religious—customs of the people, we know that liquid-tight vessels were a necessity. Hence in dipping the pieces of pottery into the glazing bath care was needful that the bottom within be thoroughly covered. Yet for its final plunge the vessel must be held somewhere. As a result, the bottom, outside, was left a veritable heel of Achilles, and many specimens show an unglazed rim near the bottom, where not quite enough of the lead glaze adhered to run down and wholly cover the sides.

*As many as half a dozen brickyards have existed at one time and another within as many miles of the pottery.

Fig. 5

Fig. 6 — Owned by the author.

Pitchers must have been in great demand, but pitchers, alas, are exceptionally subject to disaster on account of projecting handles and lips, even when one has not partaken too freely of the contents of pipe or butt. Greatly do we rejoice in a perfect example in a rather light shade of the old red ware, the cloudy splashings of a lovely brown, its height eight inches, its great age indicated further by a deterioration of the glaze in spots which was hardly noticeable when we first knew it, some twenty-five years ago. (*Fig. 4, No. 3.*)

A pitcher this that has unquestionably seen the light in three centuries, from whose unchipped rim the glaze has been smoothly worn by many rubbings, and at whose lip it is easy for a sympathetic ear to catch the murmur—

"My Clay with long Oblivion is gone dry;
But fill me with the old familiar Juice
Methinks I might recover by and by."

Fine examples of the old ware in darker red are the graceful, broad-mouthed jar (*Fig. 1*), and the straight-sided ones (*Fig. 3, Nos. 1 and 2*) which could tell us delectable tales of the rich preserves they have served to family and guests in their day:—quinces and pears cooked slowly to a clear, rich red, quite worthy of the jars that were to hold them.

Number 3 of Figure 3 is a mixing-bowl, nearly four inches deep and eleven in diameter. Its edge is somewhat chipped and its inner glaze badly worn from the vigorous stirring of many a spoon, but its black-splashed outside is handsome still.

Iantha Sammis of Huntington was married to Abner Chichester on the 26th of August, 1813, and the beautiful old red crocus jar (*Fig. 2*) was made for her before her marriage and bears her maiden name, scratched through the glazing clay before firing, between the two lower rows of creases. No doubt the fair Iantha loved flowers; perhaps she had so buried bulbs and patiently turned them to the sun that they had bloomed for her through holes cut in a rude box. Perhaps she knew better than the potter who fashioned this jar for her that, for all its distinctive beauty, a glazed jar without bottom vent for drainage might not develop crocuses successfully, and that, when her hearth fire died out at night, if the damp earth froze, her fair jar would be ruined.

At any rate, it gives no sign of hard usage and we thank its gentle owner for the care that preserved it for us.

Experience in the mixing of clays, together with the bringing of better sorts from a distance by means of the little freighting boats that sailed Long Island Sound, resulted, about 1800, in the making at Huntington of so-called stone ware, gray in color, often decorated in blue, fired in specially built kilns to a flint-like hardness, and adapted to many forms.

I look upon Figure 5 as a miracle—a fourteen-inch, five-gallon crock, which bears the stamp of *Lewis and Gardiner*. Its handles are heavy rolls of clay attached to the crock only at the ends, so that the fingers may slip through them in lifting it, and they are as sound as on the day when the crock came from the kiln, nearly a century ago. I once saw a crock of perhaps two-gallon capacity with handles like these, but it has disappeared from my knowledge. That was the only other pair of such crock handles that I have ever encountered.

Figure 6 shows a smaller *Lewis and Gardiner* crock, blue-flowered, and not exactly true, but "did the hand then of the potter shake?" No matter! And beside it stands another, a shade over two inches in diameter, two and one-quarter inches tall, bravely decked with a rich blue band around the top and with a spray of blue below it; and this was the toy of a little girl who was born in 1829. The Huntington Pottery never did neglect the children.

That gray stoneware made wondrous jugs—such tall and shapely and enduring jugs, such gloriously capacious

Fig. 7 — No. 1 owned by the author.

Fig. 8 — No. 2 owned by Miss Carrie E. Brown.

Fig. 9

jugs! It was a smaller relative of some in our collection (*Fig. 8, No. 1*) that figured in the reminiscences of a little boy of the early half of the last century. This jug must go at regular intervals to be filled with rum at the cross-roads store, a mile or two away; and the boy was trusted, with the jug in a basket on his arm, to ride a certain horse, guiltless of saddle, on this important mission. It was his joy, as soon as the barn was left behind, to plant his bare feet firmly on the horse's back, and so standing, steadied by the bridle, to gallop to and from the store, always making the journey without disaster to boy or jug or rum.

Figure 9 gives a satisfactory exhibition of individuality—a twelve-inch jug swelling to an almost equal diameter, and with a bottom broader in proportion than was common to the jugs of its period; for the potter intended this to perpetuate in its decoration the gallant sloop *Dread of Huntington*. So he must have room to outline her hull in seemly fashion, and here we see her with swelling main-sail and jib, every stick and line and seam carefully scratched, and emphasized with blue. These small-bottomed jugs, in spite of a wicked tendency to upset and waste their precious contents, persisted into the Brown Brothers' period, but they were eventually discontinued in favor of the safer broad-bottomed type of the familiar little brown jug of song, and commerce.

It is because they represent expression of individuality by the potters, that I call attention to a group of gray stone crocks (*Fig. 7*). The first, with its rolled handles attached at top and bottom, and standing staunchly—if not gracefully—out at the sides, has its decorative blue applied in a point of scallops not unlike those produced by the crochet hooks of the potter's female descendants a generation or two later. The potter who turned the second had a steady hand and an eye for grace. He carefully incised the outline of his design before applying the blue. The small third, adorned with its thrifty blue tree of no known variety, has perfectly straight sides, with no sign of rim or roll at the top, such as was common to most crocks, early or late.

I have seen an inkwell of the gray ware which had the name of the owner, I. Platt, scratched upon it in script before firing. We often come upon the name Isaac in the records of the Platt family, and the inkwell no doubt belonged to one of these.

The earthenware that developed along with the stoneware at Huntington was of varying shades of brown, these differences as well as the variations in the glaze depending much upon the firing. Pieces packed closely in the kiln and smaller pieces that were placed inside larger ones for economy of space were all affected in appearance thereby. Here are two interesting brown jugs (*Fig. 10*), and with them a soap dish of a light brownish shade, practically without glaze, so hard that it remains unblemished after unreckoned years of hard service in kitchen sinks.

A good deal of the earthenware produced by Brown Brothers had a decidedly reddish color, yet when any of it is put beside a piece of the early red ware the differences are so apparent that no one should ever confound the one with the other.

Processes in Huntington were, from the beginning, naturally, much the same as in potteries elsewhere. The clays were mixed and smoothed to proper consistency in a grinding pit, where carefully-set knives attached to a revolving frame, operated by horse power, reduced the mass to uniformity. Six wheels were in use at once in the Huntington Pottery during the period of its heaviest business, both floors of the main building being used for the purpose. Besides the pieces that were thrown on the wheels, certain others, such as covers for crocks and the all-bottom

Fig. 10 — No. 2 owned by the author.

Fig. 11

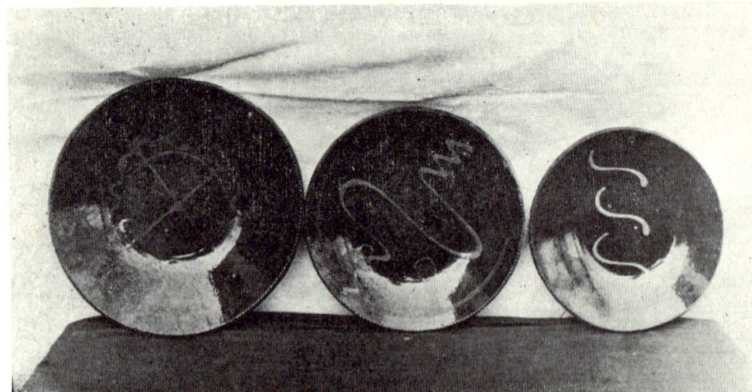

Fig. 12 — Owned by Mrs. George W. Scudder

Fig. 13 — Owned by Mrs. L. G. Carll and Mrs. John F. Wood.

pie-plates, were shaped from molds of plaster of Paris, or red clay.

Figures 12 and 13 show the round and oblong pie plates, rich in memories of mince, pumpkin, apple, and meat pies, and the deep, round one of Figure 13 is forgiven its worn appearance for the sake of the steaming, juicy, crusty clam pies it has held. These pie plates were made by rolling a mass of clay much as pie-crust is rolled, except that the roller had a gauge at either end to bring the flattened clay to an even thickness.

After rolling, the yellow decoration was applied and the sheets of clay put aside to dry further. When at just the right state, a sheet was placed over the red clay mold, pressed firmly down to shape it, and the edge trimmed round. Next, the upper surface was flowed with the glazing bath, which was not necessary for the bottom, and the plate was ready for the kiln.

The firing of a kiln remains today, as it has always been, more or less of a lottery, and the kilns at Huntington Harbor were no exception. They were about twenty feet in diameter, with walls four feet in thickness, the packing space being about twelve feet across and six in height, the flues converging at the top and their chimneys extending to a considerable height above the roof. They had eight fire-holes each, which were fed with coal every thirty minutes for twenty-four hours, then with wood every fifteen minutes for twenty-six hours. In summer about fifty hours were given to the cooling before the kilns could be opened. Less time for cooling was required in winter.

The stoneware, which had no glazing bath, acquired its glaze from the use of salt, which, after coal and wood had done all they could, was thrown on the fires.

Besides the near-by brick clays that were used at first, the pottery made use of clays found at Little Neck, Crab Meadow, West Neck, Cold Spring Harbor, Hog Island, Glen Cove, Perth Amboy, and the slip clay from Albany. In addition to articles already mentioned, water kegs, churns, stove-tubes, soap dishes with perforated false bottoms, hanging and standing flower-pots—plain and fluted, with their saucers; pipkins, bean-pots, toilet vessels, bowls, etc., were made at Huntington. But in common with all other such potteries, the business was encroached upon by the manufacture of granite-iron or enamel ware until, towards the end, flower-pots constituted the only output.

East, West, and South the teams of the pottery owners carried their wares through the length and breadth of Long Island, supplying the general stores. By boat, too, these wares went to some of the island coast villages as well as to the Connecticut shore.

Brown Brothers were very obliging to those who wanted to express their own ideas with pottery. Pitchers or other chosen shapes, when dried to the proper condition, would be turned over to them that they might scratch away the brown slip and bring out designs in the lighter body color, after which the pieces were fired. Some customers designed special shapes, which the potters would turn for them, after which they would decorate them in such fashion as they pleased. But no attempt was made by the firm to produce "art pottery" except in this way—to individual order. (See *Fig. 4, No. 2*, and *Fig. 14*.)

For myself, I would not exchange my old red jars, with their cloudy markings of brown and black, for any of the so-called "art pottery" that I know. And if you are so fortunate as to own such a jar, fill it for a season with your blossoms, from the daffodils and dogwood of springtime to the dahlias and chrysanthemums of fall, and you will agree that it has a beauty worthy of your love.

Whether red, or gray, or brown, the handiwork of the generations of Huntington potters is a heritage to be treasured, for their work has ended. Daily, as from the beginning, the light of a westering sun falls warmly on that gentle slope that stretches to the water's edge, but gray roofs and towering chimneys no longer welcome its rays. The Huntington Pottery is but a memory.

[Note — The foregoing paper was read at the December meeting of the Huntington (Long Island) Historical Society, of which the author is the president.—Ed.]

Fig. 14 — No. 2, owned by Mrs. Helen Jones.

Batter Jugs and Potters' Souls

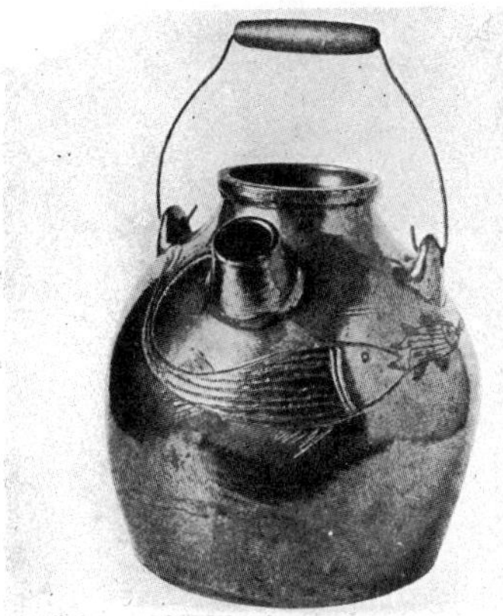

Some among the Attic circle may recall a jug of brown glazed clay with scratch decorations pictured on the cover of Antiques for May, 1924, and unfortunately described as a molasses jug. Subsequent discussion disclosed the fact that this utensil was in reality a batter jug, designed for the deliberate and perfected incubation of the buckwheat cake; though certain authorities were inclined to recognize its probable warm-weather utilization as a reservoir of cheer for workers in the hayfield. Though the specimen in question was procured in Connecticut, there remained question as to its origin.

Not long since, William Goedecke of Richmond Borough, New York City, forwarded to the Attic a photograph of a jug in his possession, which bears some evidence of having been made by the same potter that turned out the previously published example. The size of the two examples and the color of their glaze are apparently the same. Major and minor forms, particularly the shape of the ears and spout, are virtually identical. But specially worthy of note is the fact that Mr. Goedecke's jug is emblazoned with a pictorial scratch decoration which reveals the very same hand that delineated the fish of the early Attic example. More than this, the artist potter has inscribed his name, a laurel wreath, two American flags, and the date 1847 upon the inviting brown surface of his handiwork.

John Austin, 1847, is the inscription. Who John Austin was, where he worked, why his fancy turned so readily to fish, and why in 1847 he inscribed his name amid patriotic emblems upon a batter jug, the Attic knows not. But it is a fair guess that Austin, like other citizens of the Republic in 1847, was experiencing the thrill of exciting news from Mexico. General Taylor had celebrated Washington's birthday with the Battle of Buena Vista. Little more than a month later the armies of the United States took Vera Cruz by storm, and, in April, General Scott's victory at Cerro Gordo brought the end of conflict within sight.

AN AMERICAN POTTERY

The painting shown is interesting not so much for its esthetic qualities — which are not prodigious — as for its subject matter. According to some handwritten notes attached to the back of the picture, the group of buildings shown is a nineteenth-century pottery on Long Island, New York. When these notes were written it would be impossible to say. They have every semblance of age and were presumably affixed when the painting was done. That date, too, is problematical, but let us say, at least for the sake of argument, "mid-nineteenth century." The notes read as follows:

Sterling Pottery, built at Green Hill (Greenport) 1819, by Austin Hempstead and once one of the largest industries on Eastern Long Island, and supplied the early inhabitants with many useful utensils still to be seen in many old households, from the ever acceptable oldtime Pie, to the little Brown Jug. The manufacture of Flowerpots commenced with the arrival of Grant Thorburn in America followed by others in the Florist and Seed business.

Stone ware was added with great success in later years, and some of its wares will continue to compete with the arrowheads and Indian relics, down through the centuries to come.

Its many useful wares were peddled between Occobog and Oysterpond (now Riverhead and Orient) by James Osborn, with-in an Ox cart and a yoke of Oxen. No cash in circulation in those early days so the trade was mostly barter, grain, candles, wool, flax, pork, home knitted stockings, fresh ground meal and flour were among the many returned things to the factory which made it a sort of supply house from which many came after things.

A samp mortar for pounding corn was here provided free for all and its constant thud on the two last days of the week and into the night was a familiar sound as the L.I. Sunday dinner was being prepared.

Available references make no mention of a Sterling Pottery, or of Austin Hempstead, potter. John Ramsay's *American Potters and Pottery* lists a pottery at Greenport, New York, "c. 1850; stoneware; no mark," but gives Greenport as in King's County, on the western end of Long Island. If that location is correct, the pottery cannot be that in what is today Greenport, at the far eastern end of the island in Suffolk County. Here is a matter for students of American pottery to investigate.

Sterling Pottery, Green Hill, Long Island (*c. 1850*). By an unknown artist. Size, 24 by 18 inches. *From the collection of Harry Stone.*

Remmey Family: American Potters

By W. Oakley Raymond

Fig. 1 (top, left and right) — Stoneware Jar Stamped "J. Remmey. Manhattan-Wells New-York"
Obverse and reverse. The singularly abstract decoration on the reverse is incised with a free and vigorous touch. The character of the impressed lettering on the obverse suggests a relatively late date during the règime of John Remmey third.
From the collection of Madame Elie Nadelman

Fig. 2 (left and right) — Stoneware Jar and Cover, Stamped "J. Remmey, Manhattan-Wells New-York"
Somewhat earlier than the jar of Figure 1, as indicated by greater delicacy of the stamped letters and the more slender form of the vessel itself. The only early Remmey piece preserved by direct descendants of the family, but probably by John the third.
Owned by Mrs. Lillian B. Remmey

Note. The author will appreciate additional information accompanied by definitive references. He would also call attention to his article *Unmarked New York Pottery: Crolius and Remmey*, published in the *Antiquarian* for January 1930.

The major potteries of early New York were in the hands of two families — that of Crolius and that of Remmey. Each of these families was established in the country by a pioneering German ancestor from the neighborhood of Coblentz on the Rhine, where the art of potting had flourished for centuries. Each, again, produced in this country generation after generation of potters who not only were skilful in their art, but were able to turn their talents to profitable account. The saga of the Crolius tribe has already been adequately sung. It is time now to celebrate the achievements of the Remmeys.

While the first Remmey to land on these shores apparently hailed from Germany, his genealogical tree was doubtless rooted in France. We can trace these roots through Alsace-Lorraine into Picardy, whence they were torn by anti-Huguenot demonstrations and transferred to a safer soil. But the tradition of notable French antecedents was never forgotten by the Remmeys. Even as late as 1822 John Remmey the third amplified his witnessing signature on the marriage certificate of his daughter with the name *Jean de St. Remy*.

The first Remmey to come to America was John Remmey — whom we shall call the first. According to the family Bible, he was born in the town of Neuweid, on the Rhine, in the year 1706, came to New York in 1735, and presently began making pottery. His establishment was located just outside of the Indian stockade at Collet's fresh-water pond. The district, to become known as Potter's or Pot Baker's Hill, lay due north of the present New York City Hall. The Crolius pottery was on adjacent land.

Fig. 3 — Two Unmarked Crocks Ascribed to Remmey
One incised with swag and pendant design; the other with an elaboration of the incised ornament on the reverse of Figure 1. Probably by John Remmey third.
From the author's collection

No sooner had Remmey placed his business affairs in order than he took unto himself a wife, Anna Christina Corselius, whose sister Veronica had married the potter William Crolius. Three children were born to John and Anna. The first was a boy, John Remmey the second, who saw the light in New York, March 11, 1738. Twin girls followed in 1745. John Remmey the first died in 1762, leaving his pottery business in the hands of his only son and heir.

John Remmey the second was worthy of his father's trust. According to John Spargo in *Early American Pottery and China*, he operated the pottery almost, if not quite, without interruption throughout the Revolutionary War, and "when peace was at last restored . . . partook of the ensuing prosperity." Like his father he died untimely, in his fifty-fifth year, according to the family Bible. Being an industrious man, he had, in the course of thirty years, not only operated the pottery but married Elizabeth Albright and begotten a brood of nine children. Of these the second was a son, born March 29, 1765, who was duly christened John.

John the third appears to have been a man of exceptional attainments. He was but twenty-two years of age when he married Catherine Dobbs, daughter of Captain William Dobbs, for whom Dobbs Ferry is named. Ten offspring blessed the union. John the third participated in the War of 1812 as captain in the Eleventh Regiment Heavy Artillery, later a part of New York's pride, the famous Seventh. In 1817 he served as Assistant Alderman of the Sixth Ward in New York City, and was thereafter known as Alderman Remmey. He was, further, a man of literary tastes and accomplishment. Edwin Atlee Barber in *Pottery and Porcelain of the United States* emphasizes this aspect of the man. Remmey, he tells us, not only wrote a book on Egypt and contributed editorials to the current newspapers, but was a book collector whose library was considered the finest in New York. He dabbled in astronomy. Last, but by no means least, John Remmey third is said to have been a good potter. After operating the old works on Potter's Hill for some years, he changed their location to a site on Cross Street opposite Reade Street. His home was a large mansion at 9 Cross Street directly opposite the Crolius residence.

Life must have been pleasant for John Remmey third and his family. Somewhere about 1820, however, its serenity was disturbed by financial reverses. Remmey had endorsed the note of a friend, in whose eventual failure his own fortunes became seriously involved. In the upshot, he lost his business and his precious library. Thus in the third generation after the family's advent in America, the Remmeys ceased to figure in the potting history of Manhattan. Before that time, however, sundry individuals among the manifold progeny of the three Johns had established themselves as successful potters in other localities. They will be considered in subsequent installments of notes.

Fig. 4 — Motives for Brushwork Decoration on Remmey Stoneware
These odd figures in singles, pairs, triplets, and series, painted in cobalt blue, are accepted as the equivalent of a New York Remmey signature. They have been called dancing figures, which is perhaps adequately descriptive. They occur once on a South Amboy item from the pottery operated in New Jersey by the son of John Remmey third

Fig. 5 — Remmey Jars Showing the Cobalt-Blue Motives
Ordinary and probably late examples.
From the author's collection

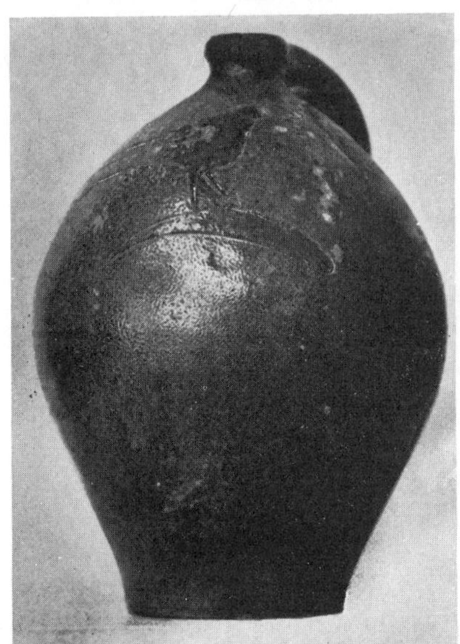

Fig. 6 (left) — Jug Ascribed to Remmey
A quite impressive item, unmarked. Apparently a trifle earlier than the jar of Figure 2. But note similar subtle spring of the outline near the base, apparently characteristic. Note, too, the incised leaflike form on which the robin perches.
From the author's collection

Fig. 7 (right) — Jug by C. Crolius
Compare with Figure 6. The Crolius ware is less stocky in form and more delicate, almost effeminate, in decoration, than the Remmey productions.
From the collection of Walter H. Powers

Remmey Family: American Potters

Part II

By W. Oakley Raymond

Fig. 1 (left and right) — Stoneware Pitcher with Incised Decoration Emphasized with Cobalt Blue (*two views*)
By Henry Remmey for Muvy P. Hall, who was a Doylestown, Pennsylvania, woman. Perhaps "Muvy" is an affectionate contraction of "Mother," and the pitcher a tribute of regard to an elderly matron rather than a sentimental offering to a maid. At the time Henry Remmey was middle-aged and married. The long, tapering neck and rotund body of the pitcher are characteristic. *Height,* 9 ½ inches.
From the collection of Judge H. E. Pickersgill

In following the history of the Remmey family of potters we must now retrace our steps to 1770, the probable birth year of Henry Remmey, fourth offspring from the marriage of John Remmey II and Elizabeth Albright. Evidently Henry learned the potting business in the paternal establishment. He married and became the father of one child, a son, Henry Harrison Remmey, born in 1794.

Sometime before 1810 Henry, with his son, migrated to Philadelphia, where on his own account he established a pottery at Marshall Street near Girard Avenue and began the manufacture of stoneware. The date of this undertaking is assumed from the statement of Henry's great-grandson Robert Henry Remmey that the earliest known marked piece produced in the Philadelphia works bore the date *1810*. From the same source Barber probably derived part of his notes on the Remmey pottery, which may be found in *The Pottery and Porcelain of the United States (1893)*.

Henry inherited the Remmey family gift for a masterful handling of his materials. A fine example of his personal handiwork is the pitcher illustrated in Figure 1. The piece carries the following dedication incised in script letters: *Muvy P. Hall/ by her frendd/ Henry Remmey.*

That Henry Remmey's style as a potter carried over into his son's régime is proved by the handsome pitcher of Figure 2, which bears the impressed mark *H. Remmey Baltimore.* Its sharply pointed snout forcibly reminds one of the similar snout on a small covered jug marked *Crolius, 67 Bayard Street, New York.* The latter piece, here also illustrated, may have suggested the form employed by Remmey. On the other hand, the credit of its devising may be awarded to Remmey. The two comparable pieces are of similar date.

Fig. 2 — Stoneware Pitcher of the Remmey Baltimore Period
An interesting piece with handsome floral decoration incised, and painted with cobalt. Mark impressed. *Height,* 12 ¾ inches.
From the collection of George S. McKearin

Like Joseph Henry Remmey, who moved to South Amboy, Henry freed himself from the major forms and decorative devices characteristic of the ancestral New York enterprise and almost immediately developed his own individual modes. The tendency was further emphasized by his grandson Richard Clinton Remmey, most of whose works may be identified at sight — an ususual circumstance.

Henry Harrison Remmey

Henry Harrison Remmey, already mentioned as the only child of Henry, was born in 1794 in New York City. On June 21, 1825, he married Catherine N. W. Bolgiano (*1802–1872*), daughter of Francis W. Bolgiano of Baltimore. Of Italian extraction, Bolgiano had emigrated to this country in the 1700's and taken up the baker's trade. Henry Harrison Remmey died at an advanced age in Philadelphia, January 18, 1878. Of his five children, the second, Richard Clinton, succeeded to the pottery business.

Evidence drawn from the Baltimore directories makes it certain that Henry Remmey, founder of the Philadelphia works, sought to command two profitable markets by placing his son Henry Harrison in charge of a Baltimore branch. In the local directory for 1818 we find the entry, "Henry Remmey, Potter, North End of Happy Alley, Fells Point." Again, in 1822–1823 the directory lists, "Henry Remmey, Stoneware Factory, N. W. corner of Bond and Pitt; dwelling Bond, West side, south of Bayard." But in 1824 the directory gives us for the first time, "Henry Remmey Jr. Stoneware Factory, Wilk, east of County Fell's Point."

Whatever the father's purpose in entering the Baltimore market, he either found, or presently developed, plenty of local competition. Charles Varle in his *View of Baltimore (1833)* remarks, "There are eight potteries in Baltimore. They have improved much in that art." This may help to explain why by September 25, 1835, the birth date of Richard Clinton, second child of Henry Harrison Remmey and his wife Catherine, we find the couple in Philadelphia. From that time on we hear no more of the Baltimore venture. Meanwhile, Henry Senior had been mending his fences at home by a process of business consolidation, as may be judged from the following advertisement published in *The Philadelphian* for May 23, 1828:

OLD STONEWARE ESTABLISHMENT

Burnett & Remmey, successors to Branch Green, respectfully inform their friends and dealers generally in that article, that they have purchased Branch Green's Establishment, near the forks of Second Street and the Germantown Road, where they manufacture and keep on hand, an extensive assortment of Stone and Earthenware, of a superior quality, and will supply orders of any amount, as low as any in the City. All orders left at J. Thompson's Drug Store, Cor. of Market & Second Street, or at Read and Gray's China Store, Market Street, third door above Fifth, will be punctually attended to.

N. B. — Country orders will be carefully packed delivered in any part of the City.

Jan. 12

Fig. 3 — Crolius Jug (*1817–1837*)
Marked *Crolius, 67 Bayard Street, New York.* Decoration in relief. The general form of the pitcher, particularly its sharply pointed snout, is not unlike that of the preceding Remmey example. *Height,* 11 inches with cover.
From the New York Historical Society Museum

Fig. 4 — Stoneware Jars, Brush-Decorated in Cobalt Blue
Unmarked but characteristic of Richard C. Remmey.
From the author's collection

Richard Clinton Remmey

We now reach the third generation of potting Remmeys in Philadelphia in the person of Richard Clinton Remmey, whose advent has already been recorded. Richard Clinton was twice married. His first wife was Agnes Smith (*1839–1882*), a Philadelphia girl, who, having borne four children to her husband, passed on to make way for a successor, Sarah Elizabeth Kaestner, her husband's junior by sixteen years. Sarah, though she gave her husband but one living child, reached the age of seventy-one, surviving her spouse by eighteen years.

Richard Clinton Remmey was a man of business ability and artistic initiative. *The Philadelphian* (*1898*) pays him the tribute of a lengthy biographical note, from which we extract the more significant features. Richard was educated in the public schools of his native city, Philadelphia. Associated at an early age with his father's business in "the manufacture of chemical and Bristol glazed stoneware," he assumed full management of the business in 1859. At the time he was but twenty-four years of age, but already married. His father, whom he succeeded, was sixty-five, but, following his retirement, lived to the ripe age of eighty-four. When the shift of management from father to son occurred, the Remmey pottery was considered one of the leading establishments in America.

In June 1896 the main plant on East Cumberland Street was destroyed by fire, but was promptly rebuilt on a larger scale, and was equipped with the latest machinery. All told, it covered some thirteen acres of land and controlled its own clay beds at Woodbridge, New Jersey. According to *The Philadelphian*, Remmey's chemical wares and bricks were world famous and preferred by industrial concerns both in the United States and in Europe.

Richard Clinton stamped many pieces of his stoneware with his initials R. C. R. over PHILA within an elongated octagon, as shown in Figure 5. Never, in so far as we know, did he use any other mark or signature. His domestic items in this ware are notable in form, with high necks predominating in both pitchers and crocks — a carry-over from Henry Remmey's distinctive manner. The decoration was chiefly, if not entirely, executed in cobalt blue applied with a brush in a gracefully sweeping featherlike design. It is the unfailingly consistent character of their shape and decoration that renders Richard Clinton Remmey's products so clearly recognizable.

Fig. 5 — Stamp of Richard Clinton Remmey: Actual Size

Probably due to the steadily widening market for chemical wares, and brick, Richard Clinton, between 1865 and 1870, gradually abandoned the manufacture of domestic stoneware, and devoted himself to the larger, and commercially more important, field in which he was an acknowledged scientific expert and industrial leader. Following a long and honorable family tradition, Richard Clinton Remmey retired in favor of one of his sons at the time of the latter's marriage. In this instance, the heir presumptive was the third child, Robert Henry Remmey.

Fig. 6 (right) — Three Stoneware Jars by Richard C. Remmey
The *R. C. R.* mark occurs on the item at the right. All characteristically brush-decorated in cobalt blue.
From the author's collection

Robert Henry Remmey
(*1866—*)

Robert Henry was married in Philadelphia, October 26, 1892, to Elizabeth Johanna Grauch, a Philadelphian. As already noted, in the same year he succeeded to his father's business, with which he had already been associated. In 1904, following the father's death, he took his brother John Bolgiano Remmey into partnership. Meanwhile, the East Cumberland Street factory, which in 1896 had been destroyed by fire and rebuilt, was again burned. This catastrophe may have encouraged the selection of a new factory location on the Delaware River at Hedley Street, a convenient point for shipping. Here the Remmey family continues operations under the corporate name of Richard C. Remmey Son Company. Robert Henry Remmey, Sr., is now inactive, but three of his seven children carry on. They are Robert Henry, Jr., his father's second child, born October 17, 1895, in Philadelphia; John Grauch Remmey, the fourth child, born October 11, 1900; assisted by a younger brother, George Bickley Remmey, the sixth child, who is ceramic engineer to the company, but not an official.

The making of stoneware pots, pitchers, and other domestic wares is for today's enterprise but a distant memory. The present generation of Remmeys are great industrialists, whose output no longer consists of individually hand-wrought objects of a minor art. The scientific investigator and the engineer have supplanted the simple craftsman. The potter's wheel, turned by foot power, and the wood-fired kiln have yielded place to huge pressing machines and giant furnaces generating temperatures that would have terrified the potters of an earlier era. The product is fire brick and other refractories, silicon carbide bricks, fire clay, high-temperature cement, and plastics. Refractory blocks weighing from seven to eight hundred pounds each are turned out in innumerable shapes to meet varying requirements. Only an extraordinary foresight capable of visioning the trend of affairs, a courage and resourcefulness that could assume fresh responsibilities and make new adjustments without dismay or confusion, have enabled the Remmey business to survive during two centuries. That each succeeding generation, building on the foundations laid by its fathers, has not merely survived but has added prosperity to prosperity constitutes something hardly less than a miracle of consistent family achievement.

Fig. 7 — Three Richard C. Remmey Pitchers: Unmarked
Narrow necks and bulbous bodies. Characteristic decoration.
Example at the left from the collection of Mrs. Isabel Ackerman; others from the author's collection

Note. The author will appreciate additional information accompanied by definitive references. He would also call attention to his article *Unmarked New York Pottery: Crolius and Remmey*, published in the *Antiquarian* for January 1930.

The New Jersey branch of the Remmey family of potters will be discussed in a later issue of Antiques.

Fig. 8 (left) — Richard C. Remmey Pitcher: Unmarked
A handsome and well-preserved piece showing characteristic free and graceful brush decoration. *Height*, 8 ½ inches.
From the author's collection

THE CHEESEQUAKE POTTERIES

By ROBERT J. SIM and ARTHUR W. CLEMENT

THE VILLAGE OF CHEESEQUAKE is inconspicuously located at the head of Cheesequake Creek in the town of Madison, New Jersey, which was a part of South Amboy until 1869. Some of the finest stoneware clay deposits in the United States were discovered at an early date along the banks of Cheesequake Creek and a number of potteries were built there. Three of them are known to have operated in the village of Cheesequake. The site of the oldest is on the south side of the present Cheesequake-Matawan highway, to the west of the residence of George Matey, its present owner. All that remains of the pottery is a few scattered bricks and a mass of fragments of discarded stoneware.

According to information obtained in the neighborhood, much waste material from this factory dump has been carted away to fill local washouts; but when excavated the layer of potsherds, wads, and batts was found to be a foot or more in depth over an area many square yards in extent. The shards are all of salt-glazed stoneware of several color shades (*Fig. 1*). The outside glaze is even more variable including dark brown. The inner surfaces are gray or have a slightly toasted appearance, but some have a dark brown slip. The fragments in the eastern (and apparently older) side of the dump have slip decorations in bluish or blackish gray. Those from the western side have various brush-on designs in bright deep blue, ranging from cobalt to nearly ultramarine.

Only ovoid-shaped crocks, jugs, or jars were found. The tops of all the jars had turned-over rims, usually with two or more raised lines just below. No jar lids were found, nor any jar neck with an inside shoulder for supporting a drop-in lid. Of hundreds of handles examined, none pressed against the necks of the jars. Most are the round, horizontal, loop type, though many jars had flattened and ribbed handles attached vertically.

To judge from the fragments, the articles produced in greatest numbers were jugs, two-handled jars, chamber pots, and beer mugs—each in several sizes. There were shallow and deep bowls with curved sides, flat-rimmed plates, soup plates, colanders, spouted field jugs, and thin cups with handles. No recognizable part of pitcher or tankard with pinch-spout, or "pour," was found.

The jugs tapered to a slightly flaring base usually with two or three encircling raised lines above it. The shoulders were noticeably sloping and the necks rather long. The mouth was ringed with a rounded lip, just below which was usually a single impressed encircling line. The upper end of the handle was flush with the mouth.

Nearly every article was decorated with blue, gray, or poured in narrow lines and small dots from a slip cup. Most favored decorations are the coiled spring and dotted fish-scale motifs. Free-hand incised designs ornament some pieces, most of them filled in with blue. There were geometric patterns, plants and flowers, strange-looking fowls and animals, or still more impossible human figures. Only one each of stamped and cogglewheel decorations was found.

A number of shards with initials, names, words, and dates were there. These are in "printed" letters or script, brushed on or scratched on. Only the years 1775 and 1776 are represented. One large jar was covered with writing but only *Daniel Holmes . . . September the 23 1775* could be deciphered. No maker's name or trade mark has been found on any of the fragments we have so far discovered.

Enough fragments were found to reassemble several heavy beer mugs (*Fig. 3*). The smaller ones held a tumblerful, the large ones a quart. All had straight sides sloping inward slightly from bottom. The handle's placement, near the middle of the mug, made for better balance. A group of raised encircling lines near the base and a similar group an inch or more from the top left a median space which was decorated with designs applied with brush or slip-cup, or incised in outline and filled in with black or blue. Scrolls, angular, geometric figures, stylized flowers and plants, birds, quadrupeds, or crudely drawn humans were used.

Except as noted, illustrations from authors' collections.

Fig. 1 — Fragments from Morgan Pottery Site. *Above,* jug necks; pale gray with deep blue or blue-gray decoration. One inscribed *Libberty/1776. Below,* examples of blue decoration. Large bird near left and incised plant near right are dull, dark blue on buff, apparently parts of same jar.

Fig. 2—Jugs by the J. Letts Potter. *Second from right,* decorated with pale blue impressed spread eagle within an oval; above this, two bands of small vertical ellipses used by all potters at this factory.

The ware fired in the kilns of this pottery was not protected by saggars, but was piled end to end and separated with various types of clay wads, batts, or "bobbs." The characteristic scars and unglazed spots left by these sometimes help in identification. Most of the articles were loosened from the potter's wheel with a twisted wire. This left fine parallel lines on the bottom, either straight across or in curves.

A contemporary manuscript record shows that General James Morgan, then a captain in the American army, filed a claim for "1 kiln of Stoneware not burnt" destroyed by British soldiers August 8, 1779. As General Morgan was then a resident of Cheesequake, and as there is no other person who is known to have made stoneware there at that early period, we feel justified in tentatively ascribing the operation of this pottery to him.

Further evidence of the Morgan connection is in a two-handled ovoid gray stoneware jar now at the Brooklyn Museum and said, thirty-five years ago, to have come "from the Morgan pottery." Eleven inches high, it is decorated with a band of light blue "watch springs" identical with the decorations on fragments found at this pottery site at Cheesequake, and the stoneware itself is of the same quality as the fragments. Hence there seems no question that the jar was made at this old pottery at Cheesequake. We have been unable to ascertain the name of the owner of the site of this pottery from 1775 to 1780.

In 1730, Charles Morgan (father of James Morgan), of Monmouth County, purchased from George Leslie of Perth Amboy, New Jersey, property located at Cheesequake and in the neighborhood of Cheesequake Creek. He was living there at the time of his death and his will, dated January 6, 1749/50, divided it among four of his sons. Fortunately, the 1730 deed from George Leslie to Charles Morgan, and the 1750 agreement between his sons by which James Morgan's share in his father's lands was set apart, are on record in Trenton and something may eventually be worked out from them.

James Morgan was the owner of the deposit of clay on Cheesequake Creek known as the Morgan bank, and widely used by other potters over a long period.

We are unable to say when this pottery ceased operation, but General Morgan had moved to Old Bridge, Middlesex County, New Jersey by 1805. July 22 of that year the *True American,* published at Trenton, printed an advertisement that James Morgan, Jacob Van Wickle, and Branch Green, under the name of James Morgan & Company, had established a "manufactury" of stoneware at South River Bridge and were offering for sale stoneware pots, jugs, and mugs. With what we already know, we are safe in saying that the Morgan pottery at Cheesequake is the earliest one in New Jersey from which any piece survives that can be definitely connected with it.

Fig. 3 — One-Quart Mugs. Reconstructed from fragments found on Morgan pottery site. *Left, right:* olive brown with blue. *Center:* pale gray with blue-gray trim.

Fig. 4 *(above)*—Jars from Warne & Letts Pottery. With fragments showing wavy-ear handles from site of that pottery. *Left,* inscribed *S Amboy N Jersy/Warne.* Right, dated *1806;* reverse decorated with cobalt brushed-on flower.

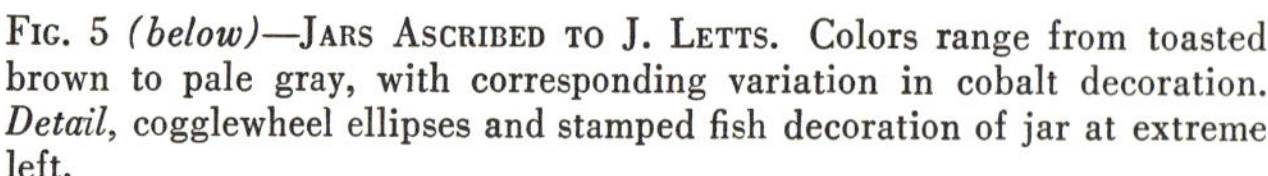

Fig. 5 *(below)*—Jars Ascribed to J. Letts. Colors range from toasted brown to pale gray, with corresponding variation in cobalt decoration. *Detail,* cogglewheel ellipses and stamped fish decoration of jar at extreme left.

The second of the Cheesequake potteries is well known for its crocks marked *LIBERTY FOR EV / WARNE & LETTS 1807 / S. AMBOY N JERSY,* or some variation of that wording *(Fig. 4)*. The site is on the property of Jacob Loesch on the north side of the Cheesequake-Matawan highway, not far from the old Methodist Church, but a considerable part of the surviving fragments was used as fill for the old landing road.

Judging from signed examples and from shards collected near the factory site, the Warne and Letts potters made, in salt-glazed stoneware, virtually every object in that material which would be used in homes and taverns. Much of the hollow ware was ovoid in form; but several cylindrical jars with angular shoulders are extant, and many fragments of such pieces were dug from the ground at Cheesequake. Parts of jugs, jars, flasks, and bottles found there give an idea of characteristics. A few marked pitchers are known.

The pottery made in those works can be assigned to four groups, according to the marks stamped on the pieces: *1, T.W.J.L; 2, T. WARNE Co. SOUTHAMBOY; 3, WARNE and LETTS,* or *WARNE. S. AMBOY; 4, Made by J. LETTS. SOUTHAMBOY.* These makers very seldom used freehand, incised decorations. All but "T. Warne" made use of several impressed motifs stamped with dies, and encircling bands made with a variety of carved cogglewheels. The potter who made the *J. Letts* ware seldom used the name stamp, but his work is distinctive and masterly. It was evidently he who produced the greatest variety of stamp and cogglewheel work (*Fig. 5*).

Fig. 6—Characteristic Pieces By Warne & Letts. Jug, inscribed *Warne & Letts 1806/S Amboy N Jersy;* light gray; the yellowish glaze thick and "curdled" on upper half, making dark daubs green-ish-blue. Jar, uniform brown; the cobalt of the crescents is blackish brown. Virtually all of this early stoneware was probably intended to be gray with blue, or sometimes puce, decorations; weather conditions, smoke, and impurities in the clay caused variations. Black specks caused by presence of iron pyrite ("fool's gold") in the clay are almost always seen in Warne & Letts stoneware. Stoneware ascribed to Morgan is virtually clear of specks.

The *Warne and Letts* pieces are more clumsy in shape. Their stamped decoration was largely limited to a serrate or dentate crescent, while the most often used wheel-made band consists of small vertical panels with a serrate line above and below (*Fig. 8*).

Nearly all hollowware made by the various potters at this factory has several impressed lines just below the top, while the base is either beveled or has one impressed line.

The jars marked *T.W.J.L.* usually have free, horizontal loop handles (*Fig. 7*), while those marked *Warne & Letts* and *J. Letts* usually had handles adherent to the sides of the jar. The latter workman sometimes attached the upper end of a jug handle well down on the neck instead of flush with the mouth. No complete piece with the *T. Warne Co* mark is known to us. On the fragments, the stamped words are covered with a broad, careless smear of blue.

Fig. 7—Jar and Jug Marked "T.W. J.L." *Left,* with typical loop handles. Both dull olive gray with dark decoration which may be maganese instead of cobalt. *Detail,* mark on jar. *From the collection of Charles Evans.*

The exact period during which this pottery operated is not known. Pieces dated respectively *1804, 1806,* and *1807* have been found. We suggest a minimum of 1800-1822 and a maximum of 1785-1830.

The records in the offices of the County Clerk and of the Surrogate at New Brunswick show facts, which, we are aware, conflict with previously published material on the subject. They are obviously at variance with the conclusions drawn by W. Oakley Raymond in his articles on New Jersey pottery in Antiques for March and July 1938 (pp. 142, 30 respectively). Yet we have found no evidence that Thomas Warne who died in 1774, or his son John Warne born in 1773, or Joseph Henry Remmey ever had any contact with the Warne & Letts pottery. Nor have we found any indication that the J. Letts of the pottery was named John Letts. Our data are as follows:

The property was owned at some period prior to October 8, 1813, by Joshua Warne (*1740-1814*). He deeded it to his son Thomas Warne, who was born in 1763 and who married March 5, 1785/6 Mary Morgan, a daughter of James Morgan and a sister of Sarah Morgan who married Jacob Van Wickle, the early potter at Old Bridge, Middlesex County, New Jersey. Thomas Warne owned the property at the time of his death but the date of his death is not known. He is described as "my son Thomas Warne deceased" in Joshua Warne's will dated October 8, 1813.

In June 1814, James Morgan Warne was appointed administrator of the estate of his father, Thomas Warne, and December 3, 1814, he deeded the property to his mother, Mary Warne, pursuant to a court order. June 27, 1815, Mary Warne deeded the property to her father, James Morgan, who owned it until his death in 1822. By his will dated November 2, 1822 James Morgan gave this property to his granddaughter Catharine Bowne, describing it as "one tract of land I bought of James Warne together with the pottery thereon."

Fig. 8—Border Designs. *Left to right: 1,* often used by Warne & Letts. *2,* used by J. Letts, T. Warne Co., and Warne & Letts. *3* and *4,* used by J. Letts.

Catharine Bowne later married William N. Jacques and retained the property until 1839. (Jacob Van Wickle was on February 1, 1827, appointed her guardian.) In 1839, pursuant to court proceedings, the sheriff of Middlesex County deeded the property to Charles Morgan, a son of James Morgan. The slightly inaccurate statement in James Morgan's will that he had bought the property from James Warne (he bought it from Mary Warne who had it from James Warne) is corrected in the 1839 deed which correctly recites that the property had been deeded in 1815 by Mary Warne to James Morgan. A deed dated 1816 from Joshua Letts to James Morgan of another piece of property in the neighborhood refers in defining one boundary line to the "old landing road that leads from the landing to said James Morgan's Potters' Shop." One further item of family history must be noted: November 30, 1805, Meleny Warne, a daughter of Thomas and Mary Morgan Warne, married Joshua Letts, whose name suggests the identity of the J. Letts connected with this pottery.

Some stoneware fragments marked *B LENT* have also been found on the site of this pottery. Of this potter, nothing is known except that there is in a private collection a jug inscribed *Made by B. LENT 1827*. We know also of two jugs with the impressed mark *B. LENT/CALDWELL*. Fragments of stoneware have also been found on this site marked *Vail & Knowles;* of them we have no information.

The third Cheesequake pottery was operated by Noah Furman from 1840 to 1856, when it was destroyed by fire (Clayton's *History of Union and Middlesex Counties*). The site of this pottery is at the edge of the meadows on the Perrine property, a mile or more west of the Cheesequake Inn. Fragments of stoneware examined there indicate that the jugs and crocks were cylindrical in form rather than the bulging egg-shape which prevailed before the 1840's. According to Mr. Perrine, most of the rejected ware from this factory was dumped into abandoned clay-pits, and so is no longer accessible.

Noah Furman owned clay deposits located near Cheesequake Creek and not far from the site of his pottery. He owned also a sloop in which his products were delivered to the New York market. His stoneware is frequently marked *N. FURMAN 39 PECK SLIP N. Y.* A crock so marked, now on exhibition at the Brooklyn Museum, is of a light brown color and has upon its side a graceful spray of black leaves. There is a tradition that the piece was purchased at the pottery at Cheesequake. Because of the New York address inscribed upon many of his crocks, Noah Furman has been supposed to be a New York potter. Proof that he made his crocks at Cheesequake is found on a straight-sided jug now in the possession of John M. Connor of Plainfield, New Jersey, which is marked *N FURMAN SOUTH AMBOY* within an oval.

The village of Cheesequake is now a farming community almost unconscious of its past. Only the stoneware remains to remind us of the skilled craftsmen who worked there over a hundred years ago.

A New Jersey Stoneware Jar

THE impressive stoneware jardinière pictured on this page is so strongly impregnated with nineteenth-century German feeling that it might easily pass for an importation from the Fatherland. Its major reliefs portray the Bacchic vines and the industrious gnomes dear to the Teutonic heart, and even the material — a hard-baked, salt-glazed, grayish-brown clay, in places washed over with cobalt blue — bespeaks the old tradition of the Rhenish potters.

Hence it is somewhat surprising to observe that the impressed mark on the bottom of the piece reads *Haddonfield New Jersey: C. W. & Bro.* For some enlightenment regarding this inscription the Attic is indebted to the generous helpfulness of Mrs. Frances Wolfe Carey of Haddonfield. It is she who has told the Attic that the initials cited are those of Charles Wingender and his brother William, both German born and both trained in their trade among the stoneware potteries of Hoehr bei Coblenz on the River Rhine. When the two brothers came to the United States has not been determined, but if, as stated by Edwin Atlee Barber in an article published in *The Clay-Worker* for February 1896, their first American association was with Richard C. Remmey of Philadelphia, we may surmise the approximate date. Richard, grandson of Henry Remmey, who migrated from New York to Philadelphia about 1810 and there established a pottery, came into control of the ancestral factory in 1859. The advent of the Wingenders must, therefore, have occurred just before, or at some time after, the Civil War, probably the latter.

But the brothers did not long remain in the Remmey establishment, whose primarily utilitarian products afforded little or no opportunity to men of artistic proclivities and experience. As soon as they were able, the pair acquired an old pottery in Haddonfield and embarked on a business of their own. In the article previously cited, Mr. Barber speaks highly of their product, which, he says, represents "some of the best work in the ordinary stoneware body, if not the most original in design, that has been produced in the United States. While their methods are essentially those of the German school, and while they have brought over with them many fine patterns . . . which they are utilizing . . . they are also producing original work of considerable merit." Mr. Barber further observes that the Wingenders were turning out pieces such as fancy flower pots and jardinières easily mistaken for articles of German manufacture. At the close of his discussion he mentions but does not name yet a third brother. The Wingender pottery is still operating in Haddonfield under family auspices, but its output is now confined largely to flower pots.

Fig. 1 — SALT-GLAZED STONEWARE JAR (*late 1800's*)
Grayish-brown with relief decoration against cobalt-blue ground. Except for the rigid egg-and-dart stamping of the surrounding bands, a handsome piece, well proportioned, free in handling, and of almost mediæval dignity. Made in Haddonfield, New Jersey, by the brothers Wingender. *Height*, 13 ½ inches; *diameter*, 13 ¾ inches.
From the collection of Dr. Karl C. Smith

The potters of Poughkeepsie

BY JOHN P. REMENSNYDER

I KNOW OF ONLY TWO published articles on the potters of Poughkeepsie, New York: "Poughkeepsie Was Also a Jugtown," by Thomas H. Ormsbee, which appeared in the *American Collector* for February 1936; and "The Caire Pottery at Poughkeepsie," by Dr. J. Wilson Poucher, originally published in the *Hudson River Magazine* for November 1939 and reprinted in the 1941 *Year Book* of the Dutchess County Historical Society. Both mention a pottery which appears on a 1780 map of the village of Poughkeepsie, and both begin the story of the Poughkeepsie potters with the appearance of John B. Caire in 1840. Mr. Ormsbee (Dr. Poucher concurring) says that although a pottery had apparently existed continuously on the original site, "just what sort of jugs and crocks were made remains a matter of conjecture down to the time when the Caire family came to Poughkeepsie to live and work."

I have not been able to locate that 1780 map. However, a pottery is clearly shown on a map in the office of the county clerk of Dutchess County inscribed *Corporation of the Village of Poughkeepsie Surveyed May 10th 1799 by Henry Livingston.* (Most of the documentary material mentioned here also came from the county clerk's office.) The pottery is located on Union Store Road about 660 feet from the edge of "Hudson's River," or on what is today Union Street extension about halfway between Water Street and the river bank.

I believe that a pottery was established here early in the eighteenth century. So far I have been unable to determine who the first potters were or what they made, though their products were almost certainly bricks and redware. I base my belief in the early existence of the pottery in part on the names which occur on documents relating to the land (later designated as Lots 9 and 10) where the pottery shown in Colonel Livingston's map was located. These include a John De Graff who sold the land in 1766 and who may well have been related to Jan a. De Graff, listed as a potter in Albany as early as 1657 (see Robert G. Wheeler's check list of Albany potters published in *New York History,* October 1944). James Winans and his wife were the purchasers, and the tract remained in the hands of their descendants until by 1804 or shortly thereafter both lots were owned by Elizabeth Winans and her husband, James Reynolds. At this time we do know definitely, from the Livingston map, that there was a pottery here; and I strongly suspect that a stoneware jug in my collection (Fig. 1) incised *Isaac Adriance* and dated *1813* was made there. Adriance is very much a local name (as witness the Adriance Memorial Library), but I have been unable to document my suspicion beyond the listing of an Isaac Adriance in the Poughkeepsie records at this period.

In May 1823 James and Elizabeth Reynolds sold Lot 10 and the northern part of Lot 9 to William Nichols. The sturdy water cooler shown in Figure 4 indicates clearly that Nichols operated the pottery; it is the earliest piece

1

2

3 4 5 6

Fig. 1. Stoneware jug incised in script Isaac/Adriance/1813 on the front, and Adriance [in printed capitals] /1813 on the back. Simple manganese decoration; height 15¾ inches. *Except as noted, all illustrations are from the author's collection.*

Fig. 2. Stoneware jug of early shape marked W. Carroll/Poughkeepsie. Decoration in cobalt; height 11¼ inches. The collection includes a small jar with the same mark. Since no documents have been found to connect Carroll with a pottery, he may or may not have made these.

Fig. 3. Stoneware jar marked J G Ball & Co./Poughkeepsie. Decorated in manganese and cobalt; height 8¾ inches. According to Smith's *History of Dutchess County* (1882), a pottery was established at Poughkeepsie by John Ball about 1820. The collection contains a jug with this same mark.

Fig. 4. Stoneware water cooler marked W. Nichols./ Po,keepsie. Decorated in cobalt; height 15⅞ inches. In 1823 William Nichols owned the Poughkeepsie pottery site shown in a 1799 map of the area.

Fig. 5. Two-gallon stoneware jar marked T. G. Boone & C. / Po'keepsie N Y. Decorated with cobalt; height 11 inches. Boone was in Poughkeepsie from an undetermined date until 1839. In 1840 he appears in the Brooklyn, New York, directory as "Stoneware Manufacturer."

Fig. 6. Stoneware gallon jar marked Po'ke'psie/ W. Reynolds/1. Decorated in cobalt; height 8½ inches. After Nichols' death in 1824 William Reynolds acquired the pottery from his estate, and apparently held it (but without necessarily operating the pottery for the entire period) until 1837.

I have been able to attribute to it. The *History of Dutchess County* (1882) says that John Ball established a Poughkeepsie pottery about 1820, and the jar shown in Figure 3 and a jug in my collection with the same mark are proof that there was such a pottery, though I have not found any other evidence of its existence. Somewhere in here, too, a local pottery was being run by Thomas G. Boone (Fig. 5). According to an article by Preston R. Bassett which appeared in the *Long Island Courant* (publication of the Society for the Preservation of Long Island Antiquities) for March 1965, Boone, who listed himself as "Stoneware Manufacturer," came to Brooklyn from Poughkeepsie in 1839 and operated a pottery there with his sons for a number of years. Stoneware has been found marked with the firm name T.G. BOONE AND SONS and SANDS ST. or NAVY ST., BROOKLYN (the pottery was located at the corner of these two streets). However, there is no indication as to how long Boone had been operating in Poughkeepsie before he moved to Brooklyn, or where his Poughkeepsie pottery was located.

By contrast, the line of descent of the pottery on Lots 9 and 10 is fairly clear. William Nichols' sister Julia was the wife of Nathan Clark, the outstanding early-nineteenth-century potter of the Hudson Valley, whose pottery had been established in Athens (across the river from the town of Hudson) in 1806. Upon William's death in 1824 Clark was appointed guardian of his children, and in that capacity conveyed the pottery and land to William Reynolds (possibly a son of the James Reynolds who had owned them until 1823). One of William Reynolds' well-designed jars is shown in Figure 6.

I do not know how long Reynolds operated the pottery. The 1831 Poughkeepsie assessments list includes the firm of Orcutt and Thompson, whose Rockingham pitcher appears in Figure 7 but no address or occupation is given and there is no way of knowing where their pottery was located; and C.W. Thompson & Co. are listed in the *New York Annual Register* for 1835 as proprietors of a stoneware factory in Poughkeepsie, but the same is true of this firm. In 1837 Reynolds and his wife conveyed Lots 9 and 10 to Solomon V. Frost, who had established a local foundry in 1831 and probably never engaged in the pottery business. In 1839 he sold the property, which was then leased by Mabbett & Anthone (Fig. 8) to William Colson and William Sanderson of Athens and Ed Selby of Poughkeepsie, they to take possession upon the expiration of the Mabbett & Anthone (Antoine?) lease in 1840. The 1839 Poughkeepsie town assessments show Selby, Colson, and Sanderson as operators of a "Pottery Bakery corner Union & Laurel" with a valuation of $1500. The gallon jug shown in Figure 9 carries the firm name of Selby & Sanderson. I know of a jug marked SELBY & COLSON POUGHKEEPSIE, and I have a two-gallon jar marked WATSON & SANDERSON/POUGHKEEPSIE. These firms cannot have been very successful: by 1841 the property was back in Frost's hands, and he sold it to Ed Selby and Levi Emigh for $3,750. I have in my collection an Albany-slip-coated jug marked SELBY & EMIGH.

By 1843 the Poughkeepsie directory listed three members of the Caire family as potters on Main Street: John, George, and "Jacob Caire & Co." Levi Emigh and Ed Libby were "potter bakers" on Union Street—the old site—and Henry Stockwell and Abraham Conover were also in the business, on Main Street. There is some confusion here. In 1842 Lilley & Sanders, of whom I have found no other record, had sold their pottery at 141 Main Street to John B. Caire, who had come with his family from Bavaria in 1839. John later conveyed this property to his son Jacob, who conducted the pottery as Jacob Caire & Co. until 1857. However, the stoneware jar in Figure 10 bears the mark of JACOB CAIRE, UNION STREET, so he must have done business at the old stand at least for a while. After this all mention of the Union Street pottery disappears; it may have been abandoned, or the railroad may have bought the site.

Examples of Caire pottery are fairly common. I show three marked pieces (Figs. 10, 11, 12) and it is very possible that the daisy-pattern pitchers in Figure 13, and the scroddle pitcher in Figure 14, are Caire products. Incidentally, Caires were working as potters in other sections as well as Poughkeepsie. Bassett, in the article cited above, says that the Boone firm in Brooklyn employed a Jacob Kair who was "without doubt, another of the Poughkeepsie family who came to Long Island to carry on his trade." He also notes that Frederick J. Caire "of the Caire family, famous potters of Poughkeepsie . . . was induced by his father-in-law to come down to Long Island and operate the [Huntington] pottery as manager."

Early in 1857 Jacob Caire was succeeded at the Main Street pottery by Thomas Lehman and Philip Reidinger (Fig. 15), and for a few months the Caires were not connected with it. However, later that same year Lehman retired and Adam Caire, one of Jacob's brothers, returned to Poughkeepsie (like Jacob and Frederick, he had been plying his trade outside of the village) and joined Reidinger. As Reidinger & Caire they ran the pottery together for twenty years, until Reidinger's death in 1878. After that, until his own death in 1896, Adam Caire was sole proprietor.

Both Ormsbee and Poucher tell a good deal about the products of the pottery under Adam Caire's management. Of particular interest to both were some mugs made offhand for commemorative purposes. Ormsbee mentions one inscribed with the signatures of fifteen members of the Vassar Class of '95; *Eleanor Gedney, 349 Mill St., Po'keepsie* is incised on the bottom of this one. Poucher mentions these mugs, but says regretfully that he has not been able to locate one. He also reports the indignant denial of a member of the Class of '95 that they were used, during class festivities, for drinking beer to the tune of "If it wasn't for beer we wouldn't be here"—a reference, of course, to the source of the fortune with which Matthew Vassar founded the college. The editor of the *Year Book* did find one of the mugs in the Adriance Memorial Library in Poughkeepsie, and appended to Dr. Poucher's article a note to the effect that one of the ladies listed on it identified the group as members of "Professor Salmon's seminar in history." Another member of the class told the editor that these mugs were not official class souvenirs, but were "acquired by girls associated with each other in small intimate groups." I am happy to be able to show here (Fig. 17) the Vassar mug owned by the Adriance Library, as well as another commemorative example. These are far from being the most important products of the Poughkeepsie potters, but they have their own appeal.

Most of the items illustrated here
are currently on display at the
Ulster County Historical Society headquarters
on Route 209 near Marbletown, New York.

7

Fig. 7. Pitcher marked *American/ Manufacture* on one side, and Orcutt & Thompson/ Pokeepsie on the other. Earthenware with Rockingham glaze, molded decoration; height 11 inches (the collection includes an identical pitcher in redware with a dark glaze). In 1835 Orcutt & Thompson apparently had leased the pottery from Reynolds, and were making these nicely molded pitchers in various sizes.

8

Fig. 8. Four-gallon stoneware jar marked Mabbett & Anthone/ Po'keepsie, N Y. Decorated in cobalt; height 14⅛ inches. Mabbett and Anthone (Antoine?) leased the pottery in the later 1830's.

9

Fig. 9. Stoneware gallon jug marked Selby & Sanderson/Po,-keepsie N Y. Cobalt decoration; height 11⅝ inches. This firm apparently operated the pottery between 1839 and 1841.

10

Fig. 10. Stoneware jar marked Jacob Caire, / Union Street, Poughkeepsie. Decorated with cobalt; height 11½ inches. Several Caires, including Jacob, are listed as on *Main* Street in the first Poughkeepsie directory, issued in 1843.

11

Fig. 11. Two-gallon stoneware jar marked Jacob Caire & Co. / Po'-keepsie. Decorated in cobalt blue; height 11 inches. The brushed-on 2 indicates the capacity of the jar, as do similar numerals on other vessels shown here.

12

13

14

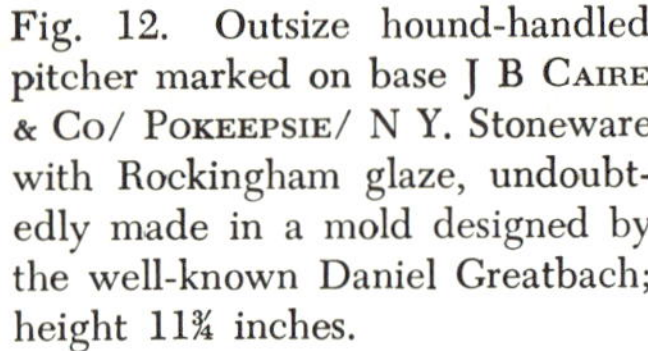

Fig. 12. Outsize hound-handled pitcher marked on base J B Caire & Co/ Pokeepsie/ N Y. Stoneware with Rockingham glaze, undoubtedly made in a mold designed by the well-known Daniel Greatbach; height 11¾ inches.

Fig. 13. Pitchers molded in an allover daisy pattern, marked on base Pokeepsie. N Y. and probably produced by the Caires. *Left*: earthenware; *center and right*: stoneware; all with brown slip; height of tallest, 6⅝ inches.

Fig. 14. Pitcher with gadrooned body; neck molded in daisy pattern. Unmarked, but probably from the Caire pottery. An extremely rare example of scroddled ware; height 7⅛ inches.

Fig. 15. Two-gallon stoneware jug marked Lehman and Reidi .../ Poughkeepsie N Y. Thomas Lehman and Philip Reidinger took over the Caire pottery in 1857 and operated it until Lehman retired in the same year. Cobalt decoration; height 13½ inches.

Fig. 16. Pint container for Post's root beer, a Poughkeepsie product of the late nineteenth century. Unmarked, but known to have been made in quantity by the Caire pottery. Inscribed *Post's* in cobalt blue; height 10⅝ inches.

Fig. 17. Stoneware mugs, unmarked but traditionally made at the Caire pottery. *Left*: inscribed *July 20th/ G.*[?] *H. Ransom/ Apokeeping* [an earlier Indian name for Poughkeepsie] / *Boat Club. Right*: inscribed with the names of nine members of the Vassar Class of 1895—Alice F. Learned, Ida H. Poppenheim, Frances Albee Smith, Christie Hamilton Poppenheim, Julia Swift Arvis, Julia Emery Turner, Mabel I. Jones, Bess Updegraff, Gertrude Witschief—a crude shield containing the year, 95, and an equally crude cipher of V over C. *Adriance Memorial Library, Poughkeepsie.*

15

16

17

GROUP OF STONEWARE from the pottery at Athens. *Left to right.* Howe & Clark, N. Clark, Clark & Fox, E. S. Fox, and N. Clark, Jr. The first and third are gray, the rest are buff; all decoration painted blue. The jug on the extreme right is unusually light in weight.

NATHAN CLARK, POTTER

By JANET R. MACFARLANE

Since 1942 Miss MacFarlane has been Curator of the New York State Historical Association museums, Fenimore House and the Farmers' Museum. She formerly held a similar post at the Rochester Museum of Arts and Sciences.

EVERY SO OFTEN manuscripts come to light which bring new information of significance for collectors of Americana. One such collection is that associated with the Nathan Clark pottery at Athens, New York, which extends the known dates of that firm to cover the nineteenth century. Invoices, broadsides, bills of lading, and letters salvaged from the pottery fifty-five years ago and stored, have just been given to the New York State Historical Association at Cooperstown, where this summer there is an exhibit of the pottery at Fenimore House. These papers, plus records in the Greene County Court House, have established the Athens pottery dates as 1805 to 1900, earlier by several years and later by many years than dates previously recorded.

In 1805—the year that the village of Athens (pronounced Aythens) was incorporated from three smaller villages situated on the west bank of the Hudson River north of Catskill—one Nathan Clark, a skilled potter from Cornwall-on-the-Hudson, came to Athens with his brother-in-law Thomas Howe, also a potter. As Howe & Clark they built on a Market Street lot the kilns and equipment required for carrying on the stoneware business. Various changes in ownership and partnership followed and we have a continuous record of the pottery from the time of Howe and Clark to the year 1892, when the business was turned over to Thomas and Edward Ryan, old retainers and potters who ran the works until about 1900 under the name "Athens Potery." The dates of the various owners are as follows: Howe and Clark, 1805-1813; N. Clark, 1813-1829; Clark & Fox, 1829-1838; E. S. Fox, 1838-1843; N. Clark, Jr., 1843-1892; Athens Potery, 1892-1900.

In 1843 Ethan Fox, who had paid five thousand dollars for the Athens works, resold it to his former partner, Nathan Clark. The latter set up in business his son, Nathan, Jr., under the favorable terms of five hundred dollars capital reduction. Nathan, Jr., continued in the pottery business until 1892, when it was turned over to the Ryans.

After the death of Thomas Howe in 1813, the first Nathan Clark continued alone in the business for sixteen years, during which period he trained apprentices, sending them at the end of their terms to manage and work in branch potteries which he founded at Rochester and the neighboring towns of Lyons and Mt. Morris. Soon he became one of the largest manufacturers of stoneware in the country.

Constant references to loads of "Morgan's best" assure us that much of the clay supply for all of the Clark potteries came from the banks at South Amboy, New Jersey, owned by James Morgan and later by Mrs. Ann Morgan. Some Long Island clay was used and at Athens a native red clay was found, good for jugs and light-weight jars.

One of the most interesting of the documents in this group from Athens is unfortunately undated, but judging from paper, ink, and script it was very possibly written by Nathan Clark. It is entitled "Rules for Making & Burning Stone Ware." The text is as follows:

1st. Let the wheelman be careful to have every piece run exactly true on the wheel. Make them of a kind precisely of the same height & width, have the ware turned light handsome shape smooth inside & outside the bottom a suitable thickness and a good top. 2nd. Let it be handsomely handled & smoothly polished in proper season. 3rd. Let the ware when dry be carefully set in the loft washed and blued. 4th. Let the plats be well made Kiln cleaned out and mended in complete order for setting. 5th. Care must be taken to set the courses plum & one piece exactly over another. 6th. Have your wood in good order raise your fire progressively neither to fast nor to slow examine well & understand the management of your Kiln so as to heat all parts alike, be carefull not throw your wood in the arches to soon or do any other act that may have a tendency to retard the heat, when fit to glaze have your salt dry. Scatter it well in every part of your Kiln (during this act you must keep a full and clear blaze so as to accelerate the glazing and give the ware a bright gloss) stop it perfectly tight and in six days you may draw a good kiln of ware.

Stoneware is made from a clay which burns to a very dense

Decorative Motifs and Dated Pieces. *Left to right,* a Clark and Fox piece, dated *1833;* water cooler, with patch on the side, made during the E. S. Fox period; gray stoneware flowerpot with applied decorative motif of branches and doves, made as a wedding present in 1807; Nathan Clark wine cask; pressed clay plaque with eagle design and dark brown glaze; pressed pitcher of late design; and an N. Clark jug made before 1829.

body at a comparatively low temperature, and colors in the fired body result from carbonaceous matters in the clay. In the Athens pottery colors range from gray to buff and red, the final color tone being derived from a variety of glazes. In this pottery works, as in most, extensive use was made of Albany slip, a good natural glaze formed in beds of laminated Pleistocene clay. Salt glaze, blue-black and brown-black glaze colors, a lead tone, chartreuse, and a tile red distinguish the ware made in Athens. Painted cobalt blue decoration, blue with incised line, and a blistered dark blue turn up frequently. The color of oxide of cobalt, or powder blue, was not affected by the kiln fires and was frequently used for brushing or quilling designs of birds, flowers, or scrolls on stoneware. According to an invoice dated 1820 it was an expensive item, for Clark was billed at five dollars for ten pounds.

The shapes are the usual jugs and jars plus household utensils, druggist's items, wine casks, hookers, water coolers, butter tub prints, soft drink bottles, and five-and-ten-cent beer mugs. Snuff jars, wash bowls, paint pots, pickle and preserve jars, and stove tubes are known to have been made. In 1815 the ten-inch stove pipes were in urgent demand from Albany. Like the stonewares produced by Cushman in Albany *(1805-1825)* and the redware of Nash in Utica *(1819-1820),* the Clark pottery is esthetically sound. The clear bright glazes of some pieces, the handsome shape of others, and the boldness of the design stand out as the work of men who knew their craft. They brought to it a conviction that they were making something more than mere pots and jugs.

The various names under which the firm operated were impressed into the collar or at the base. No other form of marking has been found on the pieces inspected. Raised designs used in the first years of the nineteenth century were made by application of coiled clay to the surface of the jar. The example in the Cooperstown exhibit is a flower pot with applied decoration consisting of entwined branches with a pair of doves, over which is centered the initials of Rhoda Titus of Athens, for whom this piece was made as a wedding present in 1807. Later molded wares gave more leeway in designing, but the results were confused and remain inferior to the early pieces created altogether by hand.

Waterways were used more than any other mode of transportation for moving raw material and distributing finished stoneware from Athens and the three western Clark potteries. Within a few years after production began, large shipments of ware were being made via Erie Canal barge, Hudson River sloop, and by ocean-going vessel to South Carolina and Georgia. The City of Hudson, directly across the river from Athens, was then a great transportation center, and quantities of stoneware, earthenware, portable furnaces, and firebrick from the Athens firm were moved from there. Toll charges were heavy, but so were those on the overland routes.

As Lyons is on the Erie Canal, these local wares and the ones from Mt. Morris on the Genesee Valley Canal were sold on the "boat exchange." Horse and wagon were put on the boat and the pots and jugs were hawked through the streets of the towns along the waterway. Evidently the firm owned its own boats, for an 1836 inventory of the Lyons property includes eight horses, three wagons, harness, and the boat *Water Witch.* Goods in trade sometimes substituted for cash, such as gin and whiskey at Bushnell's Basin, cloth and flour in Rochester.

Towns mentioned in invoices and bills of lading indicate that all of New York State and much of New England was furnished with quantities of pottery, and a broadside of 1837 offers delivery anywhere in the United States.

Wine Casks. The one on the left was made by N. Clark, Jr., between 1843 and 1892. That on the right, by his father, is dated *1820,* and is twice impressed with the words *Cogniac Brandy.*

THE POTTERS OF ALBANY

By ROBERT G. WHEELER

ONE OF THE GREAT CRAFTS CENTERS of early America was Albany, New York. Such names as those of the silversmithing Lansings and Ten Eycks, the pewterers Henry Wells and Peter Young, and the cabinet-maker Duncan Phyfe have become well known. Albany's potters as a group have, however, been largely overlooked, perhaps because their products were common workaday articles, easily broken and discarded and just as easily replaced. Yet Albany pottery does exist. From surviving examples and from old records it is possible to piece together the outline history of a craft seemingly associated with the community from its founding until the middle of the nineteenth century.

Stoneware was the product of the Albany potters. The necessary bluish clays were readily accessible. Recent soundings on Capitol Hill in the city reveal great deposits of this clay saturated with water to a depth of over one hundred feet. At hand also was one of the favorite glazes of the nation's stoneware potters. Albany slip, a common clay found only near the city, was mined and shipped all over the country. The slip, which melted under firing to fuse with the body of the vessel and form the desired glaze, was in use prior to 1800.

The simplicity of the processes involved in making stoneware was another important factor to the Albany workers. Most of their shops were small. Few potters, with the possible exception of Paul Cushman and the firm of Tyler and Dillon, were in business on anything approaching a major scale.

Albany's earliest pottery may well have been one of the first in the country. Records show that in 1653, a Johan de Hulter, one of the partners of Rensselaerwyck (Albany), embarking from Amsterdam, Holland, on a ship called the *Graef,* brought with him to America a number of freemen including several mechanics such as one "extraordinary potter" who intended to settle in the colony. Who this man was and whether he actually made pottery here have not been determined. Certainly no examples of his work have survived the years.

Fig. 1—Two-Handled Stoneware Jug by Paul Cushman (*fl. 1809-1832*). Marked with the potter's name, and decorated with incised birds, flowers, hearts, and flags.

Fig. 2 (*below*)—Stoneware by Paul Cushman. *Left,* jar, carrying potter's name. *Right,* water cooler with incised decoration and potter's name twice. *From the collection of Paul Cushman.*

There was a great need in old Albany for some such experienced craftsmen. As early as 1641, Kiliaen Van Rensselaer, first patroon, had stressed the necessity of finding a competent brickmaker for his colony. Bricks assumed great importance as building material in a region where every stream had banks of clay. Van Rensselaer did not mention pottery in his correspondence, but the colonists undoubtedly required farm and household utensils – pots and bowls made from those same clay deposits. An isolated settlement like Albany, an outpost at the edge of the western wilderness, was forced to be as self-sufficient as possible. It is hard to think that all the stoneware needed to meet growing needs and replace breakage would have been imported from Holland, particularly with a competent craftsman at hand. A list of the household goods of Cornelius Bogardus, September 1666, included no less than five little earthen platters, five great earthen platters, five earthen bowls, four earthen pots, a collander, and an earthen cheesepot.

The existence of this first pottery is necessarily based on assumption. Perhaps Albany's potter made nothing from the clay supplies but bricks. There is definite proof of brick and tile kilns in operation in the community from the 1650's, but as yet no proof of pottery kilns at that period is known.

Indeed, what appears to be the first mention of a specific individual as a potter appears in 1768. Then Stephen Van Rensselaer in defining land boundaries listed a Philip Carner, pot-baker by profession, as living just outside the city. Again working on assumption, it is possible to admit the presence of others. Someone had to be at work to experiment and establish the qualities of the Albany slip as a glazing agent.

It was not until the early years of the Republic that Albany potters really flourished and assumed a craft identity of their own, keeping step with the advance made after the Revolution by potters all over the country. We find one of the earliest advertisements in the *Albany Register,* August 5, 1800, when William Capron inserted the first of the notices that he ran for a year. He announced a stoneware factory, adding this information:

"The subscriber respectfully

Fig. 3—Albany Stoneware. *Left,* jug marked *M. Tyler, Albany/ Manufacturer. Center,* jug with blue decoration marked *Tyler & Dillon/ Albany. Right,* two-handled jar, marked *C. Dillon & Co./ Albany.* Moses Tyler worked independently as a potter in Albany 1822-1826. Charles Dillon did the same 1824-1826. From 1827 to 1834 the two were partners. From 1835 to 1848 Tyler again operated independently, making stoneware and firebrick. The firm of Charles Dillon & Co. continued 1835-1836, and thereafter became Dillon, Henry and Porter.

informs his friends & the public, that he has commenced the manufacturing of STONEWARE, of everykind, in Lyon-Street, one door west of the powder-house; where all commands in the above line, will be gratefully received. Merchants in the country will be supplied at wholesale, on the most reasonable terms."

Not until 1809 did Paul Cushman, Albany's best-known potter, set up shop. He wisely located on "Albany Hill near the divergence of the two great western avenues." Over these two roads passed supplies for the entire western portion of the state. Coshman was in his early forties when he entered this new business. Born in Charleston, New Hampshire, in 1767, he had been trained as a farmer by an uncle. A thrifty Yankee, he had saved several hundred dollars by the time he became of age. With money in his pocket, he left New England, making a circuit through Canada and into western and northern New York. Eventually he settled in Albany. Here he bought a large lot on the river front at the foot of Columbia Street and worked as a contractor. Business was good and in 1802 he married a Margaret McDonald, daughter of a Revolutionary soldier. He constructed a large part of the original wharves on the city's river side and filled and leveled the shore into business streets. Many of his contracts were entered into with Chancellor Livingston. By 1806, the city required his lot for a public market. Thereafter he changed his location and his occupation.

As a pioneer potter on Albany Hill Cushman was successful. He used two clays in making his products: first, brick, usually of a red color, glazed with lead to reveal the color of the body; and second, the bluish clays associated with stoneware, with the glassy glaze produced by salt thrown in the kiln during the baking period. His products were chiefly functional — wide-mouthed jugs and jars used to hold pickles, butter, and brine; bottle-necked ones for milk, cider, and whiskey (*Figs. 1, 2*). Old firm papers and bills list such specific products as one-gallon pitchers, half-gallon pitchers, half-gallon high and low pots, gallon pickle pots, butter pots with covers, churns, ice pots, inkstands, and in one instance that stand-by of our

Fig. 4—Stoneware From the Vicinity of Albany. *Left,* jar with black decoration, marked *N. Clark Jr.* Clarks were active in Athens, New York; Lyons, New York; and Mount Morris, New York, 1820-1890. *From the collection of Miss Lelia Heustis. Center,* five-gallon jar with blue decoration, marked *Haxton, Ottman & Co./ Fort Edward, N. Y. Right,* pitcher glazed with Albany slip, marked *J. Chapman/ Troy/ Factory.* Josiah Chapman was succeeded in Troy by Israel Seymour who worked there 1819-1865. *From the collection of Mrs. Lura Woodside Watkins.*

Except as noted, illustrations from the collection of the Albany Institute of History and Art.

modern corner drugstores, a soda fountain.

Letters show Cushman's need for workmen and reveal that he was not dependent on the Albany area for clay. Writing to A. K. Morehouse in 1829 he ordered forty loads of clay, "as good as Morgan's," to be delivered in Albany. Payment was to be made in merchandise, to be delivered the following spring, of as good a quality "as the clay you send will make."

Cushman marked his products with three known inscriptions: *Paul Cushman; Paul Cushman's Stoneware Factory, 1811;* and *Paul Cushman's Stoneware Factory, half a mile west of the Albany Gaol, 1809*. The gaol, which at this time stood on the north corner of State and Eagle Streets, seems to have been regarded by the potter as a more noteworthy landmark than the old State Capitol. His variety of marks is unusual, and helpful to posterity. Few potters marked their entire output and many never used a fixed mark. An unmarked piece of American stoneware may just as well have been made in Ohio as in Albany.

Cushman died in 1832. The following year his widow sold the pottery to Jacob Henry and Edward Selby, who operated it with Charles Dillon and Nathan Porter under the firm name of Charles Dillon and Company.

Charles Dillon had been listed as a potter before 1825. In 1826 he and Moses Tyler became partners to make the first portable furnaces in Albany. Their stoneware factory at 236 and later at 222 Washington was in operation from 1827 until 1834. A number of jugs can be found today with the words *Tyler & Dillon* and *Albany* impressed on their surfaces (*Fig. 3*). Jacob Henry had operated an earthenware factory on Washington Avenue in 1827, and from 1828 until 1834 had manufactured portable furnaces. Selby, trained under Nathan Clark of Athens, Greene County, New York, soon left Albany to work in Hudson, New York.

As Charles Dillon and Company the men continued the business at 221 Washington and on Hudson Street, west of Eagle, making stoneware and fire bricks until 1840. Then Henry left the firm to manufacture stoneware, fire bricks, portable furnaces, and flower pots at 148 Hudson. Dillon and Porter remained partners until 1842.

In 1842, Orcutt (Eleazer) and Smith (Augustus) took over. Orcutt had worked in Troy, New York, and in Ashfield, Massachusetts, before moving to Albany. He remained with Smith for two years. Smith then formed a partnership at the same location with John Brickner, which continued until 1848.

After 1850 in Albany's potterymaking, as in many other crafts, handiwork and small shops became unprofitable and were abandoned. John Brickner is typical of the small-scale potters. As it became impossible for him to compete successfully with the larger factories which were developing, he combined a grocery shop with his pottery. By 1855 he listed himself as a grocer only.

A check list of Albany potters prior to 1850 has been compiled, giving names, working dates, and the locations of the workers. Some sixty-odd potters worked in the city at various times. Their business peak was reached in 1840 when twenty different men worked simultaneously. After 1840 the number gradually decreased.

The majority were located in the two city blocks bounded by Washington Avenue and State Street, by Northern Boulevard and Lark. Many of the shops were on Spring Street. This was an ideal location. Spring Street, separating the two blocks, was named for the natural springs in the locality. Originally these would have been surrounded with banks of clay. Those first potters, then, had their raw materials, water and clay, conveniently in their dooryards. As other potters were attracted to the block, the clay supply naturally diminished and new sources had to be found, but the established location remained fixed not only in the minds of the buying public but also at the start of the overland trade routes to the West. A check of various sites on Washington Avenue shows a tendency for one pottery site to be used by a number of potters in succession.

This small area of the city must have been a civic sore spot at times. In 1838 in the Laws and Ordinances of the Common Council of Albany it was provided that any pottery upon any lane or street which might be deemed noxious or unwholesome should be considered a nuisance and conditions causing the unwholesomeness should be removed upon notice given by the Police Justice or any Alderman. A fine of $25 was set for each offense. This did much to discourage potting in Albany; larger factories moved to near-by centers.

EDITOR'S NOTE. The check list of Albany potters mentioned above was prepared by Mr. Wheeler and has been published in the October issue of *New York History,* the quarterly bulletin of the New York State Historical Association; it will be reprinted by the Albany Institute of History and Art, from which copies may be obtained for a nominal price.

New York pottery at Albany

Recent acquisitions at the Albany Institute of History and Art include a number of pieces of New York stoneware formerly part of the McKearin collection of American pottery. Illustrated in our first picture, left to right, are a brownish-gray jug, over fifteen inches high, with incised decoration of three large birds and the incised mark PAUL CUSHMAN; a water cooler of gray stoneware shaped to represent a barrel with incised and blue-painted lines for hoops and the incised mark PAUL CUSHMAN; and a cylindrical churn, gray speckled with brown, that has horizontal ribbing and the incised inscription PAUL CUSHMAN'S. STONEWARE. FACTORY. 1809 HALF. A. MILE. WEST OF ALBANY. GAOL. The last two pieces are extremely rare.

A stoneware sander, also shown, is gray with blue decoration and stands less than three inches high. An inscription, incised twice around the stem, reads ALEXANDER COPLIN TROY 1829.

Stoneware made by the White family in Utica, New York

BY BARBARA FRANCO, *Curator of decorative arts, Munson-Williams-Proctor Institute*

THE NAME WHITE should be familiar to collectors of New York State salt-glazed stoneware, for it appears frequently on crocks and jugs with distinctive bird and flower designs. By the time it closed in 1906, White's pottery in Utica had grown to be one of the largest New York State stoneware potteries, distributing wares throughout the state, New England, and as far away as California. Noah White, the founder of the White firm, left Thetford, Vermont, in 1820 and moved west to New York State, living in Vernon, in Lennox, in Westmoreland, and finally in Utica. He is first listed in the 1828 Utica directory as a laborer and later as a boat captain on the Erie Canal.

Three stoneware potteries were already in operation in Utica in the 1820's. The first was built by Justin Campbell beside the Erie Canal soon after it opened in 1825. The second, organized two years later by the firm of Brayton, Kellogg & Doolittle, was also on the canal. The third, not far away, was set up in 1827 by David Roberts. The canal system of New York State provided an inexpensive means of transporting raw materials—clay from New Jersey and slab wood for fuel from the north—which made Utica suitable for the successful manufacture of pottery. The canal also widened the potential market for finished stoneware products.

The directories indicate that in a rapidly growing city like Utica in the 1820's people changed trades frequently. The first Utica potteries were often managed by former merchants. They were small concerns with only two potters working in each shop and probably produced only enough wares to supply local needs. None of the early potteries became firmly established, and between 1826 and 1839 the three potteries changed hands every few years; the former owners either left Utica or went into other businesses.

There is no evidence that Noah White was a potter before coming to Utica, though since he was already twenty-seven years old when he left Vermont, he may have been trained as a potter there. Perhaps he first became interested in stoneware manufacture while working as a boat captain on the canal. One of the two potteries situated on the canal, that started by Justin Campbell, had been bought in 1830 by Samuel H. Addington. In 1834 White is listed in the directories as a "Stoneware manufacturer at Addington's." Three years later he was an agent for Addington and by 1839 he had bought out Addington as well as the adjacent factory formerly owned by Brayton & Kellogg and acquired by Henry and George Nash as early as 1832. The only other firm had already gone out of business, leaving White the only pottery manufacturer in Utica.

Fig. 1. *Left*, cream pot marked N. WHITE, UTICA; 1830-1850; height 9½ inches. *Oneida Historical Society. Right*, jug decorated with blue flowers and a star, marked N. WHITE, UTICA; 1830-1850; height 14 inches. *Collection of Isabelle Bergendahl.*

Fig. 2. Two examples of pottery marked WHITE'S UTICA, with characteristic bird designs in blue; 1850-1880. *Left,* jug decorated with parrot motif and with flaring collar, height 13½ inches. *Bergendahl collection. Right,* crock, height 10½ inches. *Munson-Williams-Proctor Institute.*

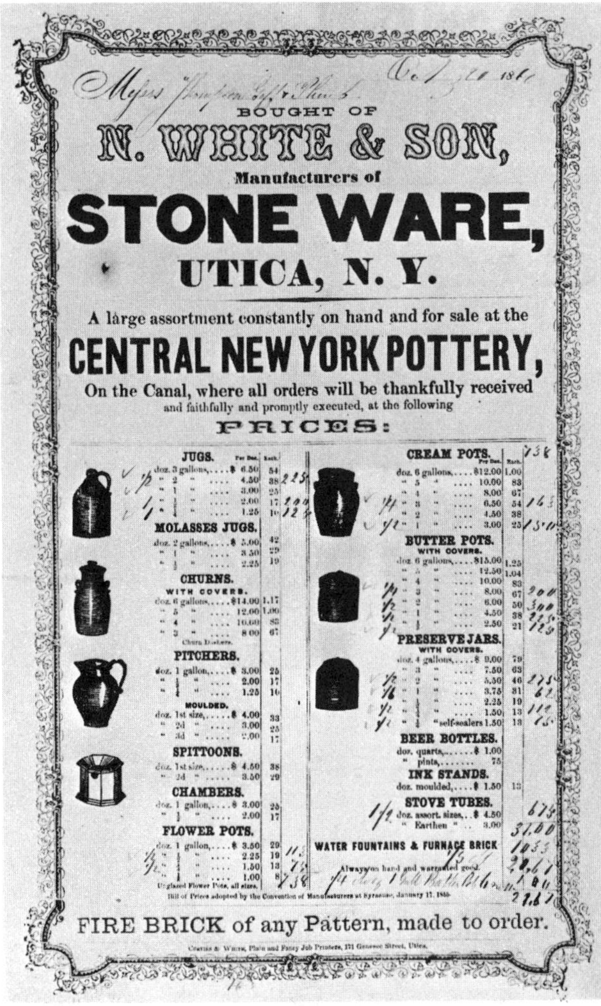

BOUGHT OF

N. WHITE & SON,

Manufacturers of

STONE WARE,

UTICA, N. Y.

A large assortment constantly on hand and for sale at the

CENTRAL NEW YORK POTTERY,

On the Canal, where all orders will be thankfully received and faithfully and promptly executed, at the following

PRICES:

JUGS.	Per Doz.	Each.
doz. 3 gallons,....	$ 6.50	54
" 2 "	4.50	38
" 1 "	3.00	25
" ½ "	2.00	17
" ¼ "	1.25	10
MOLASSES JUGS.		
doz. 2 gallons,....	$ 5.00	42
" 1 "	3.50	29
" ½ "	2.25	19
CHURNS. WITH COVERS.		
doz. 6 gallons,....	$14.00	1.17
" 5 "	12.00	1.00
" 4 "	10.00	83
" 3 "	8.00	67
Churn Dashers.		
PITCHERS.		
doz. 1 gallon,....	$ 3.00	25
" ½ "	2.00	17
" ¼ "	1.25	10
MOULDED.		
doz. 1st size,....	$ 4.00	33
" 2d "	3.00	25
" 3d "	2.00	17
SPITTOONS.		
doz. 1st size,....	$ 4.50	38
" 2d "	3.50	29
CHAMBERS.		
doz. 1 gallon,....	$ 3.00	25
" ½ "	2.00	17
FLOWER POTS.		
doz. 1 gallon,....	$ 3.50	29
" ½ "	2.25	19
" ¼ "	1.50	13
" [illegible] "	1.00	8
Unglazed Flower Pots, all sizes.		

CREAM POTS.	Per Doz.	Each.
doz. 6 gallons,....	$12.00	1.00
" 5 "	10.00	83
" 4 "	8.00	67
" 3 "	6.50	54
" 2 "	4.50	38
" 1 "	3.00	25
BUTTER POTS. WITH COVERS.		
doz. 6 gallons,....	$15.00	1.25
" 5 "	12.50	1.04
" 4 "	10.00	83
" 3 "	8.00	67
" 2 "	6.00	50
" 1 "	4.50	38
" ½ "	2.50	21
PRESERVE JARS. WITH COVERS.		
doz. 4 gallons,....	$ 9.00	79
" 3 "	7.50	63
" 2 "	5.50	46
" 1 "	3.75	31
" ½ "	2.25	19
" ¼ "	1.50	13
" ¼ " self-sealers	1.50	13
BEER BOTTLES.		
doz. quarts,......	$ 1.00	
" pints,......	75	
INK STANDS.		
doz. moulded,....	$ 1.50	13
STOVE TUBES.		
doz. assort. sizes,..	$ 4.50	
" Earthen " ..	3.00	

WATER FOUNTAINS & FURNACE BRICK

Always on hand and warranted good.

Bill of Prices adopted by the Convention of Manufacturers at Syracuse, January 17, 1855.

FIRE BRICK of any Pattern, made to order.

Curtiss & White, Plain and Fancy Job Printers, 171 Genesee Street, Utica.

Fig. 3. Price list of N. White & Son, dated 1860. *Collection of Elma Freeman.*

Combining the two factories, Noah worked with his son Nicholas A. White and two other potters. The early wares of the 1830's and 1840's are marked N. WHITE, UTICA (Fig. 1) and are very similar to the work of the earlier Utica potters. The most common forms are jugs, cream pots, and covered jars, all with ovoid bodies. The cobalt-blue decorations are usually simple, often consisting of only a figure indicating the capacity in gallons, with a flourish beneath.

The success of the White pottery was probably due to sound handling of the business by Noah White and his son Nicholas. Its history is one of constant growth and continued family management. In 1843 the works were expanded and facilities for making firebrick were added. The number of potters was increased to six with the addition of another son, William White, and one other potter. In 1849 White made his two sons partners and changed the firm name to N. White & Sons. The firm continued as N. White & Son after William White sold out his share in 1856 and moved to Utica, Illinois, where he began manufacturing stoneware on his own. When Noah's grandson William N. White joined the firm in 1863, the name was changed to Noah White, Son & Co.

Although the firm changed its name as many as ten times in the course of its history, only five different marks were used. To add to the confusion, changes in marks did not always coincide with changes in the firm's name. Fortunately, dated pots and jugs occur frequently enough to fix approximate dates for the use of the various marks.

The wares made from about 1850 to the 1870's were marked WHITES UTICA or WHITE'S UTICA. Jugs and pots with either form of this mark are characteristically different from the earlier pottery marked N. WHITE, UTICA. They are usually straight-sided rather than ovoid. The collars on jugs are more carefully finished and have a definite outward flare. The decoration, too, has become more refined. Since the mark WHITES UTICA was used for more than twenty years, wares so marked represent various stages of development. The earlier examples have

Fig. 4. Jug decorated in blue with two thrushes on a branch and dated 1864, marked WHITES UTICA; height 18½ inches. *New York State Historical Association.*

Fig. 5. Crock decorated in blue with flowers and dated 1876, marked WHITES UTICA. Y. N.; height 12 inches. The mark here is unusual because the letters N. Y. are reversed. *Freeman collection.*

rounded collars and highly stylized designs done with broad, quick strokes. The later pieces have flared collars and the designs are more realistically and carefully drawn, though still in the free style of calligraphy. A variety of bird designs began to be used in addition to many, and more realistic, flower motifs (Fig. 2). These improvements probably indicate that professional decorators were now working at the pottery. A price list dated 1860 (Fig. 3) gives some indication of the range of wares offered: jugs and molasses jugs; churns; thrown and molded pitchers; molded spittoons; chamber pots; flowerpots; cream pots without covers, and preserve jars and butter pots with covers; beer bottles; molded inkstands; stove tubes; and firebricks.

In 1865 Noah White died at the age of seventy-two, leaving the business in the capable hands of his son Nicholas A. White. The mark remained WHITES UTICA, although the firm's name was changed to N. A. White & Co. in 1866 and then again the next year to N. A. White & Son when William N. White became a partner. Under Nicholas A. White's management, the firm enjoyed its most successful period. During the 1870's the plant was expanded by the addition of a new building and the installation of a sixty-five horsepower steam engine. These improvements marked the transition from kick wheels and hand throwing to steam-powered wheels and molds. Because of this expansion and the subsequent increase in production and distribution, the addition of N. Y. to the pottery's mark became necessary. From about 1876 the mark reads WHITES UTICA N. Y. (see Fig. 5). William

Fig. 6. Crock decorated in blue with eagle and shield, and inscribed *U. S. Amerika/1886*; marked N. A. WHITE & SON/UTICA. N. Y.; height 13¾ inches. The misspelling of the word America is probably due to the fact that many of the potters and decorators during this period were German. *Munson-Williams-Proctor Institute.*

Fig. 7. Three jugs showing sequence of collar changes. *Left,* marked WHITE'S. UTICA.; 1850-1880; height 11 inches. *Center,* marked WHITES UTICA, N. Y.; c. 1876-c. 1882; height 11¼ inches. *Right,* marked N. A. WHITE & SON./UTICA N. Y.; c. 1882-c. 1890; height 11¼ inches. *Munson-Williams-Proctor Institute.*

Fig. 8. Molded water filter inscribed *Perfection Filter/Manufactured by The/Central N. Y. Pottery/Utica N Y;* c. 1890-1898; height 10 inches. *Munson-Williams-Proctor Institute.*

N. White died in 1877 and Nicholas A. White's younger son, Charles N. White, was made a partner in 1882, at about which time the mark was changed to N. A. WHITE & SON/UTICA, N. Y. (Fig. 6) .

From the 1870's on, the pottery employed about twenty people. Although three potters still worked at the wheel and continued to make handles for jugs by the hand process of pulling the clay, many more of the processes had become mechanized. The clay, prepared in rolls two and one-half feet long, was brought up from the basement by conveyer belt and put into the "jiggers" or "pull-down" molds by the mold operators. The next day other workers removed the pots from the molds and finished the bottoms by hand on the wheel. Decorating was done by young girls with artistic ability, working under the direction of a designer. Using brushes, they put freehand designs on the pottery. They also used stencils and added touches of blue to the molded wares. By this time the pottery had a kiln for firebrick and two for stoneware. The stoneware kilns were wood burning and required a full-time wood chopper to supply fuel during firing. Two or three kiln setters specialized in loading the kilns with pottery for firing.

During the 1870's and 1880's, the quality of the wares was maintained and improved. Pottery marked N. A. WHITE & SON/UTICA, N. Y. is usually recognizable by the intensity of the blue decoration, which an 1888 pamphlet, *Mercantile and Manufacturing Progress of the City of Utica,* cites as a specialty of the firm:

In color they are bluish gray with deep indigo blue decorations and in this latter attribute, this firm stands at the head of this trade in this country. Much trouble has been experienced by potters generally in this country in obtaining suitable coloring for their wares, so great indeed has this difficulty been, that some potteries have dispensed with the decorations entirely, sending their goods to market perfectly plain. This firm, however, manufactures their own coloring composition after a process known only to themselves and though frequently offered five times the price per pound asked for in the open market for ordinary potter's blue, they decline to dispose of any, but give their customers the benefit of their investigations in the way of more desirable goods at no advance in prices.

The deep-blue decorations are often fairly elaborate and carefully drawn. Another distinguishing characteristic of the pottery of this period is again found in the collars of jugs (Fig. 7). Jugs marked WHITES UTICA N. Y. have straight-sided rather than flaring collars. The collar was gradually diminished, so that by 1882 it had disappeared and only a small ridge marked the neck.

During Nicholas A. White's management, the firm operated another pottery in Binghamton, New York. Charlotte White, Noah's second eldest daughter, was married in 1843 to William Roberts, a potter who worked for her father. About 1848 the couple moved to Binghamton,

Fig. 9. German-style mug and steins, c. 1899-1906. *Left,* molded mug with buffalo design, marked WHITE'S POTTERY, UTICA, N. Y.; height 4 inches. *Collection of William C. White. Center,* large molded stein with seventeenth-century German figures, unmarked; height 10½ inches. Acquired by the owner while he worked at the White factory. *Collection of Edward Hitzelberger. Right,* molded stein with drinking scene on side visible here and buffalo on the other, marked WHITE'S POTTERY, UTICA, N. Y.; height 6¾ inches. *White collection.*

Fig. 10. Molded pitcher with a hunting scene, unmarked, c. 1889-1906; height 9½ inches. Acquired by the owner while at the White factory. *Hitzelberger collection.*

where Roberts manufactured stoneware for many years. When Charles N. White joined his father's business in 1882, he also took over management of his uncle's pottery in Binghamton, in partnership with George L. Wood under the name White & Wood. This arrangement was continued until Nicholas A. White's death in 1887, at which time Charles N. White became proprietor of the Utica pottery and dropped the Binghamton enterprise. Binghamton pottery manufactured under White's management is marked WHITE & WOOD/BINGHAMTON N. Y. or simply WHITE'S BINGHAMTON.

Charles N. White was the third and last proprietor of the firm, which was called Central New York Pottery after 1890 and then White's Pottery Inc. from 1899 until 1906. Competition from stoneware factories in Ohio and the use of glass containers at the end of the nineteenth century were creating serious problems for White's and other New York State potteries. In response to this competition, White's pottery considerably expanded its range of products to include: firebrick, cupola brick, gas and oven tile, and a wide assortment of molded wares. The manufacture of German-style beer mugs and other fancy molded wares was introduced when a German designer, Hugo Billhardt, was hired as designer from 1894 to 1901. Beer steins with pewter covers became one of the specialties of the pottery, and other molded wares designed by Billhardt were often decorated with German drinking scenes, stags, and hunting scenes, all with a definite European flavor (Figs. 9, 10).

Finally, after seventy-three years of uninterrupted stoneware manufacture, the White family's pottery was forced to succumb to competition and the less skillful management of Charles N. White. By 1907 the manufacture of stoneware had stopped. The firm continued in business as C. N. White Clay Products Co. until 1910 and then closed completely. Nothing remains of the pottery works, which were torn down soon after they closed. Only the pots themselves remain, interesting documents of a craft and of an industry that have now disappeared.

Figure 2 (Figure 1 *centre*)

Figure 3

Ohio Pottery Jars and Jugs

By Rhea Mansfield Knittle

OHIO is noted for its clay products, which range from brick and drain tile to excellent ornamental wares. Toward the close of the eighteenth century, pioneers migrating from the eastern states into the "Western Country" were quick to avail themselves of the variety of clays in which the region abounds. The first potter in Ohio of whom I have record came to the territory from Kentucky in 1795. Somewhat later, artisans from the great pottery districts of Europe were attracted to Ohio, and, during the middle of the nineteenth century, when large industries were being established, East Liverpool became for a time a world centre of potterymaking. Nearly every Ohio county boasted at least one pioneer potter, and the Ohio and Muskingum River Valleys teemed with early little kilns.

Ohio soon produced virtually all the pottery styles and techniques attempted in the coastal states, in many cases improving upon the latter in quality of clay and glaze. For stoneware it developed an ornamentation peculiarly its own. The early glazed earthenware bowls, pitchers, plates, and jars followed, in part, the Pennsylvania German and Swiss traditions and, in part, the Connecticut. *Sgrafitto* decoration on earthenware was seldom employed. Many of the old-world forms and motives likewise found their counterparts in Ohio. The later glazed ware in the Rockingham manner, manufactured at the larger potteries in eastern Ohio between 1850 and 1870, was patterned after the English product, as were the similar wares of Bennington, Baltimore, and Trenton.

Fortunately for us, it was not unusual for an early potter to inscribe his work with his name and occasionally with that of the town where he worked, together with the name of his particular patron. This inscription was customarily incised; infrequently it was applied in brown or blue slip; sometimes it was both incised and applied. Dated pieces are also found. The oldest dated jar of which I have record is marked *1804*.

The accompanying illustrations afford a fairly representative view of Ohio pottery jars and jugs. All the pieces pictured are in perfect condition and each is, in its way, a significant specimen. All but one were found by Earl J. Knittle of Ohio.

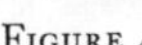

Figure 4

Figure 5

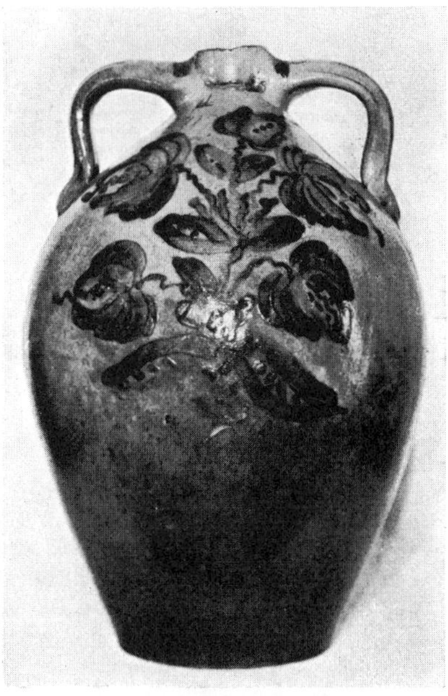

Figure 6

Figure 7

Figure 8

Figure 9

Fig. 1 — Unglazed Pottery Water Jar or Wine Cooler
Very early piece, notable for soft, natural coloring, ample proportions, and effective simplicity of decoration. Clay of blended tones of buff and a warm gray. Neck and shoulders incised with narrow reeding. Bunghole has no surrounding ornamentation, an unusual feature in Ohio water or wine jars. Sole decorative motive consists of incised and applied sheaves of wheat upon a raised circular medallion on upper part of body. *Origin:* Northeastern Ohio.

Figs. 2 and 3 — Remarkable Gray Stoneware Wine Cooler, Heavily Salt-Glazed (*1856*) (*obverse and reverse*)
Elaborate handles, splotched with blue slip and decorated with crimpings and applied buttonlike bits of clay, terminate in five large rosettes, which were applied to the body by squeezing wet clay through a funnel-like device made of heavy linen. Applied strapwork, circles, and impressed starlike forms encircle base and collar of jar. *Obverse:* Ornamented with applied flowers and foliage, hearts, clasped hands, rosettes, some of which are decorated with blue slip. Bung is in centre of a large applied heart, upon and above which are incised tiny houses. *Reverse:* High on shoulder the numeral *5* (signifying five gallons) is formed of applied circular motives. Side of jar is almost covered with large block letters incised and painted with blue slip: MADE BY E. HALL/OF NEWTON TOWN SHIP/MUSKINGUM CO: OHIO./AT W. P. HARRISES FAC/TORY. A HOLESALE AND/RETAIL DEALER IN STONE/WARE. BUCK AND BRECK/TO JOSHUA CITES. The date of the marriage of Joshua Cites, *January 13, 1856*, is scratched on side of jar. The larger letters OHIO cut above base border are likewise ornamented with blue slip. *Origin:* Newton Township, Muskingum County, Ohio.

Fig. 4 — Gray Stoneware Water or Wine Cooler with High-Domed Cover
A decorative piece, heavily salt-glazed, its major ornament washed with blue slip; inner surface is brown-glazed. Square bunghole, at base, is decorated with starlike applications. Name of purchaser, *A. A. Morgan*, blue-slipped on front and back of piece. *Capacity:* 3 gallons. *Origin:* Formerly stood in an early tavern in McConnellsville, Ohio.

Fig. 5 — Very Large Water Jar or Wine Cooler
Mottled buff and warm gray; outer surface salt-glazed; inner surface glazed with Albany slip. Octagonal bunghole protrudes from surface immediately above actual bottom of jar, which is some inches above hollow base. Bunghole ornamented with four imitation screws incised in the clay. Decoration of two kinds: flat blue slip — sprays, and inscription *Anthony Baer / Cleveland / Ohio;* superimposed clay — emblematic ornament composed of upright eagle in oval formed of two horns of plenty and ribbon bearing the words *Ne Plus Ultra.* This device is painted strong cobalt blue. *Height:* 20 ½ inches; *capacity:* 6 gallons. *Origin:* Attributed to one of the Western Reserve potters, a little south of Cleveland; made for Anthony Baer, tavern keeper, of Cleveland.

Figure 10

Fig. 6 — Gray Stoneware Two-Handled Cider Jug, Heavily Salt-Glazed
Obverse: Flowers and foliage painted in rich, cobalt slip in a large, free manner. *Reverse:* Undecorated except for the incised inscription, painted with blue slip, directly below the mouth: *J. C. Smith / Mogadore Ohio. Capacity:* 4 gallons. *Origin:* Mogadore Potteries, Ohio. Butter crocks with similar decoration, from Lancaster County, Pennsylvania, suggest the likelihood of a Pennsylvania-German prototype.

Fig. 7 — Barrel-Shaped Water Cooler of Gray Stoneware
Covered with a fine quality of salt glaze. Four hoops in applied clay encircle the barrel. Top and bottom of piece are solid, with an opening in top for filling, and a bunghole just above base. Incised sun and fish are decorated with blue slip. *Capacity:* 1 gallon. *Origin:* Attributed to Cincinnati, Ohio.

Fig. 8 — Glazed, Slip-Decorated Earthenware Jug
Rough, pitted, brown earthenware body, unevenly washed with a greenish-brown glaze. Opaque white, brilliant green, and black slip applied to each side, down the front, and on the jug's handle. The date of potting, *1831*, appears in glaze on one side. Rare. *Capacity:* 1 gallon. *Origin:* This buttermilk jug was made in new Philadelphia, by potters who migrated from Switzerland to Ohio.

Fig. 9 — Covered Cookie Jar
An outstanding piece, well-proportioned and unusually large. Yellow clay body with rich all-over glaze of mottled brown and yellow slip in the Rockingham (England) manner. Well-executed decoration in high relief, depicting a mythological group on either side of jar. Drooping handles overhang gracefully extenuated acanthus motives. A ring of smaller acanthus leaves encircles sloping rim of jar. *Capacity:* 4 gallons. *Origin:* East Liverpool, Ohio.

Fig. 10 — Harvester's Cider Jug
An exceptionally fine piece. Of chocolate-colored clay, glazed with the same color. The generous handle is ornamented with a heavy twisted vine that at one end merges into finely modeled grape leaves. Decoration in relief: below the spout, a mythological figure, probably a bacchante; below the filler, another female figure; on each side, a large medallion of grape leaves, boldly modeled. *Capacity:* 2 gallons. *Origin:* Attributed to Tuscarawas County, Ohio.

Fig. 11 — Butter or Sugar Crock with Domed Cover
Yellow clay body with rich brownish glaze. Overhanging lid topped by a finial composed of six petals. Handles in similar petal-like form attached above petal motives on the body. *Capacity:* about 10 pounds. *Origin:* Zanesville, Ohio. A typical example of everyday potting, pictured to show the excellence of both form and ornamentation exhibited by the commercial output.

Figure 11

Specimens of Ohio Pottery

From the collection of
Mrs. Rhea Mansfield Knittle

Fig. 1 (left and right) — Two Stoneware Pieces
Water cooler said to have been potted for a frontier tavern at Ravenna, Ohio, prior to 1828, the date of the tavern's destruction by fire. Body of tawny gray; deeply incised decoration colored with cobalt blue, which likewise appears around spigot hole and handle terminals. Attributed to Springfield (now part of Akron), Summit County, Ohio. About 1820–1830. Flower pot with attached saucer. Decoration not incised but stamped with dies. Attributed to Atwater, Ohio, 1835–1850

Fig. 2 — Built-Up Redware, Unglazed
Pottery is usually shaped by hand on a revolving disc, called a wheel; but it is occasionally built up, bit by bit, without turning. Built-up pieces are likely to be less symmetrical in form and less smoothly finished than those made on a wheel. The crude examples pictured were fashioned in Richland County, Ohio, about 1810–1820

Fig. 3 — Deep Bowl of Red Clay
Invested with a brilliant red glaze splashed with yellow. Similar in shape to the bowl in Figure 2, but better potted. This bowl was made on a wheel. From Steubenville, Ohio

Fig. 4 — Superior Glazed Redware
A handsome covered jar whose form recalls the work of New England potters. Red clay with a glistening, almost black, glaze, which owes its color to the employment of manganese. Made by a potter in London, Ohio. A marked duplicate is known.
Open jar of red clay with reddish glaze splashed with black, again recalling New England practice. Well-potted open jar with regularly incised wave decoration. Brown clay with brownish glaze. Precise source not specified. While the dates of the items pictured are uncertain, they are probably prior to 1850

An Excerpt from Early Decorative Arts in Ohio, Rhea Mansfield Knittle

Salt-glazed Stoneware Whiskey Jug. The large round opening with cork stopper is for filling; a small cone-shaped spout on the opposite side, stoppered with a piece of tightly rolled leather, is for pouring. A nameless quadruped with bulging eyes and long barbed tail, splashed here and there with rich cobalt, serves as a handle; it was probably meant to represent the demon rum. Found in the Western Reserve and believed to have been made by one of the numerous stoneware potters in the southerly part of this section of Ohio. Capacity, 2 quarts.

Lead-glazed Yellow-ware Water Cooler or wine jar. With caplike applied handles, and bung-hole near base. Decorated with slip of rich chocolate color. Applied ornament of eagles flanking the shield of the United States, and incised on either side of it the names *Smith & Jones* and *Slago Pottery*. These potters came to Zanesville from the Monongahela River district in western Pennsylvania. The reverse carries the further identification *Zanesville 1804. Privately owned.*

Salt-glazed Brown Stoneware Apple Butter Crock. Cobalt decoration: naturalistic depiction of apples, with letters *OK* above and *OHIO* below, and conventionalized motifs. Lid, perhaps of wood, is missing. Found in northwestern Ohio near the home of an old character nicknamed "OK" after his favorite expression. Capacity, 1 quart.

Cincinnati in 1810: "There are masons and stone-cutters, brick-makers, carpenters, cabinet-makers, coopers, turners, machine-makers, wheelwrights, smiths and nailors, coppersmiths, tinsmiths, silversmiths, gunsmiths, clock and watchmakers, tanners, saddlers, boot and shoemakers, glovers and breeches-makers, butchers, bakers, brewers, distillers, cotton-spinners, weavers, dyers, taylors, printers, bookbinders, ropemakers, tobacconists, soap-boilers, candle-makers, comb-makers, painters, pot and pearl ash-makers." *John Melish,* Travels through the United States of America, in the years *1806 & 1807,* and *1809, 1810 & 1811 . . . Philadelphia (1815).*

Salt-glazed Stoneware Sugar Crock (*probably c. 1820-1830*). Exceptionally large and handsome, potted from irregularly burning tawny-gray clays. Lid is slightly domed, and ornamented with petals in relief; raised knob handle. Rim of lid and base of crock gadrooned. Body of crock ornamented with large acorn and leaf motifs, applied, and with bands of impressed triangular patterns below a wide concave band. Handles intricately modeled in leaf and branch forms. Reverse inscribed in cobalt: *A.B. Lake/ Manufacturer of/ Stoneware/ Zanesville, O.* Such ornately decorated crocks seem to be a distinctively Ohio product. Liquid capacity, 1 gallon.

Lead-glazed Redware Jar, with rolled rim. Glaze irregularly splashed with cream, green, and yellow. Chipped, cracked, and somewhat crazed, this piece was dug up with various fragments near Mansfield, from the site where William Henry Harrison's army camped on its way northward to the Maumee Valley Indian campaign. Redware similarly ornamented is being made in Ohio today. Capacity, 2 quarts.

Cookie Jar. Deep brown stoneware. The handles were made from strands of braided clay.

STONEWARE OF RIPLEY, ILLINOIS

By MARJORIE TAYLOR

Miss Taylor's antiquarian interest stems from both family possessions—which include coverlets made by her great-grandmother with wool from her own sheep—and studies for her master's thesis on American trends (1790 to 1850) reflected in domestic arts and crafts.

Dog Doorstop. Deep brown stoneware. Showing resemblance to the Staffordshire dogs, examples of which must have been seen by Ripley potters. Stofer and Leach made such doorstops, and in all likelihood other firms produced them too.

Ripley, in Brown County, Illinois, was an important midwest "jugtown" from the time the first pottery was taken from the kilns in 1836 until the last was fired in 1913. Ten years after the town's first settler, Willis O'Neal, migrated there from Kentucky, he happened to meet John N. Ebey, a potter from Huntington County, Pennsylvania, on his way to Rushville with a load of his wares. Ebey spent the night with the O'Neal family, and the following account of this visit was published in a history of Brown County in 1882:

> During the conversation in the evening, which related to his calling, the manner of manufacture, and the kind of clay necessary to the same, someone present stated he had discovered from a tree turned up by the roots in the neighborhood, a clay that fairly answered the description given by Mr. Ebey. On the following day Mr. Ebey was taken to the place mentioned, and on investigating, it was found to be a superior quality of potter's clay. Mr. Ebey returned home, and immediately commenced preparations to remove to Ripley, which was effected the same year, 1836.
>
> A shop and kiln were soon erected, and the first pottery manufactured in the town was taken from the kiln late the same year. This was the starting point that has made this town so famous as one of the most extensive manufacturing towns of pottery in the west.

In 1847, L. D. Stofer, a merchant and manufacturer of stoneware, moved to Ripley from Summit, Ohio, and established two shops and two kilns, producing about 250,000 gallons of ware annually and employing 25 men. After his death his wife sold both potteries, one of which brought $600 in October 1891. Adam Stofer and William Shields, partners

Typical Ripley Stoneware Jugs and Jars. **Brown glaze. Note unglazed lid on third from left.**

in the new enterprise, announced their intention of manufacturing stoneware on a large scale.

The year 1848 saw another pottery established in Ripley by Francis Marion Stout, born in Kentucky in 1823, who had taught school in Illinois for three or four years. His son, Isaac Newton Stout, with whom he formed the partnership of F. M. Stout and Son in 1878, sometimes stenciled *I. N. Stout* in cobalt blue on his salt-glaze products and in yellow on his brown ware.

New potteries continued to be set up. In 1849 Charles W. Keith, a plasterer from Harrison County, Indiana, came to Ripley and continued in the pottery business there for about twenty years. Adam E. Martin, a young man of twenty, came from Stark County, Ohio, in 1852, and followed the potter's trade in Ripley for twelve years. The first native Ripley potter was W. H. Hardin, born in 1836, the same year that the first kiln was fired. One of his sons, A. B. Hardin, still lives in Ripley.

By 1870 the Geological Survey reported that "about a dozen potteries have been established in Ripley, and this number may be increased indefinitely as the wants of the community shall require, as the supply of raw material is abundant." By 1888, according to the Brown County history, the annual output was "1,000,000 gallons of various kinds of ware."

In addition to the firms already mentioned, an 1882 list includes F. M. Stout and Son, employing twenty men; Harvey Irwin, seven men; Stofer and Leach, seven men; W. A. Canada, six men; Dennis and Elett, five men; E. Warren, six men; and Crawford and Sons, three men.

Jugs were probably the most popular item, but the Ripley potteries also produced pitchers, snuff jars, fruit jars, cookie jars, crocks, salt jars, churns, and household ornaments such as doorstops. A dark brown glaze was commonly used. Lids for snuff jars were not glazed but left cream color, while those for fruit jars were made of wood, usually linden or bass, and sealed with rosin. The decorated cookie jars are probably the most interesting Ripley pieces.

The pottery business was apparently still booming in 1891, to judge from the following note which appeared in the *Mount Sterling Examiner* in August of that year:

> There has never been such a demand for stone ware fruit jars as at present exists. That is all right since B. C. Vincent and Company have just opened a kiln of nicely burned fruit jars, and can supply patrons with stone ware jars of the very best quality and any desired quantity. Let all who would put up fruit in first-class stone ware call and be accommodated.

Statements continued to appear to the effect that the "stone ware business was good" or that a Ripley man had returned home after delivering a load of stoneware to some neighboring town like Mt. Sterling, Springfield, or Beardstown.

Since there was never a railroad in Ripley, transportation of their finished products was always a problem to the Ripley potters. It was usually necessary to haul their jugs, jars, and crocks across country several miles to a railroad or river, though occasionally the small creek near the village would have sufficient water to make possible loading barges near the kilns. By the Illinois and Mississippi Rivers these barges were sent on down to St. Louis and other cities even farther downstream; according to tradition, one load went as far as Red River, Louisiana. Wares were also carried by peddlers through the countryside to farm wives and merchants in nearby towns, and some people went directly to the potteries to purchase articles they needed.

Through the years there was frequent discussion of the possibility of a railroad to Ripley, but these hopes never materialized. The transportation problem became more and more serious. In the 1890's, when the kilns were fired by coal, the potteries sometimes had to be closed temporarily because the roads were so bad it was impossible to haul in the necessary fuel. The establishment of rival potteries in nearby Macomb, Monmouth, and Abington reduced the demand for Ripley products, and the loss of market added to the transportation problem was a further discouraging factor.

Mechanization resulted in the laying off of many potters. A "large-ware jollie-machine" patented by Gaylord W. Martin on November 2, 1897, made possible the production of larger pots with fewer workmen. Martin peddled these wheels all over the country, and many potters were laid off by firms that installed the Martin wheel.

By 1913 many of those who had been most active in the Ripley potteries were too old to work any more, and the younger men gradually found work elsewhere. Today the pottery shops and kilns of Ripley have all disappeared. Only an occasional jug or pot, ploughed up in the spring gardening, recalls the days when the village was a thriving center.

All illustrations from the author's collection.

Anna, Illinois, Pottery

This pottery porker, his generous curves covered with a slightly speckled dark-brown glaze, measures eight and a half inches from upturned snoot to curly tail. He was designed to serve two purposes, according to the inscription scratched on his left side: *Latest & Most Reliable Railroad & River guide/Compliments of Anna Pottery /With a little good old Rye.* The whiskey bottle's function as guide depends on a maplike network of lines that cover the pig's back, rump, and right side, with identifying names and initials. The railroads are labeled *I C R R* (Illinois Central Railroad); *C & St L narrow Gage* (Chicago & St. Louis); *C & V R R* (Cairo & Vincennes?); *O & M* (Ohio & Missouri?). Along the hog's spine flows the *Miss. River*, and a point on its verge is identified as *St Louis. the future Capital.* Other towns spotted over the swine's anatomy are *Chicago the Corn city, Cincinnati the Pork City, Louisville the falls City, Cairo, Vincens, Centralia, Carbondale, Mound City, Grand Tower, Iron City*, and *Anna Jug City.*

Wallace Kirkpatrick, with his brother Cornwal, was busy turning out clay animals of every description in the late 1800's. One of his pieces is dated *1884*, and his Tweed jug was probably made shortly after Tweed's downfall in 1871. The period following the

STONEWARE JUG SATIRIZING THE TWEED RING

Civil War until the panic of 1873 was marked by extension of railroad lines throughout the Midwest, and consolidation of many short lines. A movement sponsored by the farmers' society, the Grange, resulted in legislation, frequently called Granger laws, establishing railroad commissions in several states. It does not seem far-fetched to surmise that Kirkpatrick's pig, a logical symbol of the farm, may have been celebrative of the passage of the Granger laws.

Paul R. Brustman of the Railway and Locomotive Historical Society has forwarded the following data regarding these midwestern roads:

I C R R stands for the Illinois Central Railroad, which was opened in September 1856. Its name remains the same today. *C & St L* means Cairo & St. Louis. Originally a narrow-gauge road, this line was opened in March 1875, changed in name to St. Louis & Cairo in 1881, and leased to the Mobile & Ohio in February 1886. Its gauge was widened to standard in November 1886. *O & M* stands for Ohio & Mississippi (not Ohio & Missouri), opened in 1857. About 1895 it became the Baltimore & Ohio Southwestern, operated by the Baltimore & Ohio. *C & V R R*, the Cairo & Vincennes, was opened in December 1872, changed to Cairo, Vincennes & Chicago in 1885, and in 1890 to Cleveland, Cincinnati, Chicago, & St. Louis (the present-day Big Four).

These facts and dates should serve to date Kirkpatrick's pig between 1875, when the Cairo & St. Louis, youngest of the roads, was opened, and 1881, when its name was changed.

VI The Potter's Craft

The ways in which American pottery was made are complex and not easily described. Most early redware was made of a clay that remained porous after firing and had to be glazed in order to be made waterproof. The dictionary defines *glaze* as a thin coating of glass. The glazing mix in which the redware was dipped consisted of either powdered sand or clay slip and a lead compound; the ingredients yielded from these materials are essentially those of glass. Since most rural potters had to conserve fuel, pots and glaze were fired together, and both had to mature at the same relatively low temperature; they also had to cool at the same rate, or the stresses resulting would craze the glaze.

With little if any knowledge of the chemistry involved, potting was a business of trial and error. Body colors could vary from gray to orange to brown; glaze, from orange to purple, depending on the amount of oxygen or carbon dioxide present in the kiln. Iron impurities could speckle the surface with brown, or produce round haloes of color in an otherwise uniform glaze. On the other hand, of course, many glaze effects were deliberate, but never very predictable.

Lead for glaze was not mined in many places in the United States—barely 1,000 tons per year before 1810—so lead ore (galena) was not the usual choice of potters; although cheap, it represented a tremendous amount of trouble to prepare. But dry goods merchants everywhere, at least as early as the mid-eighteenth century, stocked and advertised imported red and white lead, ground and unground, as ingredients,for paint, and it was such red lead (lead oxide) that most potters used.

This ingredient must have played havoc with the population when used on tableware, as the thin glaze flaked and small chips could easily be chewed along with the dinner; and, when used for food storage, the action of vinegar or other acid released lethal poisons into the contents. Potters, too, suffered a range of diseases from slow lead poisoning to silicosis, commonly called "Potters' Rot."

The answer to the redware glaze problem was stoneware—made of clays which could be subjected to extremely high temperatures, high enough to be fused (vitrified) into a body which would be dense and non-porous when cooled, and acid resistant when salt-glazed. Such a body was waterproof even without glaze. In glazing, ordinary table salt (sodium chloride) would be thrown in by the handful through ports in the crown of the kiln when the temperature was high enough to almost melt the clay. Several saltings were often the rule, usually at two-hour intervals. In the superheated atmosphere, the salt vaporizes, mixing with water produced in the kiln by combustion or brought in by air. Penetrating into the body of the ware a short distance below the surface, the soda combines with silica in the clay to form a glaze, no longer "salt" but a "soda glass," composed of as many as sixty-two complex sodium-aluminum-silicates—not a superficial skin, but a bonded part of the pots themselves.

The chloride portion rushes up the chimney as a hydrochloric acid fog, so corrosive that it eats away the bricks inside the kiln, often causing them to drip down onto the ware being fired. This accounts for the glassy green droplets that are sometimes found on stoneware, rather than any deliberate act of

Because the practice of stacking stoneware nose to nose and end to end in the kiln allowed no entry for the vapors to do their work and glaze the interiors of crocks and jugs, it was discovered around 1800 that Albany slip could provide all the smoothness and acid resistance required without much fuss or fanfare. It could be shipped dry in barrels and needed only to be mixed with water, and it fired at reasonably low temperatures. Its popularity as a lining grew, and, as time went on, it was used on exteriors as well, burning to a smooth color ranging from blue-black to red-brown. On occasion a pot, covered with Albany slip, might have been included in the kiln with other ware being salt glazed, and this combination could produce colors ranging from greenish gray to, perhaps, chartreuse. (We believe these accidental colors are what Janet MacFarlane is attempting to describe in her article, "Nathan Clark, Potter," pp. 129–130.)

The earliest decorations on stoneware were line drawings incised into the surface while leather-hard, either left uncolored or filled in with cobalt, which was at first brushed on and later trailed on as a thick slip compounded of silica, potash, and cobalt oxide. A manganese purplish black has also been reported on early Remmey pieces; and on Warne and Letts, manganese as well as an olive-brown and green have been seen. A brown slip was sometimes used by Bennington potters to paint flowers on stoneware.

A lively discussion took place in the pages of *The Magazine* ANTIQUES (July and October, 1933) as to why cobalt seems never to have been used on American redware. It can be summed up briefly here: the visual, and maybe the chemical, combination of the cobalt oxide with the lead glaze on the dark red or brown body produced an unsightly black color.

A lack of salt in the South spurred potters from Virginia southward to develop a substitute type of glaze, not used anywhere else in the country. The alkalines necessary to produce such a glaze were supplied by wood ash mixed with water (lye) or by slaked lime, or a combination of both with the addition of some sort of silica-bearing substance such as sand, clay slip, or even powdered glass. The pots were fired covered with a thick application of this mix, which could produce a glaze transparent or opaque, smooth or rough, in colors ranging from celadon to deep black. The drippy wood-ash glazes were sometimes referred to as "Shanghai glaze" and the runny dark brown as "tobacco spit." the earliest date found on a piece bearing such an alkaline glaze is 1827. Note the pictures of Southern stoneware on this page.

Most Southern stoneware was high-fired, but those of the Edgefield District of South Carolina are extremely pure and produced a highly vitrified body. Potters of this district —Collin Rhodes, Abner Landrum, T. M. Chandler, Andrew Devlin—developed a tradition of slip-trailed decoration in brown (which was derived from iron-bearing slips) and white (from kaolin), usually used on "celadon" glazed stoneware.

Two-handled jug from Edgefield, South Carolina. Dated 1848.

Much additional technical information about the potter's craft can be gleaned from *Ceramics: A Potter's Handbook* (1971) by Glenn C. Nelson, and from "The A-B-C's of Good Salt Glazing," *Brick and Clay Record* (September, 1943). Recommended as the best article to date on the subject is "Alkaline-Glazed Stoneware: A Deep-South Pottery Tradition" by John A. Burrison, *Southern Folklore Quarterly* (December, 1975).

Editors' Note: The Peabody flowerpot shown in Figure 2 of "The Making of a Flowerpot" bears a striking resemblance to those attributed to the James Pottery and others of eastern Pennsylvania, in the collection of the Philadelphia Museum of Art.

Having dealt with what American pottery was, it is fitting that this book end with an article on what it was not. The examples of European folk pottery from the Nadelman Museum, which unfortunately no longer exists, are presented to aid the collector in separating American examples from the European forms from which they derived.

Georgia alkaline-glazed pottery. Late nineteenth century.

North Carolina jar, brownish alkaline glaze streaked with white and blue, attributed to area near Hickory. Latter part of nineteenth century.

The Making of a Flower Pot

By Bessie W. Buxton

ONE of the first concerns of our forefathers, when they settled in this country, was the finding of clay beds suitable for industrial uses. First came the making of bricks for building; after that, the fashioning of utensils for cooking and eating. In 1612 brickmaking at Jamestown, Virginia, is recorded, and, in 1629, soon after Massachusetts Bay Colony was settled, Reverend Francis Higginson of Salem wrote, "It is thought here is good clay to make brickes and tyles and earthen pot as need to be. At this instant we are setting a brick-kill on worke to make brickes and tiles for the building of our houses."

Fig. 1 — Flower Pots and Bean Pots Drying Previous to Firing

In 1639, ten acres were given to Lawrence Southwick, Ananias Conklin, Obediah Holmes, and William Osborne to carry on the business of making glass and earthenware. The clay used by the potters was dug in what is now Peabody and Danvers — then a part of Salem — and some of the pits were reserved by the town of Salem for the free use of the settlers in making bricks.

The best clay was found in Danvers; but the pot industry was centred in Peabody. As the colony grew in size, the business increased, until, in 1775, the town boasted fifty-nine potteries. Sturdy men, the potters, ready to play their part in affairs, for "potters make good citizens," and a community of them is proverbially orderly, law-abiding, thrifty, and industrious. On April 19, 1775, the Potter's Company of thirty-four men left their wheels and hurried eighteen miles across country to the battle of Lexington, reaching there in time to harass the British retreat and to leave seven of their number dead on the field of battle.

Primitive methods were used by these early potters. A little water was added to the clay, which was then trodden with the feet until smooth, just as in Biblical times — "As the potter treadeth clay," says Isaiah. If stones were found, they were picked out, although good clay contains few stones. As the years went by, a rude wooden mill was evolved, in which the clay was mixed. An upright post, four feet high, from which extended flat iron blades, was set in the centre of a stationary wooden tub. A long pole was attached to the top of the post. The tub was partly filled with clay; water was added; a horse hitched to the pole walked 'round and 'round the tub. When this churning process had rendered the clay pliable, handfuls were taken out and carried to the bench, where the potter rolled the material into large balls. These were stored in a cellar to prevent their freezing, as frost would spoil the clay and necessitate its regrinding.

Fig. 2 — Early Peabody Flower Pot (*mid-nineteenth century*)
In author's family for more than eighty years. Pie-crust saucer, and rope handles

The early potters could work only in the summer, as it was impossible to heat the rude sheds in which they worked. A century later each potter usually had a little shop, which was sometimes a part of his home, the heat from the kiln warming the house. The ensuing years have brought changes; but the potter's art, one of the most ancient, has yielded perhaps more slowly to industrial change than any other. Until within the last quarter-century, pots have been made very much as they were made four thousand years ago. Now, however, the clay mill is built of iron and is run by electricity. But in the last of the old Peabody potteries, now known as the M. B. Paige Pottery, the potter still kneads his clay by hand, and still "throws his pots on the wheel."

In the morning he brings his clay balls from the cellar — enough for the day's supply. With a piece of wire he cuts a ball in halves, and, throwing it on the bench, works and kneads it vigorously, just as the housewife kneads her bread, and carefully removes every pebble or other foreign substance. When it is thus cleaned, he breaks it into smaller lumps, which he kneads again; then, raising the clay high in the air, he brings it down on the bench with a resounding slap, which drives out the air bubbles. This process is repeated until the clay has reached a proper consistency, when it is rolled into small balls, each just large enough to make one pot or jug. Sometimes these balls are weighed: a four-and-one-half-pound ball suffices for a three-quart pot, for instance. A good potter, however, can judge from experience just how large to make the balls.

The wheel has changed very little from the type in constant use since 4000 B.C. Its size varies somewhat, but the chief alteration is in the motive power. The earliest wheel was whirled by hand; later the foot was employed; and now, in this machine age, electricity does the work. Setting the wheel in motion, the potter lifts a ball of clay from the pile at his right and throws it with force on the smoothly spinning wheel; wets his hands in a pot of water and grasps the clay firmly, making sure that it is exactly in the centre of the wheel. Again wetting his hands, he thrusts his thumbs downward into the centre of the ball and draws the clay upward and outward, shaping it as it whirls. A small, square piece of wood, called a "rib," with a hole in it for the finger, is held against the still whirling pot to smooth the surface. A wet sponge is then substituted to complete the finish, and, behold! — a flower pot.

To remove the pot from the wheel, the potter uses a slender wire, about a foot long, with wooden handles, which he draws just beneath the moist clay. Then the pot is carefully lifted, and set on a long board at the potter's left. When the board is full, it is placed on the racks at the side of the shop, where its burden is left to dry. The "green" ware, as it is called when in this condition, is examined each day to make sure that it is drying evenly. In winter, pots will dry in twenty-four hours, if kept at a temperature of 80 to 90 degrees

Fig. 3 — A Modern Flower Pot
In what is known at the pottery as "Italian style." The work of John Donovan, last of the old-time potters

Fahrenheit; in summer two days or more are necessary, depending on the weather.

When the ware is dry enough to be glazed — and it must be at exactly the right stage, or else its coating will peel off — the glaze is mixed in an earthen pot. Red lead and sand are used for the common red glaze for bean pots. The black glaze, for which the Southwick pottery was noted in 1650, was made by adding lampblack to the red lead and sand; but in modern times oxide of manganese is employed. If a high lustre is desired, copper is included. Blue glaze is produced by adding oxide of cobalt to the basic components oxide of lead, oxide of tin, salt, and sand. Green is achieved with oxide of copper and ammonia; orange, with oxide of iron and ammonia. Pots to be glazed only on the outside are dipped in the liquid glaze, which, before firing, is as colorless as the clay itself. If they are to be glazed all over, the liquid is poured in and whirled about until every spot is coated. After glazing, the pots are again thoroughly dried before firing.

Setting the kiln is a busy time at the pottery. The unglazed flower pots and other hollow forms are nested — placed one inside another — and piled around the sides of the kiln. Glazed pots are separated by little rolls of clay, to prevent their sticking together and being ruined. Hollow ware of all kinds is placed upside down, to catch the heat from below, and each row is placed to cover the spaces between the rows beneath. When the kiln is full, the door is built up with brick and plastered on the outside with clay.

Early in the morning the fires are lighted under the kiln, which is still shaped much like the early Greek kiln. Four firepots, one on each side, are connected by a straight tunnel, which passes through a circular tunnel in the middle of the kiln. Wood is still the favorite fuel, about three cords being used to bake the ware. For six hours the firing is light. Then the heat is increased gradually during the day and night, until, in the early morning hours, a temperature of 1800 degrees is reached. The dampers are then closed, and no more fuel is added. This is the proper heat for flower pots, because Danvers clay will melt if the temperature rises higher. The kiln is not usually opened for forty-eight hours, unless it is necessary.

A picturesque early custom survives even to this day in the last of the old potteries. If the kiln is burned on Friday, Saturday morning finds the neighbors bringing their pots of beans to be baked by the dying fire.

The bean pots are set just inside the furnace on the hot stones, and the potter adds water from time to time, as he goes about his tasks. At the supper hour, the depositors come for their beans, which, baked by this slow heat, have all the delicious flavor of those cooked in the brick ovens of colonial days. In Salem, the small boy of the family was usually sent to the kiln to bring the pot of beans home in a gaily colored bundle handkerchief, which was tied by the opposite corners about the bean pot and thus borne by the knotted handle to avoid burned fingers. These bundle handkerchiefs, still carried by many Salem folk, were introduced by the Lascar sailors from the East Indiamen more than a century ago, in the days when Salem ships sailed the seven seas.

Fig. 4 — The Survival of an Old Custom
The Saturday beans of the neighborhood ready to be set in the pottery furnace, where they will be baked by the heat remaining after the firing of ware

Fig. 5 — Pottery Stacked in the Kiln
The kiln will presently be sealed for the firing. Shelves and supports are constructed of tile

It is uncertain when flower pots were first produced in this country. The houses of the early colonists were hardly warm enough to sustain life in human beings during the bitter New England winter, and it would have been impossible to grow plants. Even later, when dwellings were more comfortable, the stern necessities of existence absorbed so much time that little or none was left for luxuries. Probably some pots were turned out about 1800, the earliest form being perfectly plain with, of course, the usual drainage hole in the bottom. Later, a quarter-inch rim was added, and this was eventually increased to a half inch on the small pots and an inch and a half on the large sizes. This rim prevents the pots from jamming when nested. Saucers, too, have a rim — for the same reason. Quite recently, a new type of pot has been designed at the Paige Pottery, with a slightly flaring rim, copied from Italian and Spanish examples. This form has its rim, or collar, within — near the base — instead of outside. Flower pots are graded in size by half inches, from the tiny "thumb pots," an inch in diameter, to huge affairs twenty-four inches across.

Ornamented pots have been made from about the middle of the last century, among them hanging pots with a pie-crust or scalloped edge on both pot and saucer, the latter integral with the pot. Gay colors have sometimes been used: black and gold, red, green, or blue. Some pots were painted, some glazed, although plain black was the favorite glaze. (No florist approves of glazed pots; but they are so attractive, and can be kept clean so easily, that most of us use them. If one is careful to water the plants less frequently, and only when the earth is dry, glazed pots are harmless.) Because of proximity to the sea, the rope motive was a favorite.

The day of the handmade flower pot is almost at an end. Pots can be turned out so much faster and cheaper by machinery that the ancient method is nearly extinct. Today's workman is not willing to devote years to the apprenticeship necessary to become a craftsman, who, by his magic touch and the revolving wheel, can turn a flower pot into a vase, then into a jug, and back again to the homely, but useful, flower pot.

Anyone who has stood beside a potter and watched him work will never forget the experience. We see a marvel of creation before our eyes — fashioned from the earth, even as are we:

"Thus spake I to a potter on a day,
Bidding his careless wheel a moment stay.
Be pitiful, O potter, nor forget
Potters and pots alike are made of clay."

Note. The Paige pottery, whence came the illustrations for the preceding article, has had but three owners during nearly two centuries. The Osborne family was in possession from 1736 to 1866 — a hundred-and-thirty-year tenure. After a two-decade interval, the pottery passed to its present owner, who has been associated with the concern since 1872. John Donovan, maker of the flower pot shown in Figure 3, likewise has a record of more than half a century as a potter. Nowadays, it would be difficult to find men willing to devote themselves so patiently and faithfully to a single craft. — *The Editor.*

Early American Pottery

Fig. 1 — Jug. Soft green with glaze running down from top. *Height, 8 inches.*

Fig. 2 — Jar. Dark green, even glaze. Perhaps from Plymouth County, Mass. *Height, 8¼ inches.*

Fig. 3 — Jug. Olive, speckled with light brown. Probably New Hampshire. *Height, 8½ inches.*

The Methods of Early American Potters

By L. Reginald Chandler

*Illustrated by examples from the collection of H. B. Russell.**

It is fairly well recognized today that collections at large are not necessarily beautiful, but rather are interesting as recording chronological steps of development. The one in point, however, being contemporary as a whole with the first consistent efforts in this country to produce utilitarian pottery, is beautiful in many ways.

First, the housing of this particular gathering of the fictile arts within a room of old blue walls and trim at H. B. Russell's own house in Wellesley, Mass., is an achievement worthy of consideration. The shelving and niches round about this striking room are not stiff and forbidding, but rather accessible and cordial to the hand of the pottery lover, and reflect due credit to the owner's perception of things esthetic.

Secondly, grace of line and variety of shape are outstanding features of this entire collection. Many pieces oddly suggest the interesting tea jars used in the ancient ceremonies of the Japanese, while two appear to have contours similar to Chinese pieces of the Han dynasty.

*Note — In some of the accompanying illustrations the locality where certain pieces were procured is indicated. This, however, should not be accepted as other than the vaguest evidence of the actual place of manufacture.

Early American Pottery

Fig. 4 — Jar. Brick red mottled with green. Lower Connecticut valley. *Height, 10¼ inches.*

Fig. 5 — Covered jar. Terra cotta, with black splashes. *Height, 8 inches.*

Fig. 6 — Pitcher. Black, very highly glazed. Procured near Hartford, Connecticut.

Pitchers and jars of slightly amphora shape, with close or looping handles placed at the shoulders, possess a strong southern Europe flavor; but the jugs, of all pieces, seem distinctly American. So naive and yet subtle in their small necks and long sloping shoulders with the bulk well down toward the foot, these quaint containers rival those of any other country. The final attribute, of course, is color and texture, and, needless to say, although these American specimens are limited in these respects, yet it is next to impossible to find any two alike.

The conditions imposed upon early potters were such that only the most elementary formulas were used for glaze making. This point brings us to the object of this article, which, after all, is not strictly an appreciation of Mr. Russell's very interesting early American ceramics.

It would seem that much of the pleasure to be derived from accumulating pottery wares is overlooked by the average collector in his undue attention to the mere consideration of types or periods based on precedents established by textbook or museum. Yet, if we care to, we may share some of the thrill experienced by the curator if we but delve into the principles of potting during the past ages, an essential in ceramic research.

Early American Pottery
Fig. 10 — Jar. Mottled orange and green. Incised reeding and wave lines.

Developments in color or surface treatment of ceramic wares have followed closely the detection of new elements brought to light by the onward trend of civilization. In the early days of the craft, substances in use by the well advanced Orientals were sought for the attainment of excellence in glaze. Great secrecy prevailed everywhere in Europe concerning processes utilized, and little of a technical nature was allowed to pass on for the edification of other workers. So it was that cobalt, used to produce the blue decoration familiar to Dutch and Italian potters over a long period, was slow to make its appearance in the new world, and, not being a first-hand material, had to be introduced by a master potter of European training.

Cobalt was mentioned by scientists and introduced into limited use in Europe at the close of the Middle Ages, but it was not until early in the seventeenth century, that blues achieved the perfection which we encounter in the Delft ware of Holland. In reality, the successful use of this color indicates the actual advent of finesse both here and abroad.

While awaiting the evolution of these bright, pure colors which have been the last to make their appearance in any age, in any country, mankind has always had access to the brown of an element so prevalent in the substances of the earth that it is usually more difficult to eliminate it than it is to secure it. This is iron, which is calculated to constitute about four and one-half per cent of the earth's crust, and which occurs to some extent in most of the clays which the potter uses, the more notable ones being the ochres or the *Terre de Siena*. The iron and bronze ages gave to archaic man a knowledge of this metal, of copper and of tin, which,

Early American Pottery
Fig. 7 — Jug. Brilliant light green with strong green splashes. *Height, 8½ inches.*

Fig. 8 — Jar. Olive green spattered with orange and brown. Procured near Hartford. *Height, 8½ inches.*

Fig. 9 — Jug. Black with brilliant glaze. Procured in New Hampshire. *Height, 8½ inches.*

Early American Pottery
Fig. 11 — Covered jug. Reddish brown mottled with dark brown. Procured near Hartford. *Height, 8 inches.*
Fig. 12 — Jar. Purple with over glaze of strong green. *Height, 6¼ inches.*
Fig. 13 — Jug or pitcher. Intense red with black markings. Pennsylvania. *Height, 8 inches.*

although the two latter have given the most difficulty in refining, are all three foremost in every attempt to produce earthenwares of an elemental nature.

This leads to an understanding of the period in American ceramics beginning about 1750, and parallel to the great porcelain activity throughout Europe, when a few isolated men who had learned their trade across the seas attempted in a small way to start their kilns. For about a hundred years, before the flourish of porcelain generally took possession of this country, every kind of a utensil that could be manufactured from clay was turned out. There was not much recourse to the materials of foreign potters, because of both the expense involved and the ignorance of new materials. Limited to the local resources, which, of necessity, must all be mineral elements on account of the high fires to which pottery is subjected, the ingenuity of our forbears was often severely taxed to produce marketable ware.

The little group of raw materials available required some preliminary preparation before they were usable. Lead, the foremost glaze element, was best prepared for the purpose by reducing sheets of the metal in vinegar, thereby obtaining a white powder. Silica and alumina, two components of regular glass making, were easily secured in natural clay. The common mineral colorants, copper and iron, were turned into powdered salts or oxides. Clay for fashioning into shapes came down through the centuries by the disintegration of granite, but the character of each deposit is changed by much sifting and washing of the grains in each occurring torrent.

Early American Pottery
Fig. 14 — Jar. Reddish brown mottled with red and showing heavy black patches. Connecticut valley. *Height, 10 inches.*
Fig. 15 — Jar. Brick red splashed with brown. *Height, 12 inches.*

In approaching the subject of body and glaze for a comprehensive understanding of our collection, it is worth knowing that practically every clay used for body or biscuit,—as the unglazed ware is called,—is capable of being carried to the molten state. At some degree of heat, clays are more or less fusible, and certain clay will run like molasses while a near-by piece of different consistency will not sear or vitrify in the same firing. This makes possible a maturing point in the fire which is controllable by so mixing different mineral substances that the result, when baked or burned, will be an unflinching structure whose pores are filled by a semi-flowing ingredient. To include the glazing and not merely the biscuit, it would seem that a fusible clay applied over

Early American Pottery
Fig. 16 — Covered jar. Terra cotta and heavy black. Connecticut. *Height, 8 inches.*

Fig. 17 — Covered jar. Light brown marked with darker brown. Hartford. *Height, 6¾ inches.*

Fig. 18 — Covered jar. Two shades of brown with light brown glaze. Connecticut. *Height, 7½ inches.*

Early American Pottery

Fig. 19 — Jug with applied ornament. Red with darker splashes. New Hampshire.

Fig. 20 — Earthenware ring. Mottled brown. Hartford.

readily flowing material as borax or lead salts. The latter is usually chosen and such materials are added to it as will give the glaze something in common with the ware it is to cover, insuring a homogeneous fit. If great stress is not laid upon this *fitting* of the glaze, crackle or crazing follows and a network of cracks appears all over the piece with, sometimes, the loss of particles from the surface. This web-like texture of crazing appears on nearly all pottery, and, although such ware is usually considered technically imperfect, the Chinese developed the web-like pattern large or small at will, subjecting it to a dark stain for appearance's sake, that it might be more readily observed.

Colorless glazes are possible when the potter carefully makes up his glaze around a melted ingredient or flux, using mineral elements that are not discolored by iron. The natural buff or red shades of the body then have full play, as pebbles through a stream of limpid water. (*Figs. 11 and 13.*)

a more refractory or infusible clay (readily melted) would result in producing a finished piece showing a beautiful gloss and a firm upstanding contour. In some degree, this is what happens when the clay known as Albany or Michigan slip, a typical natural deposit with a high content of iron, is fired over a shape made of refractory stoneware clay. (*Figs. 6 and 9.*)

Iron in a finely divided state, or oxide, has a softening influence upon clays and imparts a deep brown color as well, but the practice is usually to build up a glaze from some such

Early American Pottery

Figs. 20, 21, 22, 23 — Soft earthenware with plates, the latter showing *slip* decoration, an application of design in various clays thinned with water to the consistency of paint.

Early American Pottery

Figs. 24, 25, 26, 27 — Typical examples of bright or high glaze derived from simple lead mixtures, shown in conjunction with common surface treatment.

It was not always desirable to procure shades of brown from the iron as found in combination with other things, and so it was often necessary to resort to the pure metal in the scale that fell around a smithy's anvil from red hot horse shoes or scrap iron. This scale was burned in a sealed pot among the stacked ware of a kiln until an oxide resulted. Then, reduced to powder, it was ground in a primitive manner between stones. Copper filings were treated in the same way and, thus incorporated in the glaze, produced translucent shades of mossy green. (*Figs. 2 and 8.*) Sometimes brown and green were combined on the same jar, or green was applied over a terra-cotta red body to produce a mottled bronze shade.

The wash of excess glaze down the shoulders of a jug will offer many methods of achieving an effect,—particularly when the oxide colorants are not ground finely, and hairlike tracks are given out behind the flowing particles. The resulting pattern is aptly called "hare's fur" on bowls from the Orient, when iron causes the markings. (*Figs. 14 and 18.*) A heavy deposit of color placed at the neck of a glazed piece yields a drip that is always pleasing in its course down the side, and many times succeeds in splashing pieces reposing below as well. (*Figs. 7, 12 and 16.*)

Early American Pottery

Figs. 28, 29, 30 — Stoneware. The large amphora shaped jar shows clearly the "orange peel" texture resulting from salt glaze, accomplished by the condensation of the vapor produced by shoveling common salt into the kiln while the fires and the earthenware are still hot.

The means of producing regulated pattern upon the surface of the ware is that either of impressing or scratching lines in series with notched sticks (*Fig. 10*), or of dabbing fantastic spots with the aid of sponge clippings dipped in some of the mineral colorants. (*Figs. 5, 15, and 17.*) Both schemes for supplying enrichment are so practical as to have been in vogue almost ever since their conception, but the more modern pieces show elaboration of the ideas. An engraved roller, bearing an incised design, for instance, supplies a neat beading in bands when pressed upon the clay pot as it is revolved. (*Fig. 13.*)

Impressions of floral motifs made of raw clay have been stuck to the unfired surface of certain pieces so as to produce a coarse modeled effect. (*Fig. 19.*) This usually necessitated a mould of some description to shape the applied part, and, in lieu of the usual plaster of Paris mould, one of porous low-fired clay was used, which partially dried and released the clay impression. The Samian ware of Roman antiquity was formed with similar baked moulds but with finer detail and finish.

The apparently haphazard manner in which glaze effects were accomplished on early American pottery may be explained by the fact that, to save time and expense, the biscuit, glaze and decoration were not secured by successive firings, as in the case of many finer wares, but, usually by a single operation of the kiln. This did not admit of many handlings, and, therefore, an unstudied, spontaneous result was produced with the effect heightened by the freaks of a capricious fire.

In the rural potteries of early America, efficient methods of washing and mixing clays for the bodies of ware were quite undeveloped, and thus, in the firing, various unexpected signs of impurity made their way to the surface, including occasional pockmarks exhibiting dark flecks within their area. (*Figs. 3 and 4.*)

In determining the region from which a certain line of pots emanated, the very simplicity of American pieces constitutes a most confusing factor. The independent potter turning out his work for simple countryfolk, had his favorite types for every vessel and, though he imbued each with homely charm, he yet stinted the finish of inside and bottom in justice to his daily bread. It will be seen that, in most ware of rural northern Europe or Colonial America, the finish of a foot or base is unheard of, until competition required something more by way of finish than just cutting through the bottom with the swirl of a wire. All handles, snouts and extraneous features are direct and businesslike,—in short, the example of early pottery derives its character from the frank realization of the purpose for which it was devised.

Distinguishing marks then, may have to be looked for among what may be considered minor details of our early American pieces. For instance, the mere method of stacking pieces in a kiln was carried on differently in different localities; and the means of supporting a glazed pot during firing may be discernible on examination, particularly if glaze was permitted on the bottom. Sometimes the lining glaze,—when it is not made from a batch of left-overs,—is always the same in one make of pottery, irrespective of what is used on the outside. Beadings, pressed work, and all moulded work are quite likely to follow the ware of one maker through many years of production. They constitute another of the many ear marks of interest to the collector in establishing identity.

European Folk Pottery

By Laura Lorenson

Illustrations from the Nadelman Museum of Folk and Peasant Arts

FOLK pottery, in common with the other folk arts, is rooted in native culture. It reveals a people's manners and customs, and sometimes even its origin. The sturdy, substantial pottery shapes, devised to meet particular needs, have the unconscious dignity of appropriateness. Their ornament is usually simple, gay, and well balanced.

Photographs by Mattie Edwards Hewitt

Fig. 1 — Italian Pottery
Jars: blue floral motives on white tin enamel.
Casket: blue, with touches of green, on white tin enamel. Mask feet

Perhaps it is the unsophisticated, primitive character of folk pottery that has delayed its appreciation by conventional collectors. Mr. and Mrs. Elie Nadelman are not to be registered in that category. That is why the Nadelman Museum of Folk and Peasant Arts, in Riverdale, New York, is unique among American private collections. The section devoted to pottery, alone, represents years spent in scouring Europe for representative examples. Now it comprehends a well-balanced selection adequately illustrating the peasant products of most of the European countries.

In studying the folk pottery of the various nations represented, covering mainly the seventeenth, eighteenth, and early nineteenth centuries, we are impressed by the evidences of an international kinship among strongly marked national characteristics, but even more by the variety achieved within the limited technical resources of the peasant potters. It was Rodin who remarked that only that is ugly which lacks character, an indirect way of saying that character is the essence of beauty. He who accepts this dictum cannot fail to perceive in the strength and honesty of modeling and the appropriateness and originality of decoration of folk pottery a beauty that lack of superficial finish fails to obscure. The potter, were he peasant or village craftsman, unconsciously bared his creative soul in his handiwork.

The decorative effectiveness of pottery was recognized even by those who were slow to accept the ware for ordinary use. Open shelves filled with colorful pieces, used only on festal occasions, and cherished by succeeding generations of a tradition-loving people, played an important part in the interior adornment of provincial European homes. The use of ornamental tile was, also, almost universal. Articles of clay, made for special occasions such as baptisms, weddings, and birthdays — aptly termed "bespoke" — and for the use of guilds, have a personal character, independent of time or place. All the skill and resources at the command of the artisan were lavished on this type of ware. The application of dates and inscriptions was apparently more typical of the northern than of the southern European countries.

A far-flung vein of homely humor frequently found outlet in folk pottery. Conscious humor was expressed in puzzle jugs, used extensively at guild festivals, and unconscious humor crept unbidden into quaint inscriptions and representations of people and animals. The following inscription on an English puzzle jug, dated *1732*, is illuminating:

"Gentlemen now try your skill
ill hold you Sixpence if you will
that you dont drink unless you spill."

Generation after generation of village potters, each adding his mite to the lore passed from father to son, have left no clear pathway of progress in technique. Similar processes were employed in widely separated places, sometimes simultaneously, sometimes centuries apart. Coarse clay, varying from buff to brown in color, was the basic material.

Lead glazes colored with metallic oxides gained a firm foothold, at least as far south as France, in the

Fig. 2 — Spanish Pottery
Plate: painted with yellow, brown, and green leaves on slip coating.
Jug: sgraffito design in yellow slip on brown body.
Animal figurine: in yellow slip touched up with brown.
Madonna statuette: mottled glaze

Fig. 3 — Spanish Pottery
Jug: pale manganese-purple ground painted in brown and green.
Lion candlesticks: splashed with green, brown, and cream

late Renaissance, either alone or in connection with relief ornament. Later these glazes were overshadowed, though never entirely eclipsed, by tin-enameled ware and its humbler relative, slip-coated pottery, which were then at the height of their glory in Italy and Spain. The slip-coated ware — variously decorated with liquid clay, known as "slip," tinted with metallic pigments — was perhaps the most universally popular of the folk pottery.

The peasant potters whose rude kilns were scattered over the countryside surrounding the famous potteries of Italy and Spain during the Renaissance, and long thereafter, in spite of similar materials and technique in both countries, endowed their ware with clearly differentiating local traits. *Sgraffito* pottery — that is, pottery whose decoration is accomplished by incising the pattern in the clay or its slip coating — as well as tin-enameled and slip-coated ware painted with metallic pigments were common to both countries. The painter's meagre palette was composed mainly of blue, green, yellow, and manganese brown and purple.

The Spanish potter's predilection for leaves, flowers, and geometrical designs betrays Moorish influence. He, however, combined these motives with landscapes, religious symbols, and animals and birds of a more or less fantastic character. An English traveler in Spain during the latter part of the eighteenth century, according to Chaffers, described Manises, near Valencia, as a pretty village composed of four streets, whose inhabitants were mostly potters making a fine, copper-colored faïence, ornamented with gilding. This ware the people of the locality employed for ornamental and domestic purposes. The small potteries near Talavera turned out a sturdy, unlustred ware, often adorned with landscape backgrounds for scenes of vigorous action. The keynote in the pungent color scheme is usually struck by a bright green derived from copper coins. A collector tells of finding in a secluded community, not far from Talavera, where straw was the only fuel, some large Talavera dishes which a housewife had transformed into a kind of fireless cooker. In the morning she would fill her ancient plates with stew, and then bury them in straw to keep hot against the midday luncheon hour.

Italian pottery betrays the mingled influences of classic art, of the native scene surrounding the potteries, and of the odd mixture of piety and fantasy with which the peasants of southern Europe were imbued. A love of rich, vibrant color was a common heritage. The color note, within the scope of a limited palette, is often distinctive. An unusual hue, once obtained, was perpetuated. Unfortunately, the early potters found red, which usually grows brighter and more prevalent in peasant surroundings the farther south we travel in Italy, a difficult color to achieve. Art was instinctive in the Italian peasant potter, and his modeling, no matter

Fig. 4 (*centre*) — Dutch Pottery (*eighteenth century*)
Buff earthenware, roof finial with dashes of yellow slip covered with a golden-brown lead glaze. Interesting to compare with a much earlier English jug illustrated in Rhead's *Staffordshire Pots and Potters, p. 71*

Fig. 5 (*below*) — English Pottery
Plate: design in light slip on a dark ground, dated *1764*.
Puzzle jug: inscription in light slip on a dark ground, dated *1732*.
Low dish: four compartments covered inside with light slip and outside with brown slip dotted with light.
Hen and brood of chickens bank: covered with dark brown glaze.
Jar: with inscription *The po bee member Whom to give aim*, dated *1610*.
Jug: applied clay medallions on ground in two shades of brown.
Plate: crab design in light slip

Fig. 6 — German Pottery
Corner stove tile and small model of earthenware stove: relief designs; covered with green glaze.
Plate: slip coating painted in colored clay and metallic pigments.
Earthenware group: decorated in slip and glaze; sacred monogram.
Earthenware bottle: in pineapple form; green and brown glaze

how humble the vessel, is satisfactory to the eye.

Delft ware, the production of which was centred about Delft, Holland, was, no doubt, influenced by the tin-enameled pottery of southern Europe, and by the porcelains of the Orient. Designs with Dutch landscapes, peasants, and domestic animals were used in conjunction with Oriental motives. Figurines of domestic animals were particularly appealing. The early blue and white ware was later varied by polychrome designs. Much of the Holland ware in the small potteries must have been intended to appeal to simple folk for decorative purposes, since wood and pewter were used in humble Dutch homes for tableware. Yet another use of clay is also suggested by the lead-glazed busts of coarse buff earthenware used as roof finials.

Detail of Figure 6

Slipware is probably the most representative of English pottery. Its charm lies in the clever use which the potters made of clay and glaze. English folk pottery includes picturesque plates and chargers, rotund jugs, friendly tygs and posset pots supplied with enough handles for several drinkers. Many bear dates and quaint inscriptions.

Various types of slipware were made in England, but trailed or dropped slip decoration, of which the Thomas Toft dishes afford outstanding illustration, appears to have been the most popular. Light designs were contrasted against darker grounds

Fig. 7 — Transylvanian Pottery (*early nineteenth century*)
Designs scratched in the clay body and outlined over the dark blue surface coating with white slip

Fig. 8 — Swiss Pottery
Plate: brown glazed surface touched up in green; decorated in white slip. Dated *1795*.
Ink well: green glaze; with sacred monogram.
Covered jar: brown ground decorated in green, yellow, and white slip, with relief ornaments and scrolled clay straps.
Fountain: green glaze; with figures in relief. Dated *1654*

and *vice versa*. Manganese was used freely to darken clay and glaze. Patterns varied from simple dots, which were none the less attractive for their tendency to amalgamate in firing, to zigzag lines, inscriptions, flowers — among which the tulip was prominent — and attempts at portraiture. The lead-glaze coating often gave the light slip a yellow tint and turned the red of the body to a rich brown.

Colored lead glazes played an important part on German pottery and stove tiles. Copper green was used extensively; but blue, brown, yellow, and manganese violet are also found. Early glazed pottery, known as "Hafner ware," frequently displayed figures in high relief, and even in the round, in niches. The white used to indicate flesh, according to Emil Hannover, was produced with tin; blue was often made opaque with an admixture of tin.

Tin-enameled and slip-coated pottery also found favor in Germany. The slip-coated ware was painted both in colored clay and metallic pigments. The tulip, said to have been introduced into Germany in the latter part of the sixteenth century, played an important part in the decoration. The oak leaf, used as a space filler, was the badge under which the German peasants fought for their faith and rights. Surviving small models and individual tiles give an idea of the monumental, glazed-earthenware stoves that occupied the centre of the main room of a German home. The stoves were frequently two-tiered, the upper part serving at night as a base for a bed. Green was a favorite color; Biblical, mythological, and historical subjects, in relief, were typical decorations.

The central European countries, with their complex mixture of races, are, or were, rich in folk art. It has been said of some of them that they decorated everything they touched from the cradle to the grave, and we can well believe it. Their pottery was influenced by Germany and Italy; but each race stamped its ware with its own traditions. A great variety of central European pottery and stove tiles is simply but effectively decorated with colored glazes, either alone or in conjunction with *sgraffito* or relief ornament, in one color or a combination of hues. Painted ornament on tin-enameled or slip-coated ware is luxuriant. The large dishes, plates, and two-handled jugs afforded the potter opportunity to express racial conceptions with a poetic exuberance and freedom of brushwork that is charming. The stove tiles are also a treasure house of designs. Gaily colored trailed and dropped slip was also used on slip-coated ware.

Pottery was made in nearly all parts of Switzerland. Slipware and ware covered with colored glazes, in which green plays an important part, are prominent. The color combinations are often daring. The Swiss were particularly lavish in their use of colored clay on both slip and glazed grounds. Orange, brown, blue, green, and yellow are frequently combined. The shapes show considerable originality. The small fountains, usually with twisted handles and flat backs open at the top, are unique. Covered bowls and tureens with finials built up with straps of clay are likewise characteristic. Also to be found are small churns, some of them decorated in light slip.

All the different types of European folk pottery meet and mingle in France. Here we encounter glazed ware, trailed and dropped slipware, *sgraffito* pottery, and slip-coated or tin-enameled ware painted with metallic pigments. Originality was shown in the combination of colored glazes. Among these, a manganese brown and violet spotted glaze is a unique contribution of French inventiveness.

Fig. 9 — French Pottery
Fountain (*right*): covered with mottled glaze; seventeenth century.
Centre fountain: with a bust of Napoleon, covered with dark brown glaze and decorated in light slip; nineteenth century.
Fountain (*left*): decorated with colored slip and glaze; eighteenth century

Index

All place names are listed by State